WAR
IN CONTEXT

GW00579434

First published 2022
Copyright © Christopher K Pike 2022
The right of Christopher K Pike to be identified as the author of this work has
been asserted in accordance with the Copyright, Designs & Patents Act 1988.

All rights reserved. No part of this book may be reproduced, stored in a
retrieval system, or transmitted in any form or by any means, electronic,
electrostatic, magnetic tape, mechanical, photocopying, recording or
otherwise, without the written permission of the copyright holder.

Published under licence by Brown Dog Books and
The Self-Publishing Partnership Ltd, 10b Greenway Farm, Bath Rd,
Wick, nr. Bath BS30 5RL

www.selfpublishingpartnership.co.uk

ISBN printed book: 978-1-83952-555-1
ISBN e-book: 978-1-83952-556-8

Cover design by Kevin Rylands
Internal design by Andrew Easton

Printed and bound in the UK
This book is printed on FSC® certified paper

WAR
IN CONTEXT
Making Sense of War

Christopher K Pike

BROWN
DOG
BOOKS

Also by Christopher K Pike:

About War

The final book of the trilogy *Making Sense of War:*

Prospects for War

will be published in Summer 2023

To the memory of

*Cpl Clifford Pike RAF, served 1940 to 1946,
UK and Burma*

'I did my bit'

ACKNOWLEDGEMENTS

Many people have inspired, helped and facilitated this book; too many to mention all individually.

I have consulted an enormous number of sources, including unpublished academic dissertations, books, articles, Wikipedia (to get dates right) and a huge number of informative and authoritative websites.

Special thanks must go to the academic staff at King's College London War Studies Department, and particularly Professor Sir Lawrence Freedman, who, over two years of hard study, put structure and insight into my concept of strategy and the political aspects of war.

Ed Handyside of Myrmidon Books provided encouragement and his percipient comments transformed a series of monographs into a coherent book.

Frances Prior–Reeves, my project editor, took a sensible business-like and supportive approach to the challenge of transforming a manuscript into a book, and that was complemented by Etty Payne of Elegant Words who did a tremendous job of proofreading.

Nicky Bird of Bird Battlefield Tours had an eagle eye for excess verbiage and historical references and Martin Dowle provided 'soft power' perspective to the subject of International Relations and cultural development, as well as a keen eyed for the odd inaccuracy.

Also, to the several college and business school colleagues who took the trouble to read the first book in the trilogy *About War* book and comment accordingly; usually in a complimentary way...

Most of all, Christine Salter, my partner, was tireless in her encouragement and support, as well as a keen eye in proofreading and research, structural comments and also, never to be forgotten, coffee at the appropriate time!

As ever, all errors, omissions and inaccuracies are mine.

INTRODUCTION

War in Context is the second book in the trilogy *Making Sense of War*. This trilogy is based on four principles:

1) Achieving peace requires a thorough comprehension of war, its provenance, prosecution and conclusion.

2) That war – a coercive act designed to change the political balance between polities – hopefully for the better – should be seen as distinctive from warfare, the practice of using physical force on the battlefield.

3) The primary responsibility of the state is the security of its citizens. The price of security is eternal vigilance. This responsibility cannot, and should not be avoided.

4) Although the state might do all it can to avoid war through diplomacy, soft power and treaties, if war is both inevitable and necessary (like WW2), then the military needs to be properly funded and professional. But this does not necessarily mean engaging in offensive military actions; there are other options, such as Peace Support Operations and counterinsurgency.

The first book, *About War*, provided a framework for the many factors that contribute to war as a social phenomenon, an activity of organised groups of people – polities.

War in Context examines how the emergence of the state both controlled war and facilitated it. The state legitimises war and war legitimises the state. *War in Context* looks at the place of the military force in general and in the context of the UK's foreign and security policy, and applies this to a sample of historical military deployments.

War changes the political balance between polities, but many commentators speak of politics, both domestic and international, as if there were a common understanding of the word. There is not, and any observer needs to ensure that politics is not used simply as a dustbin term. In this context, politics is essentially about relationships.

Having considered the case for needing military force and the place of the military in the UK's foreign and security policy, *War in Context* looks at a number of contrary views of war and the use of armed force. The starting assumption is that, although armed force is typically necessary in an anarchic world order, we should always seek stable and everlasting peace. We ask whether we can predict war and, if so, what attention might we give to the people making the predictions? And if we are to predict war, what sort of wars are we thinking of? The record of attempts to anticipate the occurrence, frequency and character of war is poor.

Terrorism is a modern preoccupation, which surged some twenty years ago after the al-Qaeda attacks on New York's World Trade Center and the Pentagon, triggering George W. Bush to launch his 'war on terror'. Terror is still exigent, and *War in Context* considers the history, the progress and the effectiveness of both terrorism and counter-terrorism.

The 9/11 attacks marked a turning point, or at least a watershed, in America's attitude to the rest of the world and to its foreign policy. Terrorism continues to be a major preoccupation for peaceful nations, the security services and the military. We provide a personal testimony for that day: 11 September 2001. We trace the consequences of the American response to those attacks and its subsequent interventions and non-interventions. We consider how the Western World might cope with less assertive United States leadership.

War in Context considers the basis for nuclear strategy: *deterrence*. This is not simply MAD (Mutual Assured Destruction) as some imagine, but 'second-strike capability', a concept that some now question. The conclusion is that nuclear strategy in general has not advanced much since the Truman Doctrine of 1948 and falls short of being truly 'strategic'.

It is often claimed that wars in the future will be fought by cyborgs, AI (artificial intelligence) and autonomous armed vehicles. This may well be true for what we called *warfare* but war itself will always be an intensely human and political preoccupation. A full examination of the implications of technology is required here and we look at the strategic implications of technology in warfare: managing the technology, in terms of long-term planning, campaign planning and battle management. We also consider the moral angles of autonomous machines and the time pressures forced on commanders and politicians by hypersonic missiles, some of which might carry a modest nuclear device – or, of course, a very large one.

War in Context has a short chapter on peace and pacifism and examines whether there are any valid arguments for pacifism, bearing in mind George Orwell's aphorism that 'pacifists can only operate if somebody else is looking after their security'.

There is an enormous amount of money to be made by researching, manufacturing or simply supplying arms and armaments. And that is only the transparent and legal part of the trade; clandestine and/or criminal arms dealing can be even more lucrative. By contrast, people who campaign for peace, irrespective of the degree of legitimacy and cogency in their arguments, invariably subsist as paupers.

Finally, we bring together all the threads of war and warfare: politics, strategy, technology and, most importantly, peace.

The appendices reproduce *About War*'s definition of War, Warfare and Strategy; an illustrative list of Britain's military inventions since 1945; 'Enough to do in our own backyard?'; The Most Notable Conventions on Banned weapons; Arms Control Treaties Concerning Nuclear Weapons and Nuclear treaties per se.

During the writing of this book, the Russian Federation invaded Ukraine. The invasion is cited in the main text; but as this is a special case, there is a supplementary chapter which provides a framework for that war, and its implications for international security.

The third volume of the trilogy, *Prospects for War*, will be published in early 2023.

London / Norfolk July 2022

CONTENTS

1. THE ROOTS OF VIOLENCE AND THE DEVELOPMENT OF THE STATE

There never was Elysium, never any Garden of Eden

The idea of a perfect land, a paradise where 'life is easiest; where there is no snow nor heavy storm' (Homer's Elysium, from *The Odyssey*) is, as one might expect from Homer, a myth. Neither did the 'noble savage' ever exist. The concept was invented as a riposte to the English philosopher Thomas Hobbes (1588 to 1679) and his idea of the 'state of nature' being 'war of all against all' and where people's lives were famously 'solitary, poor, nasty, brutish and short'. The French philosopher, Jean-Jacques Rousseau (1712 to 1778) – although he never used the term *noble savage* – largely accepted the contrasting primeval idyll of humankind living in harmony with each other and with nature. Modern scientific consensus tends to favour Hobbes rather than Rousseau insofar as it suggests that anything even close Eden or Elysium was rarely if ever achieved.

Homo sapiens, a figure we would recognise today, developed from primate predecessors between 100,000 and 70,000 years ago. The end of the Upper Palaeolithic era, about 50,000 years to 10,000 years ago, saw the Mesolithic era (literally 'middle', between the Palaeolithic and the Neolithic) and the first agricultural revolution. Instead of hunter-gathering, some groups became *sedentary*, a particular term denoting that they stayed in one place, constructing buildings, growing crops and keeping livestock. Not all hunter-gatherers settled down at the same time. In some remote tribes in Africa, Australia and South America, some were still hunter-gathering until comparatively recently. A recent news item reported that *The Sentinelese people of Andaman Islands in the Indian Ocean are a Palaeolithic people who have had no contact with outside world ...*

So, for most of the time humankind has been on earth, societies were hunter-gatherers, living a subsistent, insecure life, but – it was assumed – at peace with neighbours or 'aliens'. However, recent archaeological evidence refutes this illusion. Cave paintings show opposing sides brandishing weapons at each other, with obvious hostile intent. There are also images of animals such as aurochs (an ancestor of domestic cattle), horses and a form of deer, suggesting disputes over hunting rights.

Until roughly the 1970s, many scholars imagined that single-species groups (see panel for chimpanzees), including humankind, might have lived in this primitive state, experiencing little intragroup or intergroup violence. Some potential violence might have manifested itself in displays, something one can still see with the All Blacks rugby team haka dance, but with few injuries and even fewer deaths. The behaviour of soccer fans might fall into the same category. Remains of spears, knives and bows and arrows were assumed to be for hunting, but many prehistorical cave paintings have now been discovered showing what are evidently battles and, in some cases, both standing and prone bodies penetrated by arrows. Weapons were clearly dual purpose: for both hunting and interpersonal conflict. We use the term *conflict* rather than *war* to illuminate the extra dimension we ascribe to war.

Hobbes' view of 'the life of man' might be pessimistic, but prehistoric life could be violent and dangerous. More recently, the Kalahari Bushmen and the Inuit of the Arctic, living supposedly in harmony with nature and each other, suffered high homicide rates compared with more 'sophisticated' societies. A similar situation is found in South American tribes like the Hiwi of Venezuela, the Aché of Paraguay and the Waorani of Ecuador – hunter-gatherers who had homicide or warfare deaths of 36%, 55% and 60% respectively. As the *Journal of Human Evolution* (April 2007) comments: *'The high levels of conspecific violence and adult mortality in the Hiwi may better represent Paleolithic human demographics than do the lower, disease-based death rates reported in the most frequently cited forager studies.'* It's a small wonder that these tribes survived at all!

Fortunately for our purpose, and somewhat forgotten in terms of archaeological and anthropological research, Australia and its pre-contact aboriginal inhabitants present an uncontaminated example of the incidence of violence in hunter-gatherer societies. Even better, we have the related account of one William Buckley, who arrived on a convict ship in 1803. He escaped from Port Phillip (modern day Melbourne) and lived for thirty-two years among aboriginal people, learning their language and observing their wars and blood feuds.

Buckley was illiterate, so most of his testimony comes from a book written by John Morgan in 1852, which may contain some hyperbole. Buckley reportedly recounts that some clashes between tribes were particularly bloody, with 'many dead'. He reported that every kind of conflict existed: blood feuds, raids, ambushes and full-scale violent actions. Buckley, among other studies, also suggests that the most common type of inter-tribal attack was the surprise raid, often early morning, which frequently involved indiscriminate killing of men, women and children. Dawn raids and the surprise attack are timeless; all soldiers will be familiar with the dawn 'stand to'. The Japanese attack on Pearl Harbor on 7 December 1941 was at 8 am, one hour exactly after dawn on a Sunday. Daylight was necessary for the attack and, on a Sunday, many soldiers, sailors and airmen would be attending religious services.

Over the past forty-odd years, archaeologists and anthropologists have comprehensively changed their views on the origin, or the roots, of violence. It has been realised that intragroup and intergroup competition, up to and including lethal violence, was endemic and widespread, both in mankind and also, incidentally, in chimpanzees, our closest primate cousin (see panel).

Despite much study, and many papers and colloquiums, and although it is largely accepted that chimpanzees are indeed prone to violence, it is difficult to extrapolate this trait more generally throughout the animal kingdom. Colobus monkeys, for example, are less prone to violence, except when being chased by chimpanzees! It might be tempting to think that external factors are at play here. In *About War*, it was posited that one factor in man's historic motivation for war was the need for security: access to water, hunting grounds and shelter. A modern analogue of this would be physical security (freedom from the risk of attack), health and financial security. With man's encroachment on their natural habitat, it could be argued that the motivation for chimpanzees is also security – freedom from concern about being attacked – and access to hunting grounds. The drawback of this thesis is that, even where one might suppose that the security threat was low, chimpanzees, with little capacity for scaling, assume any threat to be serious.

CHIMPANZEES HUNT, KILL AND EAT OTHER PRIMATES.

Sociologists, anthropologists and primatologists – and quite a few other 'ologists' – debate whether primates and other mammals are naturally violent towards other members of their group, to other same-species groups and to other species. Much attention is paid to chimpanzees, mankind's closest relative.

For many years, it was thought that chimpanzees were vegetarian and foraged all day for roots, leaves and other flora. It was thought that they lived in peaceful cohabitation within their group and with other groups of chimpanzees and other animals. Intergroup or intragroup violence was confined to displays, with the pant-hoot as a well-studied vocalisation of chimpanzees, together with the thumping of feet on the ground and the banging of trees.

In the 1960s, Jane Goodall started studying chimpanzees in Tanzania, making it her life's work. She pioneered the practice of taking a detailed, scientific look into their lives and behaviours, and was struck by the similarities with human beings, including generosity, kindness, friendships and altruism.

However, after studying chimpanzees for some years, she was shocked to discover that what she thought of as peaceful vegetarians were skilled hunters, who killed other primates, particularly colobus monkeys, for food. They also fought what Dr Goodall called 'civil wars', making lethal attacks on other groups. Some attacks were group-on-group, others group-on-individual. It was certainly a shock not only to Dr Goodall but to the anthropological world. This violence was not casual or random; it has subsequently been discovered that older, more experienced chimpanzees teach youngsters how to hunt. Chasers, blockers and ambushers have been identified.

At stake is whether 'chimpanzee wars' prove that violence is innate, and, by implication, that mankind is innately violent too.

Prehistoric fighting, individual against individual, group against group and, in some instances, group against individual, was both ubiquitous and lethal, particularly given the limitations of prehistoric medicine. Yet many societies were peaceful for much of the time, which may appear contradictory. Even given the evidence of Australian aboriginal potential for violence, Buckley was welcomed into his chosen tribe and cared for.

It seems that mankind has the potential for both violence and co-operation, even kindness. Also, given the inevitable trading, the oldest form of human interaction apart from sex, we might recognise a third potential: co-operative competition. I will seek better furs so I can trade them with you for better fish. The ability to recognise the value of other peoples, in terms of trade and also fertile female partners, is among the characteristics that mark out mankind from predecessor animals.

But there are dangers here, too. Intragroup peaceful co-operation means that the members of each co-operating society, or at least a majority, must feel fairly treated or coerced both by the tribal leader and also in relation to other tribes. Peaceful co-operation between groups requires careful diplomacy in dealing with different cultures. Healthy competition means identifying the group's 'competitive advantage' (a term beloved by modern economists), which is sometimes difficult to recognise and achieve. What remains as the more tangible alternative is organised violence, requiring some investment in weaponry and training. This is the leader's challenge: a superior coercive authority may keep the peace *within* societies, but there was no such thing *between* ancient societies other than that achieved through a fearsome or formidable reputation.

The first agricultural revolution (most authorities use 10,000 BC as a marker) together with the adoption of a sedentary lifestyle was one of the several major changes in the social, economic and corporate environment for violent actions against other individuals or groups. The Neolithic settlement meant that the concentration of grain stores and livestock in sedentary farmsteads or villages made an attractive target for hunter-gatherers and other villages to attack and rob.

Thus evolved the proto city-state with its strong defensive walls and watchtowers. Rather than deterring a full-scale attack, its initial function was as defence against the surprise raid, typically conducted around dawn. So it was that the city-state became the 'political' organ for the sanction of violence, a defined contiguous area under the administration and control of a centralised government. It became the centre of economic and cultural life despite having a population that was little more than that of a modern, medium-sized town. By 2000 BC, Ur, a Sumerian city in ancient Mesopotamia, was the largest city in the world, with a population of about 65,000 souls. This is what we now know as war: organised, purposeful violence.

Not only did the state inherit some of the violent functions of the tribal group, it also restricted the right of individuals to wage war outside the state. Remnants of this can be seen in wars waged ostensibly by the Roman Republic but in reality, by maverick individuals such as Marcus Licinius Crassus, 'the richest man in Rome', against the Parthians, which ended badly at Carrhae in 53 BC, with Crassus captured and killed. Julius Caesar's campaign against the Gauls from 58 to 50 BC, was likewise essentially illegal under Roman law.

The state – initially the city-state – became the main actor and inherited many of the functions of the tribe or the group, particularly the use of organised, purposeful violence, directly from hunter-gatherer forebears. This is not the place to follow the development of the city-state through history but, for our purposes it assumed the right and determined the necessity to wage war on marauders or other city-states. City-states were necessarily led by strong leaders and it is reasonable to assume that some coercive control was involved in persuading the population to fight.

The first real civilisation, rather than empire, although some claim it was also the latter, was that of the Sumerians in the lower reaches of the Tigris and Euphrates rivers in the early Bronze Age, between the sixth and fifth millennium BC. It is deemed a civilisation because it was a loose agglomeration of city-states with a similar, developed culture. War among and between Sumerian city-states was not unusual. It is inevitable that such strong leaders would want to expand their territory and so associations of several city-states would have formed the first proto-empires. The Sumerians were succeeded by the Akkadian Empire, generally accepted to be the first real empire. Although the member city-states remained in place, they were under the control and direction of one central figure, the king, the most famous of whom was Sargon the Great, who lived from 2334 to 2282 BC. Inevitably, he wanted to expand. At one stage, his empire stretched from the Mediterranean and Anatolia, down to the Persian Gulf and the highlands of Elam. Much of this was achieved through aggressive war, whatever the casus belli.

The concept of the state as a corporate body was strengthened over the years by adopting a common system of domestic law, by the ability to enter into treaties and agreements with other states, by a shared culture, by a common currency, by a banking system – the Sumerians may have invented banking – and by numerous other in-group practices such as an accepted dress code. The state became the main actor in war and inherited many of the functions of the tribe or the group, and also the use of organised, purposeful violence – war – directly from hunter-gatherer forebears. There were many civilisations thereafter – Egyptian, Hittite, Persian, Assyrian and of course Greece and Rome – but the fundamental right of the state to wage war still pertained.

Although the 'Dark Age' is an unsatisfactory descriptor of an era in Western Europe that lasted from the collapse of the western Roman Empire until the revival of the written record, perhaps around AD 700, or the 11th century renaissance (the end date is very much disputed), and although many 'states' were sometimes no more than warlords' fiefdoms, the sense of a conferred right to determine whether and when to wage war continued. The warlords who ruled lesser fiefdoms still controlled the violence. The term state was not generally used until the end of the 12th century. Thereafter, whether labelled democratic, anarchic, feudal or capitalist, the state – a mostly contiguous territory under one, centralised government – has survived to the present day as the main agent for initiating and prosecuting war.

Thomas Aquinas (1225 to 1274) was an Italian Dominican friar, philosopher and theologian. He wrote largely from the point of view of social order and the necessity of good laws. He supported the state having a monopoly of legitimate violence (anticipating Max Weber by six hundred years), but also pointed out that the state might be more interested in protecting an elite's wealth and power (also anticipating Karl Marx's thoughts by six hundred years). Aquinas did not expound on war, or the use of organised violence, as such.

Niccolò Machiavelli (1469 to 1527), an Italian Renaissance diplomat, philosopher and writer, popularised the concept of the state in his treatise The Prince. The term, Machiavellian has come to be associated with duplicity, cynicism and expediency, and he is credited with being the originator of the maxim that 'the end justifies the means'. In fact, there is no evidence to suggest that Machiavelli was any less concerned about morality than his contemporaries. The difference was that he chose to write about what was rather than how things ought to be and, as such, is often regarded as being the first sociologist.

He wrote extensively about war, being enamoured by the Roman Republic's tradition of citizen armies, particularly as he distrusted mercenaries – known in the Italian Renaissance as Condottieri. The title of his book on war was The Art of War and it concentrated on what we would now call the practice of warfare. (See About War for a definition, or Appendix 1 in this book.) He recognised that war must be explicitly defined and that if diplomacy fails, war becomes a continuation of politics, the relationships between polities. (In Machiavelli's time, these polities were Italian city-states.)

There is a subtle distinction here between Machiavelli's dictum 'war becomes a continuation of politics' and the concept of Clausewitz (1780 to 1831) that 'war is not merely an act of policy but a true political instrument, a continuation of political intercourse carried on with other means. What remains peculiar to war is simply the peculiar nature of its means.'

Few writers make the conjunction between the state itself and war as a political act. Sir Michael Howard bemoaned in *The Causes of War* that 'the phenomenon of war as a continuing activity within human society is one that as a profession (historians) we take very much for granted.' Howard's suggestion, put in the vernacular, implies that traditional diplomatic history is pukka, whereas because war is nasty and violent it is thereby distasteful. How many times do we read the misleading observation that 'war broke out'. War does not *break out*, it is the result of human decisions and agency. As ever, we *can* learn from history, but the challenge is applying the lessons to modern conditions.

Even so, a universally agreed definition of the *state* is elusive, particularly from the point of view of purposeful violence – war. Max Weber (1864 to 1920), a German sociologist and political economist, and generally regarded as an important theorist of modern Western society, famously defined the state as 'an entity that successfully claims a monopoly of the legitimate use of physical force within a given territory.'

In 1933, countries in the Americas adopted the Montevideo Convention, subsequently joined, or at least recognised, by other states around the world. Article 1 sets out the four criteria for statehood, the most important of which is that a state is recognised as a legal entity under international law and should possess the following qualifications: a permanent population; a defined territory; a government; and a capacity to enter into relations with the other states. The European Union follows the Montevideo Convention in its definition of a state: territory; population; political authority. But although the EU mentions 'political authority', there is no mention of internal coercion or the absence of it. Implicit in these definitions is that the state can oblige its citizens (or *subjects* in the case of the United Kingdom) to take up arms and fight, though in almost all treatises on 'the state', the right to go to war with another state is not specifically covered.

It's a long intellectual stretch to see the provenance of the state's purposeful use of organised violence – war – in our hunter-gatherer forebears. However, there are parallels: how far is war, in the context of the state, inherited from the form and use of violence in the Palaeolithic era or the early city-states and what can we learn, or at least appreciate, from this analysis?

First, and most of all, in ancient societies, agricultural surpluses provided for a division of labour; the two are, of course, interconnected. Ordinary citizens were pressed or volunteered to become soldiers, usually under the command of a senior or even elected civilian. A Greek general could easily be in the ranks one year and leading the armies the next. Roman consuls led their armies as a matter of course. In the modern era, there is far more than agricultural surpluses available to fund enormous amounts of money on military hardware. The highly specialised functions within the military; their focus on waging warfare – rather than *war as a political act* – can render this huge investment dysfunctional. All military leaders will nod towards Clausewitz (see *About War*), but are simply too distracted by both technology and the problems of logistical supply and organisation, both in terms of planning and campaign management, which crowd out the political aspects.

Second, diplomacy between hunter-gatherer groups must have been fraught, with different cultures, expectations and even dialects. Diplomacy in the modern era is more or less constant and we might expect some diplomacy between the protagonists – different states or empires – and an element of negotiation before military action was taken. One might dismiss this as a statement of the obvious: in the case of the Argentinians invading the Falkland Islands in 1982, they had been badgering the British to resolve the issue of ownership for years.

After the invasion in 1982, Margaret Thatcher, the then prime minister of the United Kingdom, was asked in the House of Commons whether she would be prepared to negotiate with President Galtieri of Argentina. She famously said 'No, sir,' and she was cheered to the roof. Margaret Thatcher's refusal to negotiate with President Galtieri of Argentina and the support she had in the Commons may have been an example of war fever, given that the ownership of the Falkland Islands had been an issue with the Argentinians for many years.

Thus, the third change is that war became undemocratic, in that strong leaders of early city-states would conscript citizens to fight. The conscripted were not consulted and seldom was this put to an informed vote of those who would actually have to fight. An exception might be ancient Greece. However, the decision to send hundreds of thousands of Greek men to their deaths during World War I (or engage in World War II for that matter) was not put to a plebiscite of an enfranchised population. Nor has any war since.

The justification for invoking war in a democracy is that there is a collective decision or vote by elected representatives. This means MPs in the United Kingdom, but how free is the vote, with the practice of party whipping? And this ignores, conveniently, Quintin Hogg's (Lord Hailsham) 1970s warning that Britain was becoming an 'elective dictatorship' because of the weakness of its largely unwritten constitution.

Opinion is split over the need for a UK written constitution. Some objections to having the constitution codified may be based on a lack of appreciation of the meaning and implications of the Magna Carta, the Bill of Rights, habeas corpus, common-law, Erskine May, conventions and common practice; some objections are based on the fear that such a written constitution would constrain government actions. However, after first accepting that the government must have the right, and indeed responsibility, to invoke military action without what we might call due process, there is a good case to be made in an 'elective dictatorship' for extensive Parliamentary discussion and non-whipped voting. Indeed, when Gordon Brown became prime minister in 2007, he promised to legislate to do just that. Like many electoral promises it got forgotten in the melée of the real world: 'events, dear boy, events', to quote Harold Macmillan.

The fourth and last change is that strategy became much more important. Strategy is, or should be, a continuous preoccupation rather than the occasional distraction. Understanding the continually shifting and evolving post-war world is vital. During World War I, post-war planning by the Allies was rudimentary; they were just bent on victory, which was by no means assured. The Germans were even more cavalier. Erich Ludendorff (1865 to 1937), the chief policy maker for the Imperial German Army after 1916, had a limited strategic concept. His famous aphorism for the German offensive of March 1918 against the western Allies was that they would 'Punch a hole and let the rest follow.'

By contrast, as early as 1942 in World War II, plans for post-war Europe and Japan were already under way. Recall Churchill's concept that 'in war: resolution; in defeat: defiance; in victory: magnanimity; in peace: goodwill.'

As well as being continuous, strategy generally needs to consider what the new balance between the protagonists might be after hostilities have ended. In the case of Germany after World War II, the Allies realised that, for their own security, with the threat of Communist Russia looming and for sound commercial reasons, Germany had to 'be made safe for democracy' – and for business. The U.S. Morgenthau Plan (1944) to return the country to a peasant agrarian economy (so that they couldn't wage war) was counter-productive vengeance. In the ancient hunter-gatherer societies, there was little heed to conditions after destruction was wrought on others. If they had killed the men, abducted the women and stolen food stores, there would not be much left anyway.

So, excepting a 'Carthaginian Peace' (where the Romans simply destroyed Carthage) or Hitler's plans for the Slavs (slavery), the basic principles of war are still with us, inherited to some extent from our hunter-gatherer antecedents, developed by the early city-states and refined over the years. War became and remains *corporate* (state focused), *undemocratic, coercive* and *political*.

The Carthaginian peace has an echo in modern times in the Morgenthau Plan. This was first proposed by United States Secretary of the Treasury, Henry Morgenthau, in 1944, suggesting a Post-Surrender Program for Germany. It briefly had some influence but was not adopted. The plan envisaged stripping Germany of its industrial resources and thus its ability to wage war. The plan was dropped because Germany, with its Allied occupation, provided a bulwark against Soviet expansion. Soviet Russia had demanded, and taken – as the Allies saw it – about one third of pre-war Germany. This was East Germany, more formally known as the German Democratic Republic (DDR). It was integrated with West Germany in 1991, to form the federal German state we have today.

The state system, whether its provenance lies in the adoption of a sedentary lifestyle following the first agricultural revolution, the advent of the first great empires, Thomas Aquinas' views, Machiavelli's nod to expediency, the Westphalian arrangements or Max Weber's observations, may not be the problem, but can it be the solution? There are hopeful signs. The creation of the United Nations was an enormous leap forwards, whatever current organisational problems it faces. The United Nations banning war as such, and the 'Responsibility to Protect' agenda was inspirational. Although not instituted on anything like a sufficient scale, it is another significant step in the right direction.

Liberal interventionism and associated Peace Support Operations are currently out of fashion but may well return, strengthened, more focused and, let us hope, more successful. The world has not lost sight of the benefits of eternal peace just yet.

2. BRITAIN'S HISTORIC USE OF MILITARY POWER AND ITS LEGACY

Why resort to violence?

The use of force or physical violence has been inherited from mankind's forebears, handed down through generations, incorporated into the concept and practice of the state and thus legitimised. The use of force also legitimises the state, following Max Weber's dictum that the state is that it has a *legitimate monopoly of violence*. Historically, any state or polity not prepared to contemplate the use of force or incapable of doing so probably disappeared, vanquished by hostile neighbours, leaving no testimony.

In an anarchic international environment, where there is no higher power, no state can risk leaving itself open to hostile military action and thus risk compromising its security. Even if a vast majority of the roughly two hundred states in the world might be inclined to denounce military force and give up their weapons, those unarmed states could not and would not risk leaving themselves vulnerable to attack from secretly armed states or dissident polities within their own state. States that renounce force and disband armies usually hide behind an allied power's military umbrella.

Military force would seem a simple self-explanatory concept. But military force is different from simple lethal violence. Military force is *organised*, partly to make best use of the available equipment and circumstances, partly to protect military lives but also to minimise opponents' casualties – a slightly startling provision perhaps, but force has to be *purposeful*, which must involve achieving an optimum political balance between protagonists and a lasting peace. This is a simple extension of the security dilemma concept: *I will never feel secure when you feel insecure.* During the 20th century, Russia has been attacked several times, by Britain – Churchill's support of the White Russians – and also by the Germans. Western allies then express surprise when Russia *claims* that it feels insecure, but this may just be an excuse for hegemonic expansion.

If military force is simply about *victory* rather than peace and a better political balance, it is simply gratuitous violence. There has to be some overriding objective. War is not *just* a continuation of politics by other means. Even in defence and wars of national salvation, the goal of workable political balance between attacker and defender and the eventual emergence of a durable peace must be kept in mind. Humiliation of an opponent or an enforced armistice will scupper peace in the long term. War must be used instrumentally, to achieve political effect. Violence, the use of servicemen and women to kill and destroy is not the main function of war. The western allies and Europe as a whole, will never feel secure while Russia feels insecure. Sure, Russia may overstate the case here but until we (whoever) can work *with* the Russians on joint security, Europe will always have a problem on its eastern borders.

It might be tempting to think that we no longer need military power or that we don't need quite so much. First, though, we have to consider the changing character of warfare and its relationship to war itself.

THE CHANGING CHARACTER OF WARFARE

Until the Russian invasion of Ukraine, massive, frontal wars such as we saw during the Second World War, Korea or to a lesser extent, Vietnam seemed to be something from the past. In the modern era, it was thought troops would no longer be tasked to clear and gain control of territory as a clear measure of victory. The military task became countering insurgents, policing, peace support operations or bombing. It is tempting to say that the Russians 'changed all that' with their invasion but given that most military analysts saw Russia as the main threat to the West's security, and that Russia had built up what the analysts imagined to be a formidable military machine, perhaps it shouldn't come as too much of a surprise. Even then, the Russian/Ukraine war has some major differences from the massive frontal wars of the 20th century. To give a couple of examples: Russia's tactics seem to be destruction and terrifying the civilian population. Ukraine seems to be relying on very powerful anti-tank weapons, and would certainly be using long-range dirigible missiles and air attack if they had sufficient resources to do this. The key feature here is that this change in the *character* of warfare also affects the *nature* of war.

This changing character of warfare is a substantial subject, and indeed one that preoccupies most commentators. There is relatively less effort put into the *nature* of war, which is concerned with our security, the function of war within the international environment and our relationships with other states. The character of war concerns the way we plan for, organise and prosecute war. Oxford University has its prestigious Changing Character of War Centre, specialising in just that, and with a focus on warfare and the link between war and warfare. It's worth emphasising again that although the *character* of warfare might change, war has an enduring *nature*, in that it is the political manifestation that is important – nay, vital. The Oxford CCW Centre is unusual in this respect, in that it recognises the interplay between war and warfare. Any of their publications, particularly by Robert Johnson, are worth reading.

And this is very well illustrated by the Russian/Ukraine war. Many other states have become involved, particularly the United States and the UK, in supplying arms and ammunition; several other countries have requested that they join NATO; more troops have been deployed to the Baltic states, amid fear that they may be next. On a broader front, it is feared that if the Russians are successful in Ukraine – however described – then China may consider an early move against Taiwan. On an international political front, they are fears of a world ruled not by law and convention, but by the old power politics of yesteryear.

How does all this fit together? How much military force do we need and for what purpose? Internal and external politics, threats, risks, alliances, treaties, military lobbying, historical precedents and geopolitics all conspire to perplex anyone wishing to appreciate the scope and breadth of political and military affairs. With distracting (if true) stories about aircraft carriers without planes, about the RAF having only a small proportion of its planes ready to fly, or the Royal Navy having to change the engines on ships, or the Army being short of body armour, the work that the armed forces do around the world – such as training local troops – is largely ignored.

First though, we must question one famous trope, and that is that *the world is an increasingly dangerous place.* In his November 2020 address, the UK prime minister put it slightly differently: 'more perilous and intensely competitive than at any time since the Cold War'. We might accept the perilous, but competition? With whom? How?

There was never a time without some threat, where the military could 'stand down' or where we could confidently say there was no threat. It is almost impossible to find one year during the whole of the 20th century where we could say that the international situation was stable and not threatening. The early years of the 20th century saw an increasingly assertive Germany. The end of the Great War in 1918/1919 might have seen a few years of respite, but with the convulsions in Weimar, an increasingly militaristic Japanese and the newly formed but unpredictable Soviet Union, international security was always in jeopardy.

Following WW2, the Cold War was an ever-present tinder box, to be ignited perhaps by the Korean War (1950–53), the Vietnam War (1955–

75) or the potential Armageddon of the Cuban Missile Crisis (1962). The demise of the Soviet Union in 1990 only triggered suppressed nationalism (as in the Balkans) and a takeover of the Russian state by belligerent robber barons. The price of security is constant vigilance, but the subtleties of international relations and the lessons of history are too often missed by politicians.

Going further back into history would be no more enlightening. History and politics are inextricably bound, but historians might not be explicit enough about the context and *military* historians are too keen to get into what they call – misleadingly – military strategy, the prevailing military circumstances and battle tactics.

It is worth looking at how the United Kingdom has used military power in the years since the end of the Second World War, how useful it was, and its legacy.

THE WITHDRAWAL FROM EMPIRE

To put the use of military power into historical context, English (later we might say 'British') troops have been in action every year since Cromwell founded the New Model Army in 1645. The UK has deployed military force around the world for some purpose or another for centuries. Many lessons have been learned and incorporated into the UK's politics, foreign policy and strategic culture. The UK's current military structures reflect this legacy. There have been many successes but also some failures, but we should not be too shocked that not all interventions are successful. In general, some political scientists reckon that half of all military ventures fail to meet the original objectives, if indeed these were accurately portrayed in the first place.

Since the end of World War II, British troops have been in action almost continuously. Some examples, including resisting communists in Greece (1944 to 1947), Indonesia (1945 to 1946), Palestine (1945 to

1948), Vietnam (1945 to 1946) were a direct result of the Second World War and which hold only a few lessons for today. The withdrawal from Imperial commitments in Malaya (1948 to 1960), Oman (1954 to 1959), Kenya (1952 to 1956), the Brunei 'Confrontasi' (Indonesia/Malaya, 1963 to 1966), Uganda (1964), Oman and Dhofar (1962 to 1976), were all successes, both military and political. Kenya (1952 to 1960) was perhaps less so on the political front. Cyprus (1955 to 1959) and Aden (1964-1967) were not great successes, but not failures either.

Korea (1950 to 1953) was not really a post-Imperial war but rather one of the opening shots in the Cold War. It demonstrated to every nation that the Free World, as it was then known, would not tolerate communist expansion by overt force. The Korean War also gave succour to other South East Asian states that they would not be abandoned to communism. Although the border between North Korea and South Korea remained pretty much the same, South Korea was 'saved' from communism. The war was terribly expensive in terms of blood and treasure, with over 3.5 million deaths, as was the Vietnam War (prosecuted by the United States, Australia, South Korea and New Zealand) at over 3.2 million deaths.

One can argue about whether some other wars are in fact post-Imperial, depending on how one positions Britain's imperial ventures and the obligations to colonial citizens (sorry, subjects) that entailed. The Malayan Emergency (1948 to 1960) is considered below, as is the Sierra Leone (2000 to 2003) intervention. Again, one could argue about the Falklands War (1982), or in the extreme, the 'Troubles' in Northern Ireland (1969 to 1998) being post Imperial. Britain's armed forces performed well and 'held the line' in terms of military endeavour. If there were associated failures, these were largely political.

In the modern era, post-Imperial hubris motivated British ventures in Egypt (1956: Suez), whereas Afghanistan (2001 to 2021), Iraq (2003 to 2011-ish), and Libya (2011) were all invoked, and ultimately betrayed, by the United States, as was Suez, but it was foolish anyway. And whereas most of Britain's post-Imperial ventures were successes, the three involvements above were not only comprehensive failures, but also had a dramatic effect on perceptions of the rules-based international order, on liberal interventionism as a concept, and ultimately on strategic stability. They all had unrealistic political objectives and all had populations unused to and unlikely to develop into liberal free-market democracies within a time frame that the invading forces could contemplate.

The liberation of Kuwait in 1990, otherwise known as 'Gulf 1', involved British troops and was about safeguarding the international rules-based order. Led by the United States, the war successfully expelled Saddam Hussein's Iraqi forces from Kuwait. Action was taken under only one interpretation of a UN mandate and was based on the concept that the acquisition of territory by force was illegal. George H W Bush is to be congratulated for not having given in to some 'hawks', who wanted to 'go on to Baghdad'.

[For more details of the UK's military interventions since the end of Second World War, with dates, see Appendix A.]

We examine below two cases where British troops have won a military conflict, conducted against a backdrop of collapsing of civil power, or against competing rebel movements. It is important to recognise here that the military victory provided the space and opportunity for a political settlement which, in both cases, persists to the current day.

THE CLASSIC CASE: MALAYA AND COUNTERINSURGENCY

The Malayan Emergency started in 1948 with the Sungai Siput incident, when three British plantation workers were killed by young Chinese men. The British colonial administrators enacted emergency measures, outlawed the Malayan Communist Party (MCP) and began mass arresting thousands of trades union officials and left-wing activists.

The counterinsurgency campaign in Malaya involved British forces battling 'CT' (Communist or Chinese Terrorists) guerrillas. The guerrillas' aim was to gain independence for Malaya from the British Empire and to establish a socialist economy. It was a long war, from 1948 to 1960 – with a resurgence in 1967, when the communist leader Chin Peng renewed the insurgency against the Malaysian government that lasted, sporadically, until 1989.

It was, and still is, considered to be a classic successful counter-insurgency (COIN) campaign, but that judgement hides many facets of the 'war', such as the alleged arbitrary brutality of the British military. The conflict was called an 'Emergency' by the British for insurance purposes, as London-based insurers would not have paid out in instances of a civil war. Over five hundred British troops were killed, including, in 1951, the British High Commissioner at the time, Sir Henry Gurney. There are several aspects worth noting here about the political use of military power.

The army learned that 'jungle bashing', which involved sending out regular patrols, did not yield the expected results of finding and destroying the insurgents, who moved too quickly to be caught. Patrols are still a default activity for the British Army and armies worldwide. The 'Briggs Plan' was devised by British General Sir Harold Briggs. It aimed to defeat the insurgents by cutting them off from their support among the rural population. This involved resettlement of Malayan villagers. About 500,000 people (roughly ten per cent of Malaya's population) were forced to transfer to newly constructed settlements known as 'New villages'. Some four hundred of these settlements were built. The Briggs Plan was sound militarily, but it took another soldier, General Sir Gerald Templer, to implement it successfully. Templer had been in the post-war German administration, which gave him invaluable experience of civilian affairs.

The Malayan Emergency is also famous for the classic book, *Defeating Communist Insurgency* by Sir Robert Thompson, an experienced colonial civil servant. Though not an exciting read, it nevertheless lays out a number of key dicta for a successful counterinsurgency campaign. A full description of the Malayan Emergency would take the rest of this book, but we can summarise just a few points:

One of Thompson's underlying philosophies was that there should be civilian *political* control. This was not to say that the military could not take initiatives, but that there had to be a *political* purpose. Thompson also covered securing the support of the population, whence the expression 'hearts and minds', cultural sensitivity, systematic intelligence and, in comparison with the modern day quick in-and-out model, the campaign had to be given adequate time, while not wearing down the will of the counterinsurgency force, the legitimate local government or indeed the country providing the counterinsurgency force itself.

INTERVENTION IN CIVIL WARS – SIERRA LEONE: A MODEL
FOR FUTURE INTERVENTIONS?

The Sierra Leone Civil War started in 1991 when the Revolutionary United Front (RUF) intervened to overthrow the legitimate government. UNAMSIL (United Nations Mission in Sierra Leone) and was not succeeding. In 2000, the British government, under Prime Minister Tony Blair, decided to deploy a larger and better armed force, which eventually numbered up to 11,000 British troops. Several Royal Navy ships were also deployed and the RAF Regiment played an important role. Again, the full story would take the rest of this book, but there are aspects that contrast sharply with some more recent interventions.

After deciding that the RUF would not disarm voluntarily, the British began training the Sierra Leone Army for a confrontation. During the training mission, a patrol returning from a visit to Jordanian peacekeepers was taken captive by a militia group known as the West Side Boys (actually, just a band of criminal thugs). Negotiations achieved the release of five of the eleven soldiers, and three weeks into the crisis, British special forces launched a mission codenamed Operation Barras, freeing the remaining six. The success of Operation Barras restored confidence in the British mission; one academic even suggesting that its failure would have forced the British government to withdraw all its forces from Sierra Leone.

Eventually, the Sierra Leonean government signed an agreement with the RUF which obliged them to undergo a Disarmament, Demobilisation and Reintegration (DDR) process. On 18 January 2002, the new President Kabbah declared the Sierra Leone Civil War over.

LESSONS FROM THE INTERVENTION IN SIERRA LEONE

There are many lessons to be learned from the British efforts in Sierra Leone and several books and articles have been written about this. A summary might include:

- There was a clear mandate from the United Nations and, as member of the United Nations Security Council Permanent Five (each with a veto), Britain lobbied hard for and on behalf of Sierra Leone.
- There was a clear political objective: rather than talk of an 'exit strategy', Britain actually wanted to resolve the situation and return Sierra Leone to democratic control.
- The army commander, Brigadier David Richards (later military NATO commander in Afghanistan and then the Chief of The Defence Staff (CDS) of the United Kingdom), was familiar with the politics of West Africa and of Sierra Leone in particular.
- There was a clear international element to this conflict, which was competently dealt with. Neighbouring countries such as Liberia were neutralised if they were hostile or co-opted in the overall effort if they weren't.

- With 11,000 British troops and troops from other countries as peacekeepers, giving a total of 17,000 troops, the resources were appropriate to the task. It was, incidentally, the largest Peace Support Operation to that date. There was also a large overlap with counterinsurgency doctrine.
- There was an extensive programme of training for the Sierra Leone army.
- By intervening in some hostage situations, the British Army demonstrated that they were on the side of the Sierra Leone people and its army, and this established a good measure of political capital.

This is comprehensively dealt with by a book by Professor Andrew Dorman, entitled *Blair's Successful War: British Military Intervention in Sierra Leone.*

LESSONS FOR OTHER INTERVENTIONS ... AND FOR WAR IN GENERAL

It is tempting to compare the intervention in Sierra Leone and other British successes with subsequent interventions in Iraq and Afghanistan. The scale of those operations was much different: Sierra Leone is a country of eight million people and has an area of 72,000 square kilometres; Afghanistan has thirty-two million people and an area of 652,000 square kilometres; Iraq has thirty-eight million people in 438,000 square kilometres.

Yet there are some key lessons to be learned about the use of force to effect political change. Regarding Iraq, Afghanistan and Libya:

- There was no clear, unambiguous United Nations mandate – or any other mandate for that matter – for the interventions in Iraq, Afghanistan or Libya. Judging by the outcomes, this was clearly needed.

- In these three instances, there was no clear strategic aim, other than what the United States calls 'victory' or at least 'mission accomplished'. As we note elsewhere, military victory without a politically satisfactory outcome is simply gratuitous violence.

- In both Iraq and Afghanistan, the invading armies were careless of the political and cultural structure of those countries, leading to many unnecessary deaths. In Libya, the campaign was ignorant of the way in which Gadhafi maintained stability in his country. This is not to say that he was not an evil man, but more could have been taken into account in defining the strategy.

- Whereas in Sierra Leone, the army and peacekeepers tried, and succeeded, in getting the local population and their army 'on side', it was the opposite in Iraq and Afghanistan. In both those countries, the local population was largely antipathetic to the invading forces. Even more egregiously, the Iraqi army was disbanded by the local American Caesar, with devastating results.

- Although both Iraq and Afghanistan operations evolved into long-term commitments, this was not the original intention. ('In and out without a shot being fired' was then, and continues to be, a tragic joke.)

- The actions of contiguous neighbouring countries were either not anticipated, or downplayed. In Afghanistan, Pakistan provided sanctuary for the Taleban. Iran had a complicated relationship with both the Taleban and the official Afghan government, but saw many things through the prism of its official hostility to the United States, who had supported Iraq when it attacked Iran to get hold of its oil (the Iran–Iraq War of 1980 to 1988, largely forgotten now).

- In Iraq, Iran in particular supported some internal factions, Turkey was nervous about losing their part of what might have become Kurdistan, Syria was in disarray, and Saudi Arabia was nervous about conflict on its borders.

THE PLACE AND LEGACY OF BRITAIN'S MILITARY POWER
Great Britain created the largest, most diverse empire the world has ever seen. In 1922 it covered twenty-two per cent of the world's landmass and twenty per cent of the global population and it governed much of the seven oceans. Much of this was done by force of arms, against indigenous populations, competing European or local powers.

The British were good at recruiting other countries' young men to fight their wars. In global wars we have relied on the Gurkhas, the Canadians, the Australians, New Zealanders, and in Burma, 1942 to 1945, the Rhodesian Rifles.

The Second World War changed all that. In 1945, Britain was almost bankrupt, owing vast sums to the Americans. Manpower for the Army was short, especially against the competing demands of industry: 'get the men back into the factories'. In 1945 there were 4.7 million men and women under arms. By 1960 this had decreased to 521,000. The current number is about 150,000.

However much it might have been regretted, the retreat from Empire was inevitable, due partly to nationalist pressures within colonies and possessions, partly through British impecunity and partly through sometimes subtle, sometimes not, American pressure. (SEAC, headquartered in Ceylon (modern Sri Lanka) with an official title of Southeast Asia Command, was dubbed by the Americans as 'Save England's Asiatic Colonies'). Woodrow Wilson's Fourteen Points, set out in 1918, also contributed.

The United Kingdom managed the retreat from Empire reasonably well. Some retreats were, of course, accompanied by bloody and tragic wars of faction upon faction. The Hindu/Muslim massacres during the partition of India are often portrayed as the responsibility of the British, but it must not be forgotten that it was Hindu killing Muslim and Muslim killing Hindu. What British military action there was, was largely in their own defence. Despite this awful episode, the Raj managed to leave behind what is today the world's largest democracy, reasonably peaceful, at least internally, and on the path to prosperity for all.

Happy legacies of the British Empire are of course Canada (gained full independence in 1982), Australia (gained full independence in 1986) and New Zealand (gained full independence in 1986) among the world's leading democracies. There are many others, too many to list here. Indian, Canadian, Australian and New Zealand troops fought besides United Kingdom troops during the Second World War and were indispensable in defeating the Nazi state and expansionist Japan.

Many people imagine that these British and colonial (now, you would say 'Commonwealth') troops 'won the war' and there is no doubt that the British, with its empire, contributed mightily. Certainly we 'stood alone' from September 1939 to December 1941 but the Second World War was ultimately won with American matériel and, never forget, Russian lives.

The legacy of Empire and victory in the Second World War lives on, giving British politicians a false sense of British innate superiority. This plays well with the electorate; witness Tony Blair's 'Cool Britannia' and Tory 'Global Britain'. While pride in our history is justified and should be encouraged, there are some aspects – particularly racial discrimination – to be condemned.

The real tragedy of Britain's history, its 'retreat from Empire' and being on the 'right side' in the Second World War, is the temptation – usually taken – of resting on our imperial laurels. British superiority is an illusion, based on fond memories of the industrial revolution, an imagined racial superiority, and speaking the language of Shakespeare and Trollope.

Unfortunately, the rest of the world caught up and, while we were basking in imagined glory, overtook us. Although the UK is the fifth largest economy in the world, we are about 23rd in terms of GDP per head. As an illustration of our lack of economic performance, a substantial portion of Britain's defence spending is based on imports. Why can't we make the things ourselves?

As a member of the United Nations Security Council Permanent Five, Britain undoubtedly has a place in the world, as does its military. But that place must be tempered by the fact that there are several much larger economies, more ambitious hegemons and much larger territories than Great Britain. What military power we are left with must be used with great focus, with a clear political aim and with public support. Who, among the United Kingdom's population, really wants a 'pivot to the Indo-Pacific' region, or Ranger Regiments being 'active around the world' and operating 'globally on a persistent basis'?

The electorate might prefer better hospitals, schools and roads, but security must trump these provisions. The key questions are whether these plans for Ranger Regiments, however embryonic, contribute to our security, or whether they help trade, or promote world peace or liberal democracy in the host countries. British hubris prevents our seeing the world clearly and planning and building for Britain's new place in a changing world. Military power will have a vital part in this, but it needs to be based less on a 'gung-ho' attitude ('Global Britain'), less on expediency, less on contingency, and more on painstaking analysis and execution and a realistic realisation of our capabilities and interests. The Empire was built by force of arms but held together by competent and just civil administration. The Colonial Civil Service was the best in the world, and something to be proud of.

British arms, whether for counterinsurgency, peacekeeping, liberal interventionism or fighting wars, can make an invaluable contribution to peace within nations and between them, but only if organised violence is used *in conjunction with the aim of a just civil administration.* The intercessions in Malaya, Sierra Leone and many others demonstrate this. Afghanistan, Iraq and Libya prove it too, but by their absence. Most of all, we should never forget that war, the use of organised violence, should always be based on achieving a lasting peace.

BRITAIN AND MILITARY POWER: A VERDICT

Nevertheless, looking at the whole picture since 1945, what emerges is one of a confident, capable military with adequate capacity and reserves to intervene successfully in small wars, fight rebel armies, and engage in counterinsurgency, Peace Support Operations and policing.

Interventions in major wars are more demanding, but are usually undertaken as part of a coalition, led by the United States, or as part of NATO, sometimes with a mandate from the United Nations.

Against a record of success in Malaya and Sierra Leone and other Peace Support Operations, obvious military and thereby political failures amount to: Basra, Iraq (detailed in Chapter 7 in *About War*); Afghanistan, where there was no coherent plan or command structure, and in any case whatever objectives might have been imagined, were completely unrealistic; Libya, where the UK and others imagined that air power alone could resolve political issues; and Iraq overall, where there was insufficient influence over the Americans to insist on comprehensive post-war reconstruction, physical or political.

Since the end of World War II, Britain's hands have to a large extent been tied by decolonisation, and several other factors. The United Kingdom sees itself as one of the five or six biggest economies in the world, as one of the five Permanent Members of the United Nation Security Council, as a nuclear-armed state, as having a 'special relationship' with the United States, and as a major global player. Disengaging from this role seems to be impossible, notwithstanding the withdrawal by Dennis Healey (UK defence secretary from 1964 to 1970) from 'East of Suez' in the mid to late 1960s and, over the years, more or less continual cuts to the armed services.

The current conservative government reaffirms this global role and we cover the *Integrated Review of Security, Defence, Development and Foreign Policy* in the next section, which envisages a military presence in various locations worldwide. But there are fewer troops now than there have ever been. Given the depleted dimensions of the armed forces and the austerity cuts to diplomacy, we must wonder if the military have the physical and even intellectual resources, and the perspective to manage this to useful political effect?

LIBERAL INTERVENTIONISM

Liberal interventionism is a part of Liberal internationalism, a foreign policy doctrine arguing that the best way to peace and harmony among independent states in an anarchic system is through encouraging states to become liberal democracies. Concomitant with that, free trade and market economics will prevail, adding to economic wealth. It has its roots in British nineteenth-century political discourse. Henry Temple, Lord Palmerston, is usually credited. Liberal internationalism itself was developed in the 20th century by U.S. President Woodrow Wilson; reference his famous 'Fourteen Points', advanced at the Paris Peace Conference in Versailles 1919/1920

The hope is that, via a gradual development of international politics from anarchy to institutions such as the UN and the rule of law, democracy will emerge globally. It is essentially an idealist concept, to be contrasted with a realist outlook: isolationism and non-intervention in another country's affairs. However, we must not get carried away between the effects on foreign policy of idealism and realism.

Essentially, Liberal internationalism connects foreign policy to ethical roots. When Robin Cook was foreign secretary (1997 to 2001) under the first Blair government, he declared that, henceforth, his intention was to add an ethical dimension to foreign policy. There was some scepticism: Douglas Hurd, an old-hand diplomat retorted, 'What else?' Blair himself echoed this aspiration in his 1999 Chicago speech on The Doctrine of International Community. This is detailed in About War.

Liberal interventionism suggests that liberal, democratic states should intervene in troubled countries with aid, humanitarian assistance and support for the institutions of the state, as in Sierra Leone, and such institutions as the judiciary, the intelligence sector, the civil service and other key state institutions, if necessary, with militarily force.

The 'Responsibility to Protect' is also intended to protect civilians in armed conflict and to protect populations from genocide, war crimes, ethnic cleansing and crimes against humanity.

Implicit in the Integrated Review, which we review in Chapter 4, is that Blair's doctrine still resonates in Britain's foreign policy, but many assumptions on which it is based have changed. Commentators decrying that liberal interventionism is dead or doesn't work, usually refer to Afghanistan or Iraq, rather than Sierra Leone and other successful interventions. Blair's doctrine may be slightly out of vogue, but it is still valid. Kuwait (1991) was a great success.

3. THE DEFENCE OF THE UNITED KINGDOM

Can the United Kingdom defend itself?

We ought to begin by asking the most fundamental question of all, one that is often evaded: can the United Kingdom defend itself?

No is the answer, but we operate with and within NATO, where Article 5 of the treaty commits 'each member state to consider an armed attack against one member state, in Europe or North America, to be an armed attack against them all'. Article 5 has been invoked once: by the United States after the 11 September attacks in 2001 on the World Trade Center and the Pentagon.

But would it work in the event? In 2019, President Emmanuel Macron of France suggested that NATO was 'brain dead', but that may have been a reaction to the then U.S. president Donald Trump's ambivalence towards NATO. Popular support across Europe for NATO and Article 5 is mixed; only about half of the respective electorates felt they would support NATO in a military venture. To put it bluntly, would British parents be happy seeing their sons and daughters die defending Bulgaria? Would NATO intervene in a spat between Greece and Turkey – both of which are NATO members?

Threats no longer necessarily come in the form of foreign troops wading ashore through the surf. If hostile *military* actions – the term is *kinetic* – are the main means, non-kinetic are just as likely: cyber-attacks, assassinations (think of the Russian attempt to poison Sergei Skripal and his daughter Yulia with Novichok on British soil in 2018). The previous volume, *About War*, explained in detail 'thirteen sectors and practices at different moments and at different levels of intensity', taken from *World of War* (2020) by Paul Cornish and Kingsley Donaldson. We seem to be surprised and maybe offended by these actions – after all, it's not real war – and have only a limited concept of how to counter them.

For years, Russian submarines have played hide and seek with British submarines around the North Atlantic and vice versa. It is become something of a game, and good training, for submariners. Russian aircraft also fly close to British airspace and, in some cases, RAF jets scramble – largely to let them know we are aware of them. Again, good practice for a real emergency. But, this practice apart, can we defend ourselves?

The UK has invested in cyber capabilities, both defensive and offensive, but the degradation of conventional arms concerns military leaders and specialists. According to the *Daily Telegraph* (September 2016), General Sir Richard Barrons, former head of the UK's Joint Forces Command, sent a private memorandum to Michael Fallon, then defence secretary. In it, he laid bare the shortcomings of equipment configuration and command and control mechanisms for the armed forces. He claimed that there 'was no military plan to defend the UK in a conventional conflict.' This is particularly worrying, given the question in the Chilcot Inquiry into the Iraq debacle.

Barrons also asked who was in charge of the Iraq campaign; Downing Street, PJHQ (Permanent Joint Headquarters, Northwood), the MoD, or the Americans or the generals on the spot? He went on to say: 'The army is not equipped to fight a rival professional land force and is significantly outgunned by Russia, whose conventional weaponry is impressive.'

Barrons' last comment is chilling, given Russia's predilection for actions that are not quite cricket: *It is not necessary to shoot down all the UK's Joint Strike Fighters, only to know how to murder in their beds the 40 or so people who can fly them.* Let's hope that in a war with Russia, they do not have maps of the Officers' Messes on RAF stations ...

But security concerns have an awkward habit of turning up unexpectedly, rather like Donald Rumsfeld's 'unknown unknowns'.

What then of the future *use* of military force? How does the government address this?

Every five years, the UK government publishes a 'Strategic Review', concerning defence and security. The reception this receives from journalists, think tanks, academics and the military themselves varies considerably, the most frequent complaint being they are but excuses for 'salami slicing' the defence budget. In many cases, this jibe is justified.

Before looking at the 2020 Strategic Review (publication was delayed until 2021 due to the COVID pandemic), it is worth looking at the catchily titled *2015 National Security Strategy and Strategic Defence and Security Review*, published on 23 November 2015. This is ninety-six pages of sometimes turgid prose about threats, the government's response and how a reorganisation of the current armed forces will enable them to cope with more tasks with just the same manpower. The 2015 Review identified twenty 'Priority Risks', ranging from terrorism to Environmental Events such as animal diseases or severe air pollution. (The sceptic might grimace at the 'animal diseases' comment in the light of the COVID-19 pandemic.).

The Economist judged that Britain had reasserted itself as a 'serious military power', Professor Malcolm Chalmers of RUSI headed his verdict as 'Steady as she goes' and the then prime minister, David Cameron, claimed the U.S. president, Barack Obama, was 'clearly delighted' with the results of the UK's defence review, with American officials reported to have been concerned at the weakening of UK defence capability caused by previous cuts.

So, overall, the review was well received, but, reading the detailed commentaries, the reactions were something of a shrug of the shoulders.

NATO was not questioned, nor the UK's nuclear deterrent, other than to say that these would continue. It was only about defence and security in the (then) current environment, with a lot of explicit and implicit assumptions.

One big lacuna of the 2015 review was that it did not examine in detail what has been learnt, politically and militarily, from previous diplomatic initiatives and military deployments. For example, over the years, the British Army supported by the RAF, the Royal Navy and the Marines, has conducted many counterinsurgency (COIN) campaigns (see in particular Sierra Leone in the previous chapter). Now, despite many successes and some failures, counterinsurgency seemed to be off the agenda. Although the disasters in Afghanistan and Iraq weighed heavily, the whole notion of counterinsurgency now seemed not to be part of the military portfolio. So it didn't work? Why? How?

Peace Support Operations are mentioned several times, and Britain's military has contributed to many UN PSOs over the years. They continue to do so, in terms of both troop deployment and training exercises. But PSOs are not entirely different from counterinsurgency in that the forces will have to be deployed in far-off lands, with the associated logistical challenges. The Sierra Leone example shows that that success was down to a combined COIN / PSO operation, both components of which have challenging diplomatic and political aspects.

The key to the use of military power is to convert it into a political gain. In most cases this means a better political relationship between protagonists, who may be a legitimate government versus rebels/insurgency, etc., or between internal and external protagonists (most civil wars are influenced and even supported by external actors) or between a whole nation state and the local hegemon. Political gain must mean a better political relationship and laying the ground for an enduring peace.

There is no mention of this fundamental philosophy in the 2015 Review. Focusing on 'Priority Risks' and an essentially reactive approach to the use of military power may have indicated a fundamental change in the government's approach to the United Kingdom's armed forces.

Currently, Britain's armed forces are premised on six principles:
First, the defence of the United Kingdom and overseas territories.
This is non-discretionary. Whatever the level of the assessed threat might be, no government could reduce the size of the armed forces below critical mass, and in any case, no government could get away with it from the political perspective. Domestically, it would mean electoral defeat; externally, we would look weak to our allies, and also to our as yet undefined competitors.
Second, the defence of Europe.
Whereas we would not anticipate an attack on the British Isles, there are clear risks to NATO's eastern members and, in particular, although discounted by most experts, to the Baltic states: Estonia, with one quarter Russian ethnic population; Latvia, with about the same, and Lithuania. Lithuania has only a small proportion of ethnic Russians but is bounded by Belarus, a Russia-friendly state, and Kaliningrad, a Russian exclave. Russia also has 'previous', as the cop shows describe it, with their war with Georgia in 2008, their annexation of the Crimea in 2014 and their invasion of Donbas in eastern Ukraine, also in 2014.

A regular tactic for the old Soviet government was to 'seed' any country in the Soviet bloc with ethnic Russians. The current Russian government (well, let's say Mr Putin) might then use this as an excuse for an invasion to protect the Russian population. This is much the same as Hitler did with the Sudeten Germans in Czechoslovakia … it didn't go well for Czechoslovakia.

Russia is often held up as a major threat but it is difficult to get an objective view on this. On the one hand, there are clear Russian transgressions of international law, but no worse than the West's various adventures since the collapse of the Soviet Union. The Russo-Georgian War was nominally in support of the South Ossetians. Crimea was annexed by Russia in 2014 but many, particularly the Russians and the ethnic Russians in Crimea (two thirds) consider Crimea to be Russian anyway. Nikita Khrushchev, General Secretary of the Communist Party of the Soviet Union 'gave' Crimea to Ukraine in 1954 on the basis that they were more able to manage reconstruction and trying to do it from Moscow.

Having a predominantly Russian population, the Russians were supposedly supporting a separatist region in the Donbas in eastern Ukraine. *Third, wars or military deployments (defensive or offensive) in conjunction with NATO.*

These are discretionary commitments: out of area operations such as Yugoslavia and the International Security Assistance Force (ISAF) in Afghanistan.

Fourth, peacekeeping operations in troubled states.

This is partly discretionary; the UK does not contribute to every peacekeeping operation. But, as a permanent member of the United Nations Security Council (the 'P5'), we may feel more obliged to contribute.

Fifth, aid to civil society.

Sometimes unnoticed, but always welcome is the help and assistance that the military provides to the population in times of crisis. The RAF has evacuated UK citizens from war zones, the Army has provided security, for example, during the Olympics in London, and the Royal Navy has used its helicopters to ferry injured people from accidents.

Sixth, ceremonial duties.

Such as state weddings and funerals, guards of honour for foreign visiting dignitaries, etc.

4. GLOBAL BRITAIN IN A COMPETITIVE AGE

*The government attempts to collate foreign policy
and the use of military force*

*The Integrated Review of Security, Defence, Development and Foreign
Policy, 2021* (thankfully known as *The Integrated Review*, or IR)

The *Integrated Review* was originally announced on 26 February 2020
and was billed as 'the biggest review of our foreign, defence, security and
development policy since the end of the Cold War'. It was published on
16 March 2021, having been delayed by the COVID pandemic, followed
on 22 March by another document entitled *Defence in a Competitive
Age*, which focused more on the armed forces. Here, we deal with these
separately. The IR promised to:

> *i) Define the Government's ambition for the UK's role in the world
> and the long-term strategic aims for our national security and
> foreign policy.*
>
> *ii) Set out the way in which the UK will be a problem-solving and
> burden-sharing nation, examining how we work more effectively
> with our allies.*
>
> *iii) Determine the capabilities we need for the next decade and
> beyond to pursue our objectives and address the risks and
> threats we face.*
>
> *iv) Identify the necessary reforms to government systems and
> structures to achieve these goals.*
>
> *v) Outline a clear approach to implementation over the next decade
> and set out how we will evaluate delivery of our aims.*

Reception was cautiously enthusiastic: few, if any, pedants asked why this might be 'new' and what might have been the previous procedures for linking foreign policy and defence. *Problem-solving* and *burden-sharing* were left undefined. It was endorsed by the House of Commons Foreign Affairs Select Committee and, overall, was thought to be a major turning point in Britain's attitude to foreign affairs and the use of military force.

But it was *pre-empted* …

On 16 June 2020, the prime minister announced that the Foreign and Commonwealth Office (FCO) would merge with the Department for International Development (DFID), to become the Foreign, Commonwealth & Development Office (FCDO). This appears to pre-empt the *Integrated Review*, as one might have imagined that clause (iv) above, 'Identify the necessary reforms to Government systems and structures to achieve these goals' would come first.

This announcement was also in the middle of the COVID pandemic and, although it was thought the worst of that pandemic appeared to be over (it wasn't), better timing might have been appropriate.

Following this, in November 2020, the prime minister announced an increase in defence spending: according to RUSI's Malcolm Chalmers, this was 'an exceptional multi-year settlement that provides an extra £16.5 billion above the growth already promised in the Conservative Manifesto. Over the four years, this represents a real-term increase of between 10% and 15% in the Defence budget: equivalent to some £4 billion more annually than had been promised'. However, there was little indication of what a new or revised foreign policy might be, save some rumours in the press suggesting that the FCDO budget could be reduced by up to £4 billion in the Spending Review.

However, in a sneak preview …

In the same speech in the House of Commons, the prime minister also announced the 'first, though undocumented outcome' of the *Integrated Review* of foreign, defence, security and development policy. After recognising that 'The international situation is now more perilous and intensely competitive than at any time since the cold war', he announced eight Type 26 Frigates, five Type 31 Frigates and that the carrier Queen Elizabeth would lead a British and allied (NATO? European?) task group on 'the most ambitious deployment for two decades, encompassing the Mediterranean, the Indian Ocean, and East Asia.' One might have hoped that an increase in military hardware would have been announced *after* the publication of the *Integrated Review* but however poor the sequencing, the review itself, integrating the FCO and DFID, and the increased defence spending were cautiously welcomed by the commentariat, the think tanks, consultancies, academics and, most of all, the defence suppliers. All stood ready to benefit in terms of budgets, grants and salaries. Most of all, it was welcomed by the military itself, who could now lobby, especially among themselves, for a good share of the booty.

As part of this re-evaluation of *Review of Security, Defence, Development and Foreign Policy* – at 190 pages for the combined documents plus articles from the commentariat – it is challenging to distinguish between what amounts to continuity and what is really new. So here we just identify those provisions of the IR that affect security, defence and the armed forces. We also look particularly at the comments on the UK's nuclear deterrent.

The Main Provisions of the *Integrated Review* of Security, Defence, Development and Foreign Policy (2021)

The *Integrated Review* raised many expectations about a reset of objectives, capabilities and resources. As is usual when these reviews are published to some acclaim, the implications – or the lack thereof – sank in: reservations started to emerge.

Who could possibly disagree with seeing a UK in 2030 as 'stronger, more secure, prosperous and resilient'. But one cannot conjure these things up simply by aspiration: there must be detailed explication of the *how* as well as the *what*. At 111 pages, including the appendix, this perception of shortfall is understandable, and it's not helped by the whole document being structured in such a way as to deny easy access. There is a foreword from the prime minister, another page of the prime minister's vision and some nice graphics where one might start suspecting that one Monsieur Pangloss might have had a hand in the compilation.

This suspicion is reinforced in the next few pages where we are presented with an 'Overview' of thirty-seven paragraphs, some of which might raise an eyebrow or two. For example, Paragraph 4 says that Britain 'will play a leading international role in collective security, multilateral governance, tackling climate change and health risks, conflict resolution and poverty reduction.' Regarding poverty reduction, we have now reduced our overseas aid budget, and some would point out that we have increasing poverty at home, with the number of food banks increasing all the time. And with the current (early 2022) increasing energy prices, this can only get worse.

In Paragraph 18, *sustaining the UK's openness as an open society and economy*, is difficult to reconcile with the 'hostile environment', and lorries driving around with 'go home' on the side, invoked by Theresa May when she was UK prime minister from 2016 to 2019.

But it is *Global Britain* in Paragraph 17 that is undefined. The IR says 'this is a *practice* (sic, a policy or a strategy?) best defined by actions rather than words', which is a very good way of not bothering with any definition at all. It is all reminiscent of the old jibe 'as the mood takes him' (the minister). There is very little mentioned about how we are regarded internationally or where the 'leading international' role might operate. Where might our armed forces be forward positioned? Latin America? Unlikely. The Far East? Unlikely. The Middle East? The Black Sea? Possible, but where is the overall political objective and, dare we say, *strategy* for this region.

My own preference would be for a focus on Africa, a continent with enormous possibilities and natural resources but plagued by rebel movements and frequent coups. Many countries in Africa were also old imperial colonies, and there might therefore be some cultural and political overlap with them. Notwithstanding that, it is a tragedy that at the time of writing, the French are moving out of the Sahel and so, presumably, are the British forces. One might suspect that Tony Blair's *Commission for Africa* report has been rubbished and binned because of disdain for Tony Blair himself. My own reaction to that view would be that the source of the disdain would be that, in his time, he was a political winner, unlike many other politicians, following Enoch Powell's avowal that 'all political careers end in failure'. If the invasion of Iraq in 2003 had been a success, Tony Blair would be the hero of our time.

There is then a section on principal continuities, reaffirming our relationships with the United States, NATO, tackling crime, upholding universal human rights, sustainable development goals, and an open and innovative digital economy. One of the paragraphs has girls' education (though it's not clear whether this is a continuity or a change), and one could almost hear someone looking over the shoulder of whoever was drafting this and suggesting 'you better put in a bit about girls' education'. But then in May 2021, there was a headline saying: *UK aid cuts will mean 700,000 fewer girls get an education, NGOs say.*

Then there is another shaded section, advertising *some significant changes and shifting in policy.* Some of these are repeats, like shaping the international order, Europe, climate, but with the addition of space, but there are two new provisions: scientific technology, where the UK will be *a science and technology superpower*, a pivot to the Indo-Pacific region, and a promise to create armed forces that are '*both prepared for war fighting and more persistently engaged worldwide through forward deployment, training, capacity building and education*'. Oh, and by the way, they will have '*full-spectrum capabilities*'. (Note to MOD: please explain this term.)

And, at this point, we are only up to page 24 of the 111 pages. However, this sets the scene for the second document, *Defence in a Competitive Age*, which is concerned largely with the armed forces.

What is missing from the *Integrated Review* is any reference to previous strategic reviews: how did they fare? What lessons were learned from them? Were in fact all the changes presaged in the previous strategic reviews implemented? Were they successful? The 2015 strategic defence and security review made any number of unfulfilled and, let's face it, unfulfillable promises. Most of all, for a truly *integrated* strategic review there should be some mention of budget. Let's accept that the government has committed to spending £188 billion on defence over the next four years – an increase of £24 billion, or fourteen per cent – many governments seem to fall into a habit of announcing such things, and then rowing back on them later. Forty new hospitals were going to be built – still? HS2 extensions, overseas aid commitments all fall into this category. We just wait until the defence budget does the same.

What did we spend over the past five years? How did we spend it? Was it worth it? Did we get value for money? And most of all, are we improving in this particular field? The MOD does not have a great reputation for budgetary consistency. Various headlines over the years claim that the MOD has a vast black hole of commitments without any obvious source of filling it – up to £35 billion it is said. Even more mysteriously, it disappears, but then any competent accountant can turn a profit into a loss … it's slightly more difficult to turn a loss into a profit though.

Let us accept that the government has committed to spending £188 billion on defence over the next four years and that this is a genuine increase of £24 billion … There is another niggle – easy to pass over, but absolutely vital …

Almost every paragraph in the introduction, vision, overview, principal continuities, significant changes and shifts involves the word *will*. Now, in terms of strategic planning, it is absolutely vital to get a clear idea of the overall objectives, but past history, current performance, the environment, operational constraints, overall policies, strategy, plans, implementation, process, control mechanisms and, as mentioned above, budget, should all have a look in. They don't. This document would not pass a first-year MBA exam.

Also, some of the current ministers in the government cut their teeth in the white heat of front-line journalism. One can only imagine what the sub-editors would have thought of the *Integrated Review*, but one suspects they might have got through quite a few blue pencils …

DEFENCE IN A COMPETITIVE AGE

The *Integrated Review* was published on 16 March 2021, closely followed by the second document, focusing on the armed forces and their use, entitled *Defence in a Competitive Age*.

At first sight, this is an impressive document. The foreword, from the Secretary of State for Defence, recognises the *massive change* that has occurred over the past few years, but he warns against *previously battle winning but now outdated capabilities.*

- Just a note about organisational change: having helped many different types of organisation *change*, I note one common feature. Almost everybody in an organisation will recognise the need to *change*, will advocate *change*, and even lay out exactly what *change* needs to happen. But the other remarkable thing is that none of this applies to themselves. Armed forces, please note.

One can immediately see that this document is slightly at odds with the *Global Britain*, problem-solving and a force-for-good agenda of the *Integrated Review*. *Defence in a Competitive Age* seems to be more 'assessing and dealing with threats' orientated. It might be churlish to identify this, but there does seem to be a divergence here. This is especially so since after claiming that 'the armed forces, working with the of government, must think and act differently, that they should no longer be held as a force of last resort but become more present and active around the world, operating below the threshold of open conflict to uphold our values and secure our interests, partner our friends and enable our allies, in both the Euro Atlantic (not defined) and the Indo-Pacific (not defined) or, (heaven help us), 'beyond'.

Perhaps the Secretary of State has watched too much *Star Trek*. The UK seems to have dropped everything to do with liberal interventionism as such, with Peace Support Operations focused more on training other forces than in participating.

Over the years, strategic reviews have claimed to be oriented in subtle and sometimes not so subtle ways. For example, some are threat-orientated, some are capabilities-driven, some effects-based (though one might find it difficult to imagine what 'non-effects-based' effort might be) and some foreign-policy led. Sceptics – and there are many in this particular area – might point out that the real driver for strategic reviews has always been constraints imposed by the Treasury.

Defence in a Competitive Age puts the various threats at the very heart of its philosophy. And there are certainly enough of them: eighteen in all. Some of these are to be expected: state-based threats or violent terrorist groups. Some might simply be new weapons technology, such as high-energy weapons and electromagnetic rail guns. One surprise is that there is no mention of battlefield nuclear weapons. These are weapons with a smaller yield that could be used against an airfield, port or a large carrier. Whatever the conflict, it is the problems associated with an enemy's use of a battlefield nuclear bomb that is probably the most serious threat we face if we ever get into a hot war.

Inevitably, *Defence in a Competitive Age* says that the armed forces will need 'new doctrines, new operating methods, new capabilities and new partners' if they are to counter our enemies.

Commentary on the *Integrated Review of Security, Defence, Development and Foreign Policy, 2021* and *Defence in a Competitive Age*

Professor Malcolm Chalmers, deputy director-general of RUSI, published his first comments on the review as: *The Integrated Review: The UK as a Reluctant Middle Power?* He concluded that 'the *Integrated Review* accepts that UK foreign policy needs to be based not only on permanent institutions and alliances but also on flexible issue-based coalitions more suited to a multipolar world. It also acknowledges the importance of integrating economic security and prosperity into a strategy for national security'. This was one mark of distinction, but he also concluded that the IR 'fails to fully acknowledge the depths of the challenges – economic, political and military – that will face the UK in the coming years or the necessity of making difficult choices in the allocation of scarce resources'. However, he concedes that 'In comparison to its predecessor reviews in 2015 and 2010, the Review is a marked step forward, and provides an articulate contribution to the national conversation. But there is much more to be said, and disputed, in the years to come.'

Intriguingly, given the objective of being a 'problem-solving and burden-sharing nation' as part of the 'Global Britain' agenda, Chalmers also declared that 'The Doctrine of the International Community', expounded in Tony Blair's 1999 speech, supporting a rules-based international system no longer applies. The Blair doctrine is explained in my previous book, *About War*. This doctrine reinforced, rather than invented, the concept of liberal interventionism, detailed in the panel at the end of Chapter 2. It *appears* that the whole idea of liberal interventionism is now dead, though it may make be a resurgence.

Neither does Chalmers refer to the excellent article by his colleague, Peter Roberts, also of RUSI (also detailed in *About War*), entitled 'Designing Conceptual Failure in Warfare, the Misguided Path of the West'. This is a complementary view to the Cornish / Donaldson book *War 2020* (also detailed in *About War*). *War 2020* described 'Thirteen sectors and practices at different moments and at different levels of intensity' to an enemy's potential hostile actions, which means on the one hand a different configuration of our forces, but mainly differently focused political control. There is little, if any, recognition of this in the *Review*.

Professor Paul Cornish, of Cityforum, in his review of the *Integrated Review* also observes that it is difficult to disagree with the foreign policy agenda, with the implication that it is all too good to be true. He also points out the difficulty of making predictions, suggesting that 'the very last thing that the IR needs is the pretence of certainty'.

Leading and managing strategic workshops – which I have done often – frequently shows that assumptions generally held to be true can always be, and should be, questioned. An intriguing exercise is to demand of strategic practitioners what assumptions they have made in coming to their conclusions and thus plans. Usually, there is little that cannot be shaken about and sometimes turned on its head.

Cornish also questioned whether the *Integrated Review*, or at least the defence document, was *genuinely strategic*, concluding that the 2021

UK defence review would 'invite criticism in terms that have been heard too often in the past – that the UK's national strategy is incoherent and the defence posture is both under strength and over stretched'.

From an MBA / Business School point of view (no apologies for that) the *Integrated Review of Security, Defence, Development and Foreign Policy, 2021* looks very much like a product without a market. The avatar for the product might be military force, but what of the market? What of the 'customers' (avatar: the enemy)? What might our armed forces be called upon to do in the future? The *Integrated Review* suggests 'war fighting on a frontal basis', but also mentions our 'little used tanks'. Under the slogan of 'permanent and persistent global engagement', a new Ranger Regiment (a force of four battalions) will become 'more present and active around the world'. Operating 'globally on a persistent basis' from their bases in 'strategic hubs', these troops will 'support and conduct special operations discreetly in risk environment's and take on 'some tasks traditionally done by special forces'. It all sounds exciting but … what for?

One must ask if our armed forces have the resources for this, given that they will also have to support Peace Support Operations. And, again, what happened to counterinsurgency? Sierra Leone was an exemplar of a combined approach: PSO and COIN. Is this now all in the past? Any campaign requires that military force must be integrated with political and diplomatic efforts. What of these?

Professor Cornish concluded that *Defence in a Competitive Age* and, by implication, the *Integrated Review* itself was 'Incoherent, under strength and overstretched'.

The overall verdict on the *Integrated Review* and, by implication, *Defence in a Competitive Age* is best left to Max Hastings, writing in *The Telegraph*, the house journal for the Tory party. He disdained both Boris Johnson and the *Integrated Review*, stating (slightly modified): 'but while he' (Boris Johnson, the prime minister) 'excels at articulating such objectives, he lacks the application, and sincere concern for others, to pursue them effectively. The government's *Integrated Review* of defence exemplified this. It represents an admirable statement of where Britain would like to go, bereft of plausible explanations of how it might get there, especially since the prime minister has led us into isolation' (presumably a reference to Brexit). Hastings made no mention of budget, but we can be sure he would if asked.

The *Integrated Review* was conceived and produced as if surrounded by a wall of mirrors (Cornish suggested 'an echo chamber'). While there is a place for inspirational leadership, such documents and plans must face up to circumstances when, as the Americans say, the rubber meets the road. Various Tory party manifestoes have advanced the idea of 'Global Britain', but without any rationale, diplomatic or financial, to back it up. There are vague, unquantified references to trade, ignoring a discernible trend to partial defence autarky. One point to pick up from Professor Cornish's comments about whether the review is truly strategic, is the concept of 'Grand Strategy'.

GRAND STRATEGY: FUNDAMENTAL OR A CHIMERA?
Some military leaders bemoan the lack of any 'Grand Strategy' for the UK's armed forces. Do we need an overarching template of what we're all about, how we make our way in the world and what use we will we make of military power?

An exemplar of this is an article entitled 'Reclaiming the Art of British Strategic Thinking', in the *RUSI Journal* (February/March 2010). Major General Sir Paul Newton, one-time Assistant Chief of the Defence Staff, Air Vice-Marshal Paul Colley and Brigadier Andrew Sharpe – all, one might expect, experienced military leaders – assert that the UK's policies lack any detailed and enduring 'grand strategic manifesto'. Furthermore, they suggest that we (Who? *We?*) have let slip both the mechanisms and more importantly the grammar with which to conduct the relevant strategic discourse within and around defence. This intellectual decay extends well beyond the Ministry of Defence, to Whitehall's machinery and culture. The rest of the article has the usual references to Clausewitz, political objectives, grammar, nature, etc. They illustrate the poverty of thinking in the British military today. Since they are all one-star generals and above, one is bound to ask of them: what exactly were you doing, general, when you took the Queen's shilling?

Any military deployment must be congruent with achieving a better relationship between the protagonists (even if the military is a third party) and providing a basis for a lasting peace. This must be based on exhaustive political, cultural and military intelligence. Most of all, the conversion rate of military success and political change – or at least a good estimate of it – must be imagined before any action is taken. This represents a major challenge, and when British lives are at stake, to say nothing of civilian lives, considerable effort should go into this analysis. Who, then, is actually leading the political campaign?

Some of the successes of the British military in counterinsurgency have been where there is a clear political vision and an undisputed political leader: Malaysia, Sierra Leone and Northern Ireland are good examples. We can be sure that the current conservative government would claim to have a clear Grand Strategy, manifest in 'pivot to the Indo-Pacific region' or 'Ranger Regiments' and 'strategic hubs', even if they do operate 'globally on a persistent basis'. But recall the original promises made when the *Integrated Review* was announced:

'Global Britain'. What exactly does this mean? Achievable or not? Are we prepared to make whatever investment? Is it worth it?

'A problem-solving and burden-sharing nation'. There are about two dozen real problems, some quite close to home that need addressing. Do we have a plan, or even an opinion?

'Determine the capabilities.' There's very little about diplomatic and political insights.

'Identify the necessary reforms to Government systems and structure'. As ever, but there needs to be more political control for military deployments. (Consider Chilcot.)

COMMENTARY ON THE FUTURE USE OF MILITARY POWER
Every New Age is heralded largely through historical retrospection rather than contemporaneous scrutiny. Yet every New Age faces new and different challenges: political, economic, social and thereby military, many not recognised at the time. Whatever New Age we are now in, we can never be confident that a hostile force would not threaten the British Isles or our dependencies. There have been periods of relative peace in world history, but none lasted.

The 'Long Peace' describes the period following the end of the Second World War in 1945 to the present day. Although the Cold War, 1945 to 1991, saw the absence of a major war between the United States and the Soviet Union – the major powers – there were many other wars around the globe, many of which were proxy wars, sponsored by one of these two superpowers.

Unless and until we can safely say that there is no risk to the mainland United Kingdom or its dependent territories – and the consensus is that will be never – we will need military power. But you cannot have a little bit; the lead times are too long. The United States did a phenomenal job in rising to the industrial challenge of a war against Japan *as well as* Germany but only because it was protected by vast oceans to the east and west and was therefore more or less immune to attack.

The United Kingdom has a responsibility to see that our armed forces go into battle in foreign lands to face indeterminate threats properly prepared, well led and equipped with the best we can do.

Equipment needs to be planned, designed and sourced. This is becoming an increasingly lengthy process – ten years or more. Nuclear ships can take up to fifteen years to build, long after threats during the planning stage have evaporated or changed. Also, it takes time to train a military force. They need to be familiar with sophisticated electronic equipment, yet still be able to take 'traditional' offensive action against an enemy and to defend themselves. There is simply no substitute for field experience. Sending untrained troops into any deployment, one involving kinetic action or simple patrolling, would be irresponsible.

Training officers takes many years; senior generals evolve, they cannot be manufactured or recruited. Generals have to lead troops while managing and defeating a wide range of threats ranging from 'conventional' enemy troops though to insurgencies and ISIS-type movements. Modern threats cannot be met though militias or yeomen, as of old, or by raising an army by mobilising the freeman, through the fyrd, as was done in Anglo-Saxon times.

The public are rightly proud of our armed forces, but a younger generation in particular finds war irrational, messy and distasteful. We should not resist this sentiment, but construct a credible narrative as to why military force is necessary, what it can be used for, and what it can and cannot do. 'Send in the troops' has been a familiar refrain throughout modern history, but it needs to be credible to itself and to whatever opponent comes our way.

Is there a responsibility to stand shoulder to shoulder with the United States, whatever the cost? Yes, according to the latest *Integrated Review*. But the question is moot. It is an open question whether there is a parallel responsibility to the international community – insofar as that exists. Judging by the historical record, the United Kingdom has faced up to that responsibility well, with respectable results. The *Integrated*

Review suggests that the government has decided that we do indeed have such international responsibilities, but they are couched in the language of threats to ourselves, rather than to any notion of peace or justice for the billions of people who live under repressive regimes. But do we have the resources – military, economic and political – to face up to this responsibility?

The primary and overriding responsibility of the government, of whatever political persuasion, is the security of the United Kingdom. This may well best be achieved by co-operating wholeheartedly with Europe and the United States, and by playing a full role as one of the five permanent members of the United Nations Security Council. It will not be achieved by eschewing peace support operations, counterinsurgency and, ultimately, liberal interventionism. The forward-placed Ranger Regiment operating on a persistent basis seem to be going in another direction.

A Sceptical End Note on the *Integrated Review of Security, Defence, Development and Foreign Policy, 2021*

The *Integrated Review* makes several comments that are at odds with the current policy of the current government.

The IR indicates that the government will:

- '… sustain the UK's openness as a society and economy, underpinned by a shift to a more robust position on security and deterrence. This runs alongside a renewed commitment to the UK as a force for good in the world – defending openness, democracy and human rights.'

Where? How? Ranger Regiment? Becoming 'more present and active around the world'? 'Operating globally on a persistent basis'? It is difficult to see how these all match.

- 'To hold to account those involved in serious human rights violations and abuses.'

- This seems in contrast with our relationships with Saudi Arabia, Burma, Belarus, Russia, China, Syria, Somalia, Turkmenistan, Libya, Cuba, Bahrain, Sri Lanka, Sudan, Zimbabwe, Venezuela and Turkey.
- 'Contribute to our global reputation as a force for good and an S&T power'.

This seems to ignore that we import a substantial proportion of our Defence equipment.

- 'As a force for good in the world, the UK will remain sensitive to the plight of refugees and asylum seekers.' Hardly compatible with sending them to Rwanda!

This is difficult to reconcile with the government's hostile environment concept and buses bearing the slogan 'go home'. Most of the discourse about immigrants does not distinguish between refugees, economic migrants on one hand and legal and illegal immigration on the other.

The future is, of course, unknowable. The *Integrated Review* envisages a 'pivot' to the 'Indo-Pacific' region, as if we have little to do in Europe and the near abroad. But the potential flashpoints in a crescent from Svalbard to Yemen yield quite enough to be getting on with, politically, diplomatically and militarily.

Surely, there is enough to do in our hemisphere. A more sensible and achievable geographic focus for our diplomatic and military efforts might be Europe, the Mediterranean, the Near East and North Africa. In the Appendix, we lay out twenty geopolitical security risks. Clearly, being geographic, we exclude terrorism and threats like al-Qaeda or Islamic state, which are substantial. This is not to say that any of these are likely, but it would be comforting to know that the concepts outlined in the *Integrated Review* and *Defence in a Competitive Age* can comprehend and manage these threats.

5. CONTRARY VIEWS

Not everyone agrees that the world is an 'increasingly dangerous place' or that we should have the level of military power that we have.

Over the years, there has been a healthy pacifist movement, saying that military force is wicked, in that it inflicts death, destruction and misery on many people, or indeed unnecessary, in that many wars fail to meet their original objectives. We cover pacifism in Chapter 16 of this book. Insofar as pacifism is an idealist movement, a more structured argument is to be found from several academics and think tankers. First up is Steven Pinker, who claims that, in general, the world is more peaceful now.

In 2011, he published his book *The Better Angels of Our Nature*, the title taken from Abraham Lincoln's inaugural address in 1861. In it, Pinker argues that, over the long and even short term, human violence has declined. He claims, among other assertions, that the nation state's legitimate monopoly on the use of force has prevented individuals from seeking revenge; that commerce means that other people and peoples are more valuable as customers alive than dead and that the people in modern, civilised states take a more humanitarian approach to the victims of conflict.

He examines four 'inner demons' that might drive humans to violence. First, perhaps using Machiavelli's 'means to an end', is to use *violence* to steal what we want. Second, is *dominance*: the urge for authority, prestige, glory and power – very Roman. Third, is *revenge*: retribution for historic grievances – President Putin today.

Finally, comes *ideology*: a shared belief system, usually involving a vision of utopia that justifies violence in pursuit of unlimited good. We might be sceptical of *ideology*, as it may just be a belief system promoted by a leadership caucus of the nation state seeking power rather than for the benefit of the population. It rarely works anyway: even if we write off Fascism and Soviet era communism as simply extensions of the egos of Hitler and the USSR's leaders from Lenin to Brezhnev, and Mao Zedong, the classic example would be Islamicism (and within that, Sunnis v Shiites) – which seems to affect most Muslim states to some degree or other. Other religions, too, of course: Modi's growing Hindu state or the militant form of Buddhism that has caused so much trouble in Myanmar. In Afghanistan there are signs of strife between the Taliban and new strains of IS for whom the Taliban are seen to be dragging their feet in implementing extreme Islamic law. It's a moot point: is this ideology, being true to the cause, or simply an excuse for the acquisition of power and the perpetuation of the regime. The latter stages of Soviet communism witnessed a complete abnegation of the revolutionary drive.

Pinker's four 'angels' are: *empathy*, where we might feel someone else's suffering; *self-control*, where we might avoid acting on impulses and take a more measured approach; *moral sense*, where we think something just might be morally right (humanitarian assistance) or morally wrong (mass murder in another country) and *reason*, where humankind can examine things logically and objectively, an inheritance of the Age of Enlightenment.

Pinker's book was received enthusiastically by people such as Bill Gates, who stated that it was 'one of the most important books he had ever read.' Perhaps he ought to get out more. To some people it was 'convincing', 'well argued', 'marvellous' and a 'monumental achievement'. There were, however, many criticisms, some based on the statistical methodology, some more philosophical. The most edifying *negative* review came from theologian, David Bentley Hart, who wrote that 'in Pinker's book, one encounters the ecstatic innocence of a faith unsullied by prudent doubt. Furthermore, it reaffirms the human spirit's lunatic and heroic capacity to believe a beautiful falsehood not only in excess of the facts but in resolute defiance of them'. Finally, Hart says: 'by all means praise the modern world for what is good about it but spare us the mythology.'

So, is Pinker right? Has violence declined? And if we think it might have done, what time period should we use? Particularly if we are considering war, how do we define war? And how do we group massive, multinational conflicts with smaller border disputes?

Neometrics.com is the website run by Matthew White, an American author who wrote *The Great Big Book of Horrible Things*, published in 2011. White collates and reconciles various sources concerning violent deaths. According to his analysis, the 17th century saw some forty-four million violent deaths, the 18th century, eighteen million violent deaths. This sounds as if Pinker might be right, but then, the 19th century saw some forty-five million violent deaths. Both were trumped by the 20th century, with 200 million violent deaths. For reference, in the 21st century so far, there have been over one million violent deaths. Of course, these numbers are for violent deaths, not necessarily through war, and on the basis of a much larger population.

It is tempting to think of the 20th century as being a statistical anomaly, but humans driving violence is not something that we can easily measure. It is, however, difficult to sustain Pinker's argument about decreasing violence. We can discount both Matthew White and Steven Pinker. Even if we could reconcile the number of deaths and the destruction that wars and violence had caused, and even if the numbers cited were halved, the numbers of dead would still be appalling. Perhaps it is a matter of entropy. Some criminal gangs, particularly in the drug trade, are unrestrained in their violence, as the death toll in Mexico will show, whereas casual violence in most developed societies might empirically be declining – we no longer have to suffer highwayman when travelling! Steven Pinker's analysis is interesting and useful, but it's not a basis for foreign policy, or the use of military power.

Sir Simon Jenkins …

… is an author, journalist and the UK's national iconoclast treasure. He has persistently questioned whether we need quite as much military as we have, or whether we need it at all. *Guardian* headlines such as 'My once in a generation cut? The Armed Forces. All of them'. Or 'it is delusional to think Britain should be a global military power'. Or 'Does Britain really need the military?' All tell a similar story. One of his observations is that the existence of the military and its configuration has more to do with lobbying from the generals, the MoD and arms manufacturers than anything to do with strategy.

In June 2018 he wrote: 'No armed force threatens the United Kingdom, or has done for more than half a century. The idea that British nuclear missiles and "global reach" have kept our islands intact for that time is rubbish. So, the generals battle with the Treasury about being a "tier-one power" and "global influence for good", requiring "full-spectrum capability" and a "seat at the top table". Sources tell me that when Theresa May (British prime minister 2016 to 2019) asked Gavin Williamson (the then defence secretary – 2017 to 2019) what "tier one" actually meant, he had no answer. The emperor's clothes were made of clichés stitched with jargon.'

Paul Mason...

… is a journalist who writes about security. In an article in the *New Statesman* in January 2019, Paul Mason bewails the idea of Britain being a global power. 'Thanks to a combination of conservative cant, inter-service buffoonery and woefully illiterate MPs, we have this fantasy of 'global reach', an 'Imperial fantasy'. (as was Brexit, he adds). He suggests that 'global Britain' cannot be realistic 'with the Navy comprised of just nineteen big ships and an army that cannot even fill its manpower without employing migrants'. He adds that 'we don't want, or need, to fight Vladimir Putin, we simply need to deter his attempts to weaken our democracy, show leadership to a Europe full of tin pot crooks and redesign our Armed Forces in a way best adapted to meeting this threat.' Given misadventures such as Afghanistan and Iraq, not to mention Libya, he suggests that expeditionary wars should be off the agenda, and that we really need to concentrate on defending Europe.

Regarding NATO, Mason claims that the commitment to mutual defence is becoming 'dangerously undeliverable', particularly, he says, if it were 'preceded by a chaos-inducing hybrid warfare campaign, mobilising organised crime, propaganda outlets, high finance, corrupt politicians and the money of the American alt-right.'

He might well be right about that, but there is another angle. According to a recent international YouGov study, the support for NATO overall is declining in the UK, Germany and France, fortunately not accompanied by opposition movements. I say *fortunately* in that there is no obvious substitute for European security, and also that if there were to be a movement among European countries to leave NATO or to separate from NATO, it might well result in the Americans walking away. They've done it before. And although support for NATO has not fallen quite so much in America, it is still pretty low, at under half the population. In general, most people in NATO countries look favourably on their NATO commitments, but part of that depends on which country they were asked to defend. We ask elsewhere whether Scottish parents would be happy seeing their sons or daughters killed defending Bulgaria. (This has nothing to say about the natures of Scotland or Bulgaria, they simply represent the geographic extremes of Europe.) Chamberlain's infamous 1938 one-liner summing up Czechoslovakia (a far away country, between people of whom we know nothing) springs to mind at this point.

In a throwaway comment at the end of his piece, Mason also opines that we don't actually have the political capability to design strategy. However, he's wrong to assert that we lack a cross-party community of politicians, experts, academics and military capable of having an informed debate. There is a healthy and well-informed caucus of think tankers, consultants and academics perfectly capable of providing informed comment. It's just that ministers don't ask them to and don't listen when they do. One can almost hear Colonel Puffington of Much Binding in the Marsh harrumphing into his gin and tonic about lefties and the need to bring the natives under control.

The demise of the Soviet Union in 1990 gave the world an opportunity to go back to basics, consider foreign policy opportunities and constraints and, for the UK, to reset our position in the world for the 21st century. Instead, overtaken by American triumphalism, NATO was extended up to the border with Russia, deliberately, so it seems, to annoy the Russians. This is the basis of President Putin's chagrin. He claims that the United States has broken the guarantee it made to the Russians in 1990 that NATO would not expand eastward. After 1990, Some writers announced the 'end of history', meaning that liberal, free-market capitalism had won the ideological war. Some American commentators suggested that it was time for the Russians to 'eat their greens', meaning that they should acknowledge the comprehensive failure of socialism as practised by the Soviet regime and become a liberal, free-market democracy under American tutelage. One hardly needs to comment that the Russians did not subscribe to the same view. Anyway, socialism, in whatever form, was dead.

In fact, although budgets were cut, thinking on foreign policy, strategy (such as it was), did not change much. Defence spending in the UK declined from 4.1% of GDP in 1990 to a current figure of about 2%, only just reaching the benchmark set by NATO. But instead of it being predicated on a new vision, the defence cuts were done in what the MoD and military men saw as 'salami slicing', which they found frustrating and they made their views plain.

Both Simon Jenkins and Paul Mason miss an important point, one concerns NATO itself. NATO was conceived as a deterrent, against the USSR. In the famous words of NATO's first secretary general, British General Hastings 'Pug' Ismay, NATO's mission was 'to keep the Russians out, the Americans in, and the Germans down'. So far, it's been successful in that quest – rather more than was bargained for in the case of the Germans. To be fair, other NATO activities might include observation, patrolling, humanitarian assistance (the delivery of food and other supplies) and sponsoring and facilitating and protecting peace talks.

Edward N Luttwak …

… is an author, historian and strategist. One of his claims to fame is a book entitled *Coup d'État: A Practical Handbook*, a how-to manual for those wishing to take over a state. It was written and published in 1968 and revised in 2016. Some commentators suggest it is semi-satirical book, in the same vein as John Updike's *Coup*, or Evelyn Waugh's *Black Mischief*, but it is really deadly serious, in the Machiavellian tradition. In a 2016 article in *The Guardian*, Luttwak was dubbed 'the Machiavelli of Maryland'.

He is also famous for his seminal book *The Logic of War and Peace*, citing the ancient aphorism 'if you want peace, prepare for war', a useful aphorism but one that seems to contradict the problems raised by the security dilemma. Luttwak's writings have enthused about the concept of 'grand strategy' where every aspect of a nation or state, including armed force, are aligned to achieve an overall political goal. He also suggests a *paradoxical logic* that applies to all aspects of conflict. In a nutshell, this is about the fact that the more territory you conquer, the more people you might have to keep under control. Looking at the way that large empires fell apart, there is probably some merit in this thesis.

It is difficult to position Luttwak's views within the vast parade of hawks and doves, pacifists, military people and professional commentators. On one hand, he can appear to be the ultimate realist, and on the other, deeply committed to peace. In 1999 he published an article in *Foreign Affairs*, the journal of the American think tank, the Council on Foreign Relations, entitled 'Give War a Chance'.

Deliberately iconoclastic, Luttwak suggested that war does have one saving grace, namely that it can resolve conflicts and lead to peace. Wars, he says, have not been allowed to run the natural course, that is the victory of one side over the other. Imposing ceasefires and armistices only allows the protagonists to regroup their forces and to re-arm. He admits that such expedients are useless unless peace negotiations start immediately, which is not always the case.

Luttwak's particular ire is for peacekeeping (see panel), citing wars as far back as the Arab–Israeli war of 1948 to 1949, the various Balkan adventures and, one imagines, countless interventions in Africa. The most egregious example was Srebrenica, where Dutch peacekeepers, constrained by the injunction for them to be politically neutral, allowed 8,000 Bosniak Muslim men and boys to be massacred by VRS, the Bosnian Serb Army of Republika Srpska under the command of Ratko Mladić.

GIVE WAR A CHANCE AND PEACEKEEPING
One of the roles of Britain's armed forces is to participate in peacekeeping operations authorised by the United Nations. Peacekeeping represents a range of activities designed to create political and military conditions in order to allow competing factions within a failing state to resolve their differences and negotiate a lasting peace. There may be serious rebel incursions or

insurgencies from other coherent polities within the state. Quite often these are sponsored and supported by other states, hostile to the 'home state', meaning that the political aspects of peacekeeping become more challenging. When considering peacekeeping, everyone should keep in mind that you cannot keep the peace where there is no peace to keep. Maybe this seems to support Luttwak's position, but he is generally known as a maverick.

So far, so plausible; Luttwak's ideas may deserve to be taken seriously. But, and it's a big 'but', he goes on to suggest that Palestinian refugee camps have prevented Palestinians' absorption into local societies. Indeed, he suggests, the various Palestinian refugee camps may have made it easier for their enemies to exact reprisals, such as with the appalling massacres in Sabra and Shatila camps in 1982, where Phalange militia massacred up to 3,500 civilians, mostly Palestinians and Lebanese Shiites. In a different scenario, further from home and attracting less attention from the press, he mentions the enormous refugee camps along the DRC/Rwandan border. Peace, Luttwak says, only takes hold when war is truly over.

He also suggests that peacekeepers in general are keen to avoid combat, partly to be seen as impartial and partly to avoid their own casualties. His article in *Harper's Magazine* February 2007 'Dead End: Counterinsurgency warfare as military malpractice', had a go at almost every aspect of conventional COIN, from 'Integrating Civil and Military Activities', through 'Intelligence in Counterinsurgency' to 'Intelligence, Surveillance, and Reconnaissance Operations.'

Finally, he does mention some instances of historical success in COIN but, as he quotes one of Rome's enemies – a Caledonian by the name of Calgacus, who lost the Battle of Mons Graupius in AD 83 – as saying: 'of robbery, slaughter, plunder, they give the lying name of empire; they make a solitude and call it peace'. (Often abbreviated to 'they made a desert and called it peace' – very Roman!) We might doubt Luttwak's perspective. He also suggests that the Nazis were very good at keeping order in occupied countries like France by the simple expedient of reprisal massacres. He does have the grace to admit this is not an option for any western army.

Luttwak's views were rejected by other commentators, citing instances of COIN success. It seems to have been generally accepted that his time, and views, were past. However, and the reason we quote him in this book, both he, and to a large extent the militaries concerned, have forgotten what war is all about. War is a hostile act of coercion, the use or threat of organised violence designed to change the political balance between polities. Implicit in this is that changing this political balance must mean a lasting peace for both sides. It is not simply about winning (a) the battle or (b) the war. A good example of this is that after the invasion of Iraq in March 2003, President George Bush flew to a U.S. carrier declaring 'Mission Accomplished'. If your concept of war is just winning battles, Bush was right. But the war was not over: the Americans finally left in 2020, seventeen years later. Even then, there was only a limited *political* balance between polities and a lasting peace may be some way off yet. Luttwak makes the same mistake: counterinsurgency is only one step along the road to a lasting peace, which can only be brought about by this better balance.

David Kilcullen …

… is a professor at Arizona State University and at University of New South Wales, Canberra, Australia. He has been involved in COIN for the past twenty years and is something of a guru on COIN. In his rebuttal of Luttwak's notions, he mentions a conversation he had with a member of a tribe that sits astride the Afghan-Pakistan border. His interlocutor said: 'You want to bring us "democracy" at the national level, but we already have democracy within the khel (a clan or family connection – a grouping somewhere between the tribe and the family). What we want from the government is security, honour, justice and prosperity. If anyone offers us those things, we will fight for him to the death. If democracy only brings elections, what use is it?' Kilcullen's conclusion is that this is a fairly widespread view in both Afghanistan and Iraq.

We therefore repeat: war, to be called 'successful', must change the political balance between polities, not just involve the 'victory' of one side over the other. This must mean a lasting peace for both sides. It is much more than winning battles. If that means taking control of the defeated country's government, particularly if that was weak in the first place, then so be it, and this should be built in to any invasion, peace support or counterinsurgency initiatives. Germany was devasted at the end of World War II but Allied civil / military control was imposed until Germany's civilian administration could stand on its own feet. Germany recovered rapidly, but full sovereignty did not happen until after the reunification of Germany in October 1990. Technically, Germany remained under Allied military occupation until this date, with many American bases in West Germany. Japan had a parallel experience, and although military occupation ceased in 1952, there are still seven American facilities in Japan.

6. PREDICTING WAR

Given that war has been with us forever, should we just accept it and prepare accordingly, or can we predict it in some way?

The previous volume of this trilogy, *About War*, started with the observation that war has been a constant theme and backdrop for all groups, clans and civilisations. Throughout history there have been many years of peace, some lasting hundreds of years, some only a brief interlude in between wars.

Does war have a future as a means of resolving differences between states? In short, will wars increase or decrease in frequency and intensity? When answering that question, we must be sure that we are addressing just that point, and not some apocalyptic vision of war such as autonomous killing machines taking over and deciding to destroy mankind or some authoritarian body achieving worldwide hegemony. Given the historic persistence of war, it is notable that few futurists or popular gurus address this key issue: will wars increase in frequency or will mankind 'come to its senses' and banish – or seriously reduce – war as a means of achieving peace?

Futurists tend to focus on dreadful scenarios rather than the actual number of wars we might expect.

And, whatever the scenario, what can we or should we do about it? How might we avoid war? The usual assertions are that 'we live in an age of uncertainty', or 'the world is an increasingly dangerous place', as if previous ages were more stable and predictable than the present. There is also the conviction that we are currently facing a period of discontinuities, from 9/11 to Trump, populism, and the resurgence of Russia, China, etc. There is also 'post-truth', as if politicians and journalists have always (ever?) been models of probity. Indeed, there are few sources of what the future for war and warfare might hold and even fewer about how we might approach this issue.

These apocalyptic scenarios are overstated. Every age has its own perceived threats and fears. Try this: take the years of your parents' birth and look at the threats, domestic and international, at that time: what were the major concerns then? Try it out with your grandparents – or even try a random number generator. At only a very few points in history can we say that there was not 'enough to worry about'. After the Second World War, there was a fear that war would break out again. In the 1960s, CND (the Campaign for Nuclear Disarmament) had us worrying about 'the bomb'. Then there were the hard years of the Cold War, AIDS and now the new COVID-19 scare. Throw in climate change for good measure.

Notwithstanding enormous differences in incomes around the world, too many countries struggling to become modern states, terrorism, and populist autocratic governments, humanity has survived and, dare we say, prospered.

So, uncertainty? Yes. Despondency? No. Yet, despite all the periods of peace and stability over the years, war, with all the blood and treasure it costs and it being so easy to start, difficult to control and challenging to end, has a nasty habit of 'breaking out'. More than that, let us recall that many wars fail to achieve their original objective for either or all the protagonists.

Can we predict war? Could we assemble all the factors that we think might cause war? Could we agree with, say, a panel of experts on which were the major factors and how they interact? It is unlikely; different disciplines would have different views on almost every aspect of any model that might be proposed. Yet this is something that we need to address. Recruiting, training and equipping an army, navy and air force can take years. Training officers might take longer. Although it took many years to defeat Nazi Germany, one of the reasons was that the existing cadre of British Army officers was simply not large enough to lead the new, larger armed forces.

WHAT HAPPENED IN THE PAST?

The ancients in Greece and Rome did not have to concern themselves with predicting the future: this was all in the hands of the gods. Fate could be expiated by sacrifice or propitiation, but it was largely useless. Now, in a supposedly more enlightened age, we worship different gods: money, technology and consumer goods. The problem is that technology – such as AI – fools us into thinking that it can provide better answers to what are essentially human problems: how to assess and anticipate other countries' and their leaders' moves; how to arrange, organise and control intelligence gathering and, most of all, how to control (in its comprehensive *managerial* sense) the progression from data to knowledge and wisdom. For example, there is no evidence that 'the West' has got the measure of President Putin, despite a vast range of information about him.

There is, though, one parallel. In ancient times, you could not call up any particular god – there were many – and ask for an opinion or a forecast. This had to be done via an intermediary, such as a priest or an oracle. You'd also have to pay: in those days, by sacrificing a goat or, for really important decisions, an ox.

The parallel lies in supposed expertise: priests or oracles were governed by a central authority and they abided by a stringent set of rules about how to interpret and understand a smattering of freshly eviscerated chicken's innards and what they might represent. We now know that this is nonsense, but in the modern world, rarely have consumers tested experts' accuracy against later actuality. Some studies have confirmed that, in terms of prediction, experts perform only as well as any layperson. In one study, various supposedly informed groups were pitted against where cows left their cowpats in a sectioned field. Rather appallingly for the predictions business, the cows won.

The assumed expertise of priests and oracles also has parallels with modern forecasters. In ancient times, it took years to be accepted as a priest or an oracle, if you managed it at all. In the modern world, experts are those with an education in the relevant discipline, typically as part of an institution such as an academic think tank. It is interesting to note that most institutions and think tanks always have disclaimers at the top or bottom of their staff's articles saying that this does not represent the view of the corporate whole. Why on earth not? Don't they have views themselves? Might not a considered consensual view from the academic department or the think tank be more useful than an individual view? Answers come there none. With no disrespect to a learned professor, any politician would have to be pretty sure of his subject to disagree with a professor working in that particular field, and yet, strangely, and by their actions, they do.

At the time of writing, for example, Liz Truss, the UK's Foreign Secretary, is off to Moscow to give the Russians a wigging about building up their forces on the Ukrainian border. It would be intriguing to know how many non-partisan experts on Russia she consulted, how much understanding she has of the Russian psyche. Would she have any idea of the scale of sacrifices that the Russians made in winning the Second World War for us?

Other academics may be no more successful. Indeed, according to Ariel Colonomos in *Selling the Future*, academics suffer penalties for thinking outside the disciplinary box and would rather be wrong within conventional approaches than correct in a general, non-conventional way. Think of economics, the only discipline where you can get a Nobel Prize for a study, and someone else get a Nobel Prize the next year for saying something entirely contrary. Under the current research regime in the United Kingdom, grants are awarded based to some extent on the number of papers published. It's difficult to believe that there is not an insidious political influence here. Numbers of publications are necessary essentials for securing tenure and promotion.

WHAT, THEN, OF THE FUTURE OF WAR?

In his ground-breaking work *The Future of War: A History*, Professor Sir Lawrence Freedman asserts that attempts to predict the future of war have not gone well: 'virtually without exception, they get it wrong'. He suggests that the modern world failed to predict, and has thus not prepared for, the increasing number of intrastate conflicts and the developments of insurgency and counter-terrorism. The extraordinary thing about this finding is that in the Correlates of War list of wars between 1900 and 2000, of the 343 wars listed, some 210 are designated intrastate – over sixty per cent.

Before we analyse the process by which forecasts and predictions are made, we might look at a rationale for doing it at all. Many people in positions of authority in any organisation disdain planning, of which forecasting and prediction are a part, because 'the future is unknowable'. Fifty years ago, all the talk in industry was of automation, which has indeed, to a large extent, come about. Yet insufficient measures have been taken by the government to alleviate the plight of those people who are no longer employed because of automation: so what was the plan?

In a recent study of the use of robots in manufacturing businesses, China came top with 140,000 robots installed during 2019, followed by Japan and the United States. United Kingdom did not even make the list of the top fifteen countries. If automation is an essential theme of British industry, and we might also say society, then the United Kingdom needs to take automation much more seriously. Think of relative economic performance of 'the North'. In a more recent example, we are all told that we need to 'save the planet' and stop driving diesel cars. That's fine. I get the message. But for the several hundred cars in my little corner of London, there are just two charging points within reasonable walking distance. I have not yet investigated whether they have the same type of charging plug.

WAR IS UNIQUE

But, GDP growth, automation and electric cars aside, war is unique in terms of human experience and takes us into a new dimension. Obviously, we need to predict which wars we might be involved in and plan accordingly in terms of defence capability and general military equipment. Manpower, in terms of numbers and technical capabilities is also vital. Currently (in early 2022) both the RAF and the Royal Navy have a shortage of technicians to service their planes and ships.

The security of the British state is obviously the first priority for the United Kingdom government. Plans are made in conjunction with NATO, where an attack on one is deemed to be an attack on all, and other members of NATO are obliged to come to the aid of the attacked state. Although this is still the case, it is not necessarily popular across Europe's population. The '… attack on one …' provision is least popular when it comes to defending Turkey, perhaps the most wayward of all NATO members. Now, despite it not being strictly within NATO's remit, NATO may decide to intervene in conflicts outside the Euro Atlantic area, such as Afghanistan. What might be the rationale for such interventions? The rationale may be one of the following.

First is moral outrage, in that poor civilians are suffering in war-torn countries. Second, there is always the danger of ungoverned space, which may provide a haven for terrorist groups who may wish to attack neighbouring countries or the mainland of Great Britain. Third, many civil wars are supported, or at least influenced, by neighbouring or allied countries, either by providing troops for one side or the other or providing safe havens. Finally, and a particular current problem is that of refugees. According to the UNHCR (the United Nations High Commissioner for Refugees), the global number of forcibly displaced people, including refugees, has doubled since 2010, and now amounts to 82.4 million souls – about the same as the population as Germany. This would clearly be a political decision but there may be good reasons why we might wish to intervene, as many of these conflicts represent security risks to our, or Europe's, well-being.

In *About War* we distinguished between the future *of* war and the future *for* war and advanced the thesis that most forecasts about war were actually based on forecasts *for* war, in that they concerned the mechanisms of warfare rather than the political framework *for* war itself. It is a fine distinction, but an important one. Let us therefore examine how we fare in terms of predicting future wars. Here, let us make it clear that we are talking about wars as political acts, and not primarily warfare, though they are, of course, closely linked.

FORECASTS OR PREDICTIONS?

These two terms are most often used synonymously, but there is an important distinction, and usage in the literature varies. Forecasts are usually based on past data, extrapolated into the future. The best example is weather forecasts, although the concept can be used for any factor, such as GDP, where we have sufficient data. So, for the avoidance of doubt, as the lawyers say, forecasting is about collecting, analysing, understanding and to a large extent extrapolating existing and past data.

One can immediately see there are value judgements all over the place. Whence is the data collected? Are correlations weighted? How? Is each piece of data given equal weighting or are they weighted exponentially?

Is it a moving average? What about outliers? On that subject, and although there are well understood statistical methods for identifying outliers, these may indeed be the most important ones. Looking at data going back many years, any statistician would claim that the Second World War, with its horrendous casualties of between fifty and seventy million souls, was a statistical outlier. But the sources and causes of that war are vitally important, as witnessed by the enormous amount of literature on the Nazis, the Third Reich and the general progress of the war. Despite ending some seventy-six years ago, we are still living with the consequences.

Forecasting is a precarious pastime; estimates are almost bound to be inaccurate and may provide little comfort for the forecaster or the user. Statistical analysis would back this up, though correlating forecasts with outcomes and attempting to learn from the experience is not a common pursuit. More than that, most forecasts are one-dimensional, focusing on just one aspect, or too few aspects, which go unreferenced and uncoordinated: many 'futurists' seem never to have heard of systems thinking or the concept of a dynamic. This is particularly true of political punditry. Many self-proclaimed experts are often no better than uninformed speculators. In many cases forecasts are what Bill Gates called 'random' guesses.

Prediction, on the other hand, is a more general concept, based on forecasts, but tempered with the idea of the probability of various other inputs, plus – and this is the important point – human agency, which may be influenced, albeit subconsciously, by wishful thinking. There is nothing we're going to do about the weather tomorrow, but we might well influence a political leader who is thinking of taking military action against whomever he or she sees as an enemy. Forecasts are essentially inputs to a model where predictions are the output. One academic wag held that political analysis was as unreliable as weather forecasting.

He then suggested that this was an insult to weather forecasters. Mischievous perhaps, but it underlines the scepticism with which we should approach all predictions. But it's not quite as simple as that ...

PREDICTION AS PERSUASION

Nigel Gould-Davies of St Antony's College, Oxford, in a review essay entitled *Seeing the Future: Power, Prediction and Organisation in an Age of Uncertainty* in *International Affairs* 93:2 (March 2017) reviews a number of recent books on how the future, particularly for war, is seen. His first suggestion is that: 'forecasting is not merely useful but usable, a form of persuasion about how the future should look. It helps legitimise the preferred future of powerful interests.'

As an illustration, few senior policemen would turn up in the Minister's office and declare that, since they've done such a good job in reducing crime, they can manage on a smaller budget next year. We can be sure that no senior military officer would turn up in the Minister's office and suggest that they could manage with last year's tanks, ships or planes. Predicting the future, particularly for war, is fundamentally political, with considerable implications thinking about war and thereby, incidentally, warfare.

SELF-FULFILLING PROPHECIES

There is also the danger of the self-fulfilling prophecy, where the act of predicting an event may bring it about. For example, predicting that a bank will become insolvent could cause a run on its deposits. The same might apply to starting a war. 'You think war may be probable? Better arm up!' was AJP Taylor's diagnosis of the reason for the First World War. Many suffer from the same syndrome, believing that they could not possibly achieve this or that. In the event, they're probably right. As Henry Ford famously said, 'If you think you can do a thing or think you can't do a thing, you're probably right'. The same might be said of people: I had a distant cousin once who grew up in a toxic household, being told that she was no good, and a lot of trouble. Hardly surprisingly, she grew up in just that way, and died young.

It always amazes me how military power is considered the principal dimension of the relationship the United States has with Russia and with China. One cannot help but feel that there is a major antipathy towards both their systems of government, coupled with a complete lack of understanding about the problems, both geopolitical and social that these countries face. After all, Russia is the largest country by area in the whole world and China has over 1.4 billion people. One wonders how American politicians and civil servants would cope with such problems.

Certainly, the United States security establishment has always seen Russia as a security threat, on memories of the USSR. Indeed, they were confident in predicting the Russian invasion of Ukraine. The European security establishment seems not to have expected the invasion, on the old maxim 'hope for the best but plan for the worst.'

BIG DATA: SALVATION OR DISTRACTION?

Many publications today celebrate the potential benefits of 'big data' and thence artificial intelligence, suggesting it will transform almost every, if not all, aspects of political, social and business life. Umm, yes, but … can big data and AI improve the prediction of wars? Indeed, can big data and AI improve international relations?

In an internal report published some years ago, when the FCO was simply the Foreign and Commonwealth Office (it is now the FCDO, the Foreign, Commonwealth and Development Office), the authors made the point that: 'Business has woken up to the transformational potential of big data. The FCO has not. The FCO is not yet in a position to mine even its own internal data for insight, which means we miss important patterns and trends.' This is, incidentally, an intriguing comment about the FCO. The FCO / FCDO's budget has been progressively cut over the past years, and with the current practice of shifting civil servants around on a regular basis and the consequent loss of an enormous and hard-won bank of experience, the FCO is a shadow of its former self. This leaves a gaping vulnerability in terms of political judgement. Coupled with an increasing shift of emphasis onto trade, the FCDO's role is becoming more like a sales office than a diplomatic mission .

First, we should be wary of investing too much faith in the power of 'big data'. Data is simply that: just data. To transform this into information requires judgement and experience as much as it does computing skills. To transform that information into knowledge is even more difficult, requiring a greater depth of experience, with progressively more human and, one might say, intuitive intervention. Transforming that knowledge into wisdom depends absolutely on a human approach.

Second, and something one sees ever more frequently is what the Americans call a 'category error'. Although 'big data' and massive computing power can provide any number of correlations, probably too many, it is much more challenging to establish causal links. William of Ockham died 670 years ago, but he should not be forgotten. Computers can at least appear to think deductively, but do they 'think' inductively? Eventually, everybody will know everything, or at least have access to the data, and perhaps some information, curated by who knows whom. They may manage to transform some of that information into knowledge, but their access to the data / information may persuade themselves that they have knowledge and hence wisdom. This is the main, and perhaps the overwhelming, problem of 'big data', apart from who gathered it in the first place. And, yes, in the military sense, this could also be applied to the C4ISR (Command, Control, Communications, Computers, Intelligence, Surveillance and Reconnaissance) concept, part of the JBI

(Joint Battlespace Infosphere). Inductive reasoning is one of the key essential features in thinking objectively about the future, and certainly about running a war or a battle.

Gould-Davies's analysis is astute and percipient, and his conclusions very close to my own interest in organisational behaviour. The main conclusion he draws from his review is that the key is *not from better method but from better organisation.* He seems, thereby, to suggest that, as long as the forecasting models and protocols are robust, it is the *organisation* that is the constraint, something with which any experienced manager would agree.

But he slightly undersells his case: to many, *organisation* simply means the hierarchical arrangements of various functions and the processes that link them. In fact – and something that Gould-Davies will know well as being experienced in both academic and corporate life – an organisation covers functions and hierarchies but also leadership, values, clearly defined roles, reward mechanisms, expectations and a shared sense of corporate goals (the last applies even in a government department). For example, the term 'strategic culture' in governmental departments is subtly different from what the business community would recognise as 'culture' or 'business culture'. It's not a serious contrast, but one that needs to be borne in mind. Anyone who has worked in business will be familiar with the potential discomfort of suggesting that budgets are too optimistic or too pessimistic. It is a resurgence of the 'shoot the messenger' idea of years past.

Another recent academic source comes from the late Colin S Gray, a professor in the Politics and International Relations department at Reading University and author of many books on war and strategy. His book *Another Bloody Century* (2005) starts by quoting Carl von Clausewitz: 'war is a permanent feature of the human condition'. He goes on to outline six connecting threads, the first two where, reflecting Clausewitz, he asserts that 'war will always be with us'. His second is that 'history is our best guide'. The other four threads are the usual suspects around the political context; the social and cultural angles; strategic surprises and international efforts to control or modify war.

Early on, after acknowledging that 'definitions can be a blight', he reminds us of 'the difference between war and warfare be flagged', and explains that 'War is a relationship between belligerents, not necessarily states. Warfare is the conduct of war, primarily, though not exclusively, by military means.' The two concepts are not synonymous. This is absolutely correct, and a central theme of this trilogy, yet Gray goes on to say that 'Because this book is mainly concerned with strategic topics, which is to say with matters bearing directly or indirectly on the use of force, it addresses the future of warfare rather than war'. This seems to contradict his previous comment. Strategy is about all aspects of a state's capability, not just its warfare making ability. Curiously, he then asserts that 'because war in its many grisly guises ... a permanent blot on, and contributor to, the course of human history, warfare is thus deemed the more profitable subject to pursue.'

The second concern is that Gray's thesis, which depends so much on the past for predicting the future, ignores the fact that our understanding of the past is rooted in the concerns and interests of the present. It is currently the 100th anniversary of the First World War and historians are still arguing about the root causes, citing motivations all the way from Germany's desire to be on a naval par with Great Britain through to AJP Taylor's railway timetables. It is doubtful whether Gray could assemble any thesis based on this last point!

Although we need to forecast and thus predict demographics, economic performance, investment, trade and other factors of the state, there is a very good case for forecasting the conditions of war and predicting when any individual war might break out.

ORGANISATIONAL MOMENTUM AND INERTIA

Big data, AI, forecasts, predictions, conventional wisdoms, experts, gurus, strategic culture and a sometimes comprehensive misunderstanding of other cultures crowd in, occasionally to help, more often to inhibit contemplating what wars might break out in the future. Surely, every society wants to be a modern, liberal, free-market capitalist society. Surely, every other society in the world wants to live in a consumer paradise? Maybe not. They are dying out now, but many older Russians still miss Stalin.

A big danger is organisational. In the UK and NATO, there is no Dissent Channel, which is a United States Department of State framework for Foreign Service Officers through which they can express constructive criticism of government policy. Unfortunately, there is no current intelligence (sic) as to whether this functions as planned.

Imagine rocking up at the meeting before Afghanistan was invaded or Libya bombed. Imagine somebody sitting in a corner saying, 'Please sir, we cannot convert Afghanistan to a liberal free-market by forcing them.' *Beatings will continue until morale improves* is not a good strategy for anything. Imagine the same scenario in planning for Libya: it must have been known, and if it wasn't, it should have been, that Libya would simply descend into warlordism. The invasion of Iraq in 2003 was seen in terms of conquest, rather than strategic persuasion.

The chosen, or maybe politically indicated, solution takes on an organisational life of its own; actually, a blight on most forms of planning. To follow the example of Iraq, 'We're going to invade this country, destroy any form of governance and disband their army.' What could possibly go wrong?

COMMENTARY

We can agree with Colin Gray that the only guide we have to the future is the past. His assertion that history is our best and, by implication, *only* guide is credible. But *history is a constant dialogue between past and present.* Our understanding of the past is rooted in the concerns and interests of the present. But what exactly *do* we and what exactly *can* we learn from the past?

What, for example has Europe learned during the 20th century? Scores of millions of people, largely civilians, but also military personnel, died during it. It is no wonder the Americans talk about European 'civil wars'. What has Europe learned from that experience? Four times in that century the Americans came to Europe's help, first in the First World War when there were two million doughboys in Europe helping the Allies in their war against Kaiser Bill's Imperial Germany. In the Second World War, FDR brilliantly nudged his country from being the 'arsenal of democracy' to his 'Europe First' policy with wholehearted help with men and materials in defeating Nazi Germany. The Marshall Plan was, according to Churchill, 'the least sordid act in history'; though it is disputed that he referred to it in this context, it put Europe back on its feet again. And then Europe recovered under the power of the United States' nuclear umbrella.

Yet Europe has still to navigate a political and diplomatic route between maintaining good relationships with the United States, consensus and consistency among themselves, and their own individual and collective security.

In essence, Europe doesn't 'get it'. It is proving overwhelmingly challenging to get a common view on foreign policy, security and defence, much less come to terms with any associated spending. Poland – of all countries – has remained sceptical of the EU's common foreign and security policy and Brexit was quintessentially petulant. Perhaps, as Talleyrand is reputed to have said of the Bourbons, 'they have forgotten nothing and learnt nothing'. He probably did not say any such thing, but we can be reasonably sure that he had such a sentiment.

There is a clue, though, in Gould-Davies' essay, *Organisation*. Call it OD, or Organisational Dynamics if you want to impress, or even governance. It is no surprise to me that, of all security and defence analysts, he stands out as having a deal of commercial organisational experience. This is not something that is particularly emphasised in security and defence, other than changing how the Army, Navy and Air Force be configured, but, considering all the different aspects of an organisation *apart* from hierarchy (which is obvious) – governance, process, audit and dissent, span of authority, span of control and dozens of other factors that make up a successful corporate whole – the key to prediction lies here, with organisational and interactional experience, rather than with gurus, experts and statisticians.

Yet there remain many pitfalls. In establishing and accepting forecasts, as defined above, we can interrogate the sources of past data, examine how it has been 'cleaned' and critique the statistical methodologies for whatever extrapolations are used, but even that requires some knowledge of the forecasters' craft. Many observers are happy to accept false origins on graphs, logarithmic scales and weighted averages without querying the underlying protocols. And, I wonder, how many forecasts and predictions are subject to a post-audit, with the actual result correlated with the original forecast? Not many, I would think.

Prediction, again as defined above, requires human intervention with functional biases, conventional wisdom and political views all contributing to, or detracting from the result. Any prediction should invoke the questions: Who said that? Why did they say it? How did they say it? What sources did they use?

We cannot live without forecasts and predictions. At the very least, as in David Mamet's play *American Buffalo*, we have to have something to deviate from. Any forecast or prediction will stimulate discussion and debate; assumptions will be questioned, methodology interrogated and the results inevitably challenged.

Forecasts should always be treated with a keen analytical eye; predictions should always be treated with a sceptically raised eyebrow.

7. CLASSIFYING WAR

No two wars are the same

The use of organised violence to achieve a political aim may be a common characteristic of war in general, but almost every other factor is particular to that war. Cyber war is a non-violent form of war but there may be violent consequences such as an unplanned nuclear launch or an interruption of electricity supplies. Overall, there is no general model of war.

Classifying wars is important for both long-term planning for war and for preparing for any particular war. Clausewitz's advice that 'no one starts a war – or rather, no one in his sense ought to do so – without first being clear in his mind what he intends to achieve by the war and how he intends to conduct it' is apposite.

If expeditionary wars are in prospect, such as Afghanistan or Iraq, where the troops might be fighting in a foreign land far from home, transport, logistics and communications will be vital. The stakes might be quite low – you can always declare victory and leave. This is quite different from defending the homeland, where politicians would be at hand to advise or negotiate, and the whole nation might be involved. World War II was an existential war, with the fighting literally on the doorstep. The stakes were very high.

Classifying any prospective war is important. Fighting one sort of war when the enemy is fighting is another is folly. One of the problems during the Vietnam War was that the United States fought an insurgency war, when in fact they were fighting a civil war on behalf of one of the parties – and the one least likely one to succeed at that. Recently released papers reveal that the Americans were aware of this but continued with counterinsurgency and supporting the side least likely to succeed. The

Americans might have been inspired by the British experience in Malaya, a true counterinsurgency war, but with dramatically different issues. Nevertheless, both in Vietnam and Malaya, the threat of communism was thought to be very real at that time.

We also need to consider the possible outcome of any proposed war. Will victory in the war improve our security? Since we don't want a defeated though disgruntled enemy on our doorstep, will they accept defeat and feel secure? Germany, after the allegedly harsh terms imposed on them after World War I at Versailles in 1919, was ripe for Hitler's manipulation whereas, after World War II, Germany accepted their defeat and the aid and assistance offered by the victors to rebuild their economy. War must facilitate a better political relationship between protagonists, or at least a more stable arrangement. One exception to this is the 'Carthaginian Peace' outlined in Chapter 2.

We need an analytical framework. We need a structure and a process that can systematically analyse the prevailing political balance between likely protagonists and the public's appetite for war. War is a political act, and we must distinguish it from warfare (see Appendix 1 for a definition of both). There is no doubt that considerable political planning in the U.S. and UK went into recent wars, but it was planning about internal politics, party politics, interservice rivalry and logistics. There was evidently a dearth of advance political analysis and planning before the wars in Afghanistan, Iraq and Libya. Consider the invasion of Afghanistan in 2001. Was it really conceivable that Afghanistan would return to, or even reach, a stable, democratic government? In 2007, Paddy Ashdown was in the frame to be the local Caesar, but he demurred, saying:

'We do not have enough troops, aid or international will to make Afghanistan much different from what it has been for the last 1,000 years – a society built around gun, drugs and tribalism. And even if we had all of these in sufficient quantities, we would not have them for sufficient time – about 25 years or so – to make the aim of fundamentally altering the nature of Afghanistan, achievable … the realistic aim in Afghanistan, with current resources, is not victory but containment.'

Tragically, this advice, from such an experienced and distinguished soldier and diplomat, went unheeded.

The sheer number of wars, campaigns, battles and conflicts in history is daunting. Brave readers might be tempted to flick through the *Collins Encyclopaedia of Military History*, by Dupuy and Dupuy. It is over 1,600 pages long, and opening any page at random reveals that there was a battle, a war or a campaign recorded in almost every year since the first entry in 1469 BC. Wars stretch back to the start of recorded history and certainly beyond that.

Every war since the beginning of time is a labyrinth of geopolitical considerations, international relations and domestic politics, all of which might be realised, but tempered, encouraged or constrained by human agency. It is this aspect which makes classifying war difficult but not impossible. It depends on as much understanding of the potential enemy's politics as your own.

CLASSIFICATION PITFALLS

Having made a case for some sort of classification, we must be aware of the pitfalls.

First, many wars before Napoleon were fought by fairly small semi-professional armies. Ordinary citizens might live quiet, peaceful lives without ever actually experiencing war or being bothered by it. In Chapter 1 we examined Machiavelli's distaste for mercenaries and his affection for the ancient memory of the Roman Republic's citizen army. Wellington's troops at Waterloo included troops from Prussia, Hanover, Brunswick and Nassau. They were not exactly mercenaries, but it was the British who funded many of those other countries' troops. Victory, certainly in Machiavelli's time, went to the richest cities, those able to afford the best mercenaries.

Prior to the Napoleonic wars (1792 to 1815), few people thought war particularly unusual. Summer was the time for campaigning, though the troops had to be home in time for the harvest. The aristocracy would use winter for hunting as a substitute for war, and to keep themselves and their horses in good condition for the next summer campaigning period.

Secondly, until the advent of the tank in World War I, many wars were often sieges or wars of attrition, not the wars of manoeuvre that we would expect in the modern era. Until the final assault on the German lines, World War I was essentially a mutual siege war with the British naval blockade, and troops on both sides stuck in the trenches moving backwards and forwards by a few yards for every offensive. There were no castles involved, but German defensive positions could be almost as formidable. The Napoleonic wars and the American Civil Wars involved manoeuvres, but this was greatly constrained by transportation arrangements. Often, these battles were over in a day.

WHAT IS A 'NECESSARY' WAR? WHAT IS A 'JUST' WAR?

AJP Taylor (1906 to 1990) was a British historian, famous for his 'talking head' polemics on television and neat, if sometimes tangential, aphorisms, such as 'no war is inevitable until it breaks out'. For our purpose here, his assertion that Bismarck (German Chancellor 1873 to 1890) fought 'necessary' wars and killed thousands, the idealists of the 20th century fight just wars and kill millions' is either trite or deeply profound.

He was referring to the 'necessary' wars of German unification, the German Empire having been proclaimed in 1871. The supposed 'just' wars were against fascism in the 20th century. But what exactly is 'necessary'; what exactly is 'just', and for whom? Would this help with classification? Different protagonists would have different views on what was necessary or what was just. Even Hitler thought he had God on his side, and that his wars were just and necessary!

Thirdly, many historic wars, were fought by troops who were required to fight by coercion or by obligation to their lord. There was no democratic process involving the whole population. The men 'pressed' into service in the Georgian Royal Navy did not have a vote about it. The absence of a democratic process does not disqualify the war from being a true political war, but it does give a different perspective to the modern mind. In the absence of any democratic process, then as now, one might recall Marx's maxim that the state maintained the hegemony of the ruling and aristocratic class and was coercive and parasitic. A minor current distraction is that the UN prohibits war as such, so modern wars tend to be described as 'police actions', 'pacification' or even 'humanitarian assistance'. The bombing of Libya in 2011 was described at the time as 'humanitarian intervention'. But it was really about regime change, which is illegal under the UN Charter.

CATALOGUE OF TYPES OF (POLITICAL) WAR

Let us then attempt the classification of different wars, considering them from the political perspective. This approach, of course, raises the question as to whether there are wars that *do not* meet the 'war is a political act' criterion. This might seem fatuous, but World War I is a case to consider. What were Imperial Germany's political objectives?

Recall the comment mentioned in Chapter One from Ludendorff: 'We'll punch a hole and let the rest follow.' Political contact and negotiation between protagonists was limited, ironic when one recalls that the guru of political war was a Prussian, Carl von Clausewitz. The list is deliberately short, and is intended as an illustration of widely differing types of war rather than anything like a comprehensive survey.

WARS OF RELIGION: DEFINITION

'Religion is the main cause of wars,' is a popular refrain, but the facts do not bear this out. A religious war is motivated by differences *of* religion, such as Christianity and Islam, or *within* a religion (Roman Catholic versus Protestant or Shiite versus Sunni). Current thinking, however, suggests that, although religion may be a factor in what is otherwise viewed as a religious war, other factors such as social, political, economic, ethnic or territorial aspects may be as important and may even predominate; religion may just be the tip of an iceberg or a pretext. In Charles Phillip's *Encyclopaedia of Wars*, he calculates that of 1,763 known wars, just 123, or seven per cent, had religion as their leading cause.

Other authorities, such as Matthew White's *The Great Big Book of Horrible Things* (2011) suggests that just ten to fifteen per cent of the world's 'one hundred events with the largest man-made death tolls, regardless of who was involved or why they did it' had religion as the main cause. There are dissenters: some people believe that nationalism and religion were, and remain, the main causes of war. But whereas we might find a good consensus for the meaning of religion, patriotism, and its more aggressive parallel nationalism, are more difficult to pin down. Given such restrictions, identifying examples of purely religious and supposedly religious wars is open to debate.

THE CRUSADES

One might suggest that the Crusades, dated nominally from Pope Urban II's proclamation in 1095 to about 1271 were principally, perhaps only, about religion: the Roman Church versus Islam. But not quite. According to Wikipedia, 'Historians now debate the combination of the Crusaders' motivations, which included the prospect of mass ascension into Heaven at Jerusalem, satisfying feudal obligations, opportunities for renown, and economic and political advantage.'

One website (WriteWork: Essays and Writing Guides for Students) has the fascinating line: 'But the Crusades were merely religious for political reasons' – which says it all! It justifies this point by pointing out that Pope Urban II promised Crusaders' estates in the Muslim lands they conquered, an important opportunity to the second sons of the nobility who would not inherit their ancestral lands. The Crusaders fought for glory, for land, and for economic benefit; the Islamic forces fought for their spiritual survival, but also to achieve hegemony – political control – over other lands. Discuss, as they say.

THE THIRTY YEARS WAR (1618 TO 1648)

This was one of history's most brutal wars and was fought mostly in central Europe. There were eight million casualties, fewer from battles than from resulting famine and disease. Alliances and participants shifted over the course of the war. On one side was the Imperial Alliance, nominally Roman Catholic, comprising the Habsburg Monarchy, the Spanish Empire, the Electorate of Bavaria and the German Catholic League. This war, between Catholic and Protestant states of the Holy Roman Empire, centred on Germany. But recall Voltaire's verdict in 1756 that: The Holy Roman Empire was neither Holy, nor Roman, nor an Empire. Prior to 1870, 'Germany' was a basically a patchwork of states and principalities.

The Anti-Imperial Alliance, nominally Protestant, comprised Bohemia, Sweden, the Electoral Palatinate, the Duchy of Savoy, the Principality of Transylvania, the Dutch Republic, Denmark-Norway, the Heilbronn League, the Landgraviate of Hesse-Kassel, Brandenburg-Prussia, the Duchy of Brunswick-Lüneburg, the Electorate of Saxony and, in the latter stages, the Roman Catholic Kingdom of France, led, interestingly, by Cardinal Richelieu.

Originally, it was seen as a German civil war and one of the European wars of religion. CV Wedgwood, an English historian (1910–97) suggested that the war was really part of a wider European conflict, whose underlying cause was the continuing contest between the Austro-Spanish Habsburgs and French Bourbons. As it evolved, the war became less about religion, Catholic against Protestant, and more about power, and about which states would dominate and govern Europe. The war changed the geopolitical face of Europe and the role of both religion and nation states in society. The Thirty Years War ended with the Peace of Westphalia in 1648, which established the principle, still current, of agreed borders and non-interference in the domestic affairs of sovereign states: 'Westphalian Sovereignty'.

MODERN RELIGIOUS WARS
Despite popular wisdom, it is difficult to find any modern war that has religion as its main *apparent* cause, as in the Holy League and the Ottoman Empire above.

ISRAEL AND PALESTINE
The Israel (Jewish) – Palestine (Islam) conflict has starkly different religions on either side, but their differences are more to do with the Palestinians' bitterness at being displaced from what they thought of as their homeland by the newly formed Israeli state, returning to what they

thought of as *their* homeland during the 1947–1949 Israeli–Palestine war, part of the wider Arab–Israeli conflict.

The current Israeli-Palestinian territorial situation followed Israeli military occupation of the then Palestinian territories in the 1967 Six Day War. It is now recognised as the world's 'most intractable conflict', Israel having occupied the West Bank and the self-governing Palestinian territory for fifty-four years. The 'Peace Process', such as it is, proceeds glacially, if at all.

INDIA AND PAKISTAN

India, nominally the Republic of India, a secular state, and its neighbour, Pakistan, nominally the Islamic Republic of Pakistan, would seem obvious candidates for a religious war. In fact, there are different routes.

In 1947 the British 'quit' India, the word coming from the Indian nationalists' Quit India Movement. The British and, incidentally, one of the leaders of the movement, Mahatma Gandhi, wanted to leave a unified state, but the All-India Muslim League, led by Mohammad Ali Jinnah insisted on a separate Islamic state, Pakistan, covering modern day Baluchistan, Punjab, Sindh, Khyber and Pakhtunkhwa. Jinnah also wanted to include Bengal, geographically distant from metropolitan Pakistan, to be called East Pakistan. The British demurred, pointing out that East Pakistan would be some 2,000 km distant, but Jinnah insisted again, saying that this was Pakistan's problem, not that of the British. We mention this here because we cover the secession of East Pakistan, now Bangladesh, shortly.

The British left, leaving behind, 'the finest army in the world', according to Louis Allen (who wrote *Burma: The Longest War, 1941 to 1945*). The army was divided between India and Pakistan. Since independence, India and Pakistan have fought four main wars (1947, 1965, 1971 and 1999) and a number of border skirmishes. The causes have been water supply and insurgencies but the status of Kashmir has been central to their antipathy. Fighting between two parts of such a hitherto fine army would inevitably result in many casualties on both sides. The total amounts to something like 70,000 souls. However, the verdict must be that, although India and Pakistan have quite different religions, that in itself has not been the main cause of the various wars.

YUGOSLAVIA

After the collapse of the Soviet Union in 1991, the Socialist Federal Republic of Yugoslavia, known usually as just 'Yugoslavia', fell apart. The constituent republics declared independence, though there were unresolved antipathies between ethnic groups within the republics. Many war crimes were committed during the wars, including crimes against humanity, genocide and maltreatment of prisoners of war. Rape was also used as a 'weapon of war', planned and organised by the military command, rather than the tragic consequence of undisciplined troops. During the various wars, the multi-ethnic Yugoslav People's Army (JNA) suffered desertions of Slovenes, Croats, Kosovar Albanians, Bosnians and Macedonians. The rump became the Serbian Army, directed by the infamous Slobodan Milošević (1941 to 2006). As president, Milošević invoked Serbian nationalist rhetoric to further his cause, that of a 'Greater Serbia'.

The seeds of conflict were political, nationalist and religious – with a jumble of Christian (Orthodox) Serbs, Christian (Catholic) Croats, largely Muslim Bosnians and Herzegovinians, Muslim Kosovans and largely Muslim Albanians. However, the various ethnic groups had lived peaceably enough under Tito's firm Yugoslavian government. But that peace did not survive his death. Leaders like Milošević and many others, invoked dormant ethnic and ethno-religious differences to further their malign cause. Religion was exploited as a tool to further political ends.

COMMENTARY

No war is about religion alone. Even where the rationale offered is religion, other motivations, admitted or not, will always be present. But what is the opposite? The corollary of a religious war might be a secular war, instituted and prosecuted by a secular state. There are roughly 196 states in world, half of them secular. In Islam, there may not be a such clear distinction between religion and state. Indeed, many Islamic countries style themselves 'The Islamic State of, say, Afghanistan, Pakistan, Iran etc.' That does not necessarily mean that their wars are based on religion. They all have political agendas, driven to a greater or lesser extent by religion, but it's still politics.

IDEOLOGICAL WAR

Most of the ideological differences between the communist bloc – Soviet Union and China and others – were played out during the Cold War, which we consider subsequently. There were many proxy wars, but the deadliest, and most clearly ideological, was between communist North Korea (supported by China and the Soviet Union) and a western-oriented South Korea. It was a nasty and brutal war with horrendous casualties: approximately three million war fatalities and a large civilian death toll, comparable with World War II or the Vietnam War. Almost all Korea's major cities were destroyed and there were many war crimes on both sides.

South Korea was supported by the United States, Great Britain, and several other countries under a United Nations mandate. Following clashes along the border and insurgency in the south, North Korea invaded South Korea on 25 June 1950 and the war ended on 27 July 1953 in an armistice. Technically, the war continues to this day, but there have been no major military incidents since the armistice.

The ideological angle is best illustrated by one small cameo: when

North Korean prisoners of war were returned to the north in western clothes and shod with western shoes, they discarded them at the border, not wishing to have anything 'capitalist' about them, not even clothes.

ANCIENT AND MODERN WARS

Few foresee the calamity of the consequence of war or grasp its significance at the time. Did Carthage realise that their war with Rome was existential? Did Harold Godwinson appreciate that a Norman Conquest would change England forever in 1066?

King Philip II of Spain believed that his Armada of 1588 would restore the Catholic status quo in England, but did he appreciate the cataclysm for Spain: some would identify the demise of the Spanish Armada as the start of Spain's long decline. Certainly, Elizabeth I, inspired and diverted by nationalistic fervour, fully grasped the threat to England's political and religious future, and also herself.

The generals who planned the mobilisation of World War I were concerned with railway timetables; attritional war was neither intended not foreseen. Only Kitchener predicted a lengthy war, that it would not be 'over by Christmas', while Britain's lonely Foreign Secretary, Sir Edward Grey, was among the few who predicted tragedy.

Prime Minister Robert Walpole, nearly two centuries before, had been similarly prescient. When war broke out against Spain in 1739 (War of Jenkins' Ear), he said, with foresight: 'They may ring their bells now, before long they will be wringing their hands.' He was not deaf to that ruse of so many specious orators: the appeal to patriotism, saying, 'The term has been prostituted to the very worst of purposes. A patriot, sir! Why, patriots spring up like mushrooms!'

The list of unintended consequences of war or declarations of war are legion. Did the South fully appreciate the likely outcome of their secession from the United States in 1861 for the cause, as Rhett Butler says, of 'living in the past'? Did they fully appreciate the industrial might of the North? Clearly not.

Germany's industrial base in 1941 was considerable, but nothing like the potential of the United States. Yet Hitler, blinded by that same 'Victory Disease' that corrupted Japanese strategy, declared war on the U.S. on 11 December, four days after Pearl Harbor. This ignorant miscalculation, together with his ultimately calamitous attack on Russia, would lead to the nemesis of the bunker.

WARS OF ATTRITION

A war of attrition is where each protagonist tries to wear down the enemy through continuous losses of personnel and matériel, weapons, ammunition, vehicles, aircraft and all the other paraphernalia of war. Attrition also wears down the willingness of the protagonists' populations to support the war.

However, in the absence of a democratic government and a free press, populations may be coerced into supporting a long attritional war. Such was the case in North Vietnam: they suffered something like 3.2 million casualties (military and civilian), but were prepared to go on to the end. The Americans did not have that luxury. There were many civil protests, particularly on college campuses, as it was that age group that were being drafted, and eventually the Americans were obliged to make their humiliating withdrawal. Politicians generally prefer a quicker solution, using fewer resources and, more importantly, causing fewer casualties.

A quicker solution also plays better with the population. Military leaders would prefer manoeuvre warfare, with the usual tactics of concentration of force, deception and outflanking the enemy's forces. The protagonist with access to greater resources such as a superior industrial base and a larger population to draw on usually wins.

But greater resources do not always mean victory. A theoretically weaker side in terms of personnel and an industrial base may deliberately seek out attrition warfare to wear out the enemy or to persuade that enemy that it is simply not worth the effort to defeat the other side. Until comparatively recently, Switzerland had a strategy based on not being able to win a war against any near competitor, but they could make it very expensive in terms of personnel and equipment to defeat them. The natural fortress protection of the Alps would deter all but the most determined!

There is no clear distinction between 'conventional' and 'attritional' warfare: there is usually an element of attrition in any war. Few wars are started as attritional wars but might become so. Even then, when the enemy is sufficiently worn down, more conventional warfare usually provides victory. We could identify many wars in history where attrition played a part, but two examples illustrate the principle well.

In World War I, although firepower and targeting, as well as aerial reconnaissance, improved, mobility did not. The war settled down to a long and bitter slogging match between the trenches, resulting in horrendous casualties. However, the Allies' victory was achieved with a great offensive in the autumn of 1918 involving all arms co-operation and mass manoeuvre.

The campaign on the Eastern Front in World War II, between Germany and Soviet Russia, 1941 to 1945, was an existential struggle with terrible casualties: some thirteen million. Red Army staff work was superb, logistically. They moved men and machines efficiently, even ruthlessly, but were careless about casualties. The western Allies did not have that political luxury. Russia's access to new recruits was almost unlimited. Attrition does not merely apply to matériel, though we might also remember that the United States and Great Britain supplied Soviet Russia with nearly eighteen million tons of equipment during World War II, most in her ultimate hour of need, without which Mother Russia might have perished.

The political angle of a war of attrition is that the population must support the war and tolerate the casualties, as well as the diversion of resources to the war effort. The government must be prepared to justify any war, but a long war of attrition is more difficult to sustain politically.

Sun Tzu, the Chinese general, military strategist and philosopher, lived around 600 BC and his seminal work *The Art of War* is still read today. His famous aphorism that *There is no instance of a nation benefitting from prolonged warfare* still has resonance.

WARS BETWEEN STATES AND WARS WITHIN STATES

So far, we have considered states as the main agent for war; state versus state. A recurring and increasing trend is for armed conflict within states or intrastate war. This includes civil war, secession wars, rebellion, revolution and insurgency. We might also add crime syndicate war, warlordism and terrorism, the last of which we deal with in the next chapter. Ideology and religion may also play a part. According to the Peace Research Institute in Oslo, '2017 was one of the most violent years since the end of the Cold War. While violence levels decreased slightly from the all-time high of 2016, non-state conflicts and internationalised intrastate conflicts continue to challenge the international community's ability to achieve global peace' Taking their data from Uppsala University's Department of Peace and Conflict Research, PRIO also reckon that interstate wars declined from fifty-three in 2016 to forty-nine in 2017 (the latest figures available), whereas intrastate conflicts increased from sixty-two in 2016 to eighty-two in 2017.

Definitions are important. For example, the various conflicts in Colombia from 1964 to the present day have involved over a dozen far-right paramilitary groups, about the same number of far-left groups, as well as crime (drug-related) syndicates, all armed, and all with a slightly different agenda. FARC, the Revolutionary Armed Forces of Colombia, is the best known. Given such a melee of groups, we might hesitate to define the aim or objectives of any faction in Colombia. Civil war? Revolt? Rebellion? Crime syndicate war? Perhaps all of these. And, while we should not expect a definitive answer, some broad categories are useful.

For a general definition of intrastate war, the aim of each party provides a guide. This might be to maintain or to overthrow an unpopular government, to resist a government's restrictions or to secede from the state altogether.

CIVIL WAR

A war between organised polities within the same state or country or between an organised polity (sometimes several) and the legitimate government is civil war. The aim of either side is to take control or to maintain control of that country.

But it's not quite as straightforward as that. Patrick M. Regan, in his book *Civil Wars and Foreign Powers* (2000) reckons that most civil wars involve other countries, either openly with military assistance or covertly with arms or intelligence support. The statistic is surprising. Regan estimates that about two in every three of the 138 intrastate conflicts between the end of World War II and 2000 experienced interventions by other countries, with the United States intervening in thirty-five (one in four). Each intervening power will have its own agenda.

Civil wars differ from rebellion in that both sides need to be reasonably well organised and resourced; mere rebels are easily crushed. Civil wars are thus high-intensity, large-scale and bitter conflicts and usually result in large numbers of casualties. The American Civil War (1861–65) resulted in 700,000 dead (though most from disease). They also consume significant resources. Spain suffered about half a million deaths during their civil war (1936–39). The continuing war in Syria has cost nearly half a million deaths to date, with over seven million internally displaced and over five million refugees.

REBELLION AND REVOLUTION

Whereas the aim of a rebellion is resistance to an established government, a revolt seeks a revolution, which aims to involve a majority of the population in overthrowing an unpopular ruling class. The French Revolution is a good example. The revolutionaries aimed to end the Ancien Régime, represented by the monarchy, and institute a republic. They were successful in doing away with Louis XVI, executed in 1793, but a true republic did not emerge until a century later. Revolutionary France then suffered a rebellion in the Vendée in 1793, the suppression of which cost something like 200,000 dead.

SECESSION

Secession is where a polity within a larger sovereign state attempts to break away and form a new sovereign state in its own right. The breakaway polity is almost always geographically contiguous. Sovereign states are generally very reluctant to lose territory and the two sides frequently descend into civil war.

BANGLADESH

A tragic example of secession and the intervention of another state is the Bangladesh Liberation War. After the partition of India in 1947, the Pakistani state divided itself into two: West Pakistan, now simply Pakistan, and East Pakistan, which covers most of Bengal. In reaction to a Bengali independence movement, West Pakistan launched Operation Searchlight, which involved systematic killing of nationalist Bengalis, students, intelligentsia, religious minorities and armed personnel. This became known as the Bangladesh Genocide, which alienated Bengali opinion. With assistance from the Indian Army, Bengal declared independence from the union of Pakistan to establish the new nation of Bangladesh. Like many secessions, it was very bloody; military casualties amounted to about 50,000 killed and wounded, with civilian death approaching 300,000. The People's Republic of Bangladesh has been an independent state since 1971. Despite being 90% Muslim, it is officially a secular state.

In the event of internal strife, the sympathy of the international community will generally lie with the legitimate government of that country. The government will not wish to give up its position and suppression of revolts, rebellions and insurgencies is usually ruthless. Much legitimacy is conferred by virtue of the government being established and recognised by the international community (see further comments on the Montevideo Convention). The government will not wish to give up its position and suppression of revolts, rebellions and insurgencies and is usually ruthless. Also, individual governments might be wary of their own position and exhibiting too much sympathy for rebels might encourage their own. In short, with revolts, rebellions and insurgencies as well as civil wars, 'the state must win'.

Peaceful secessions are possible. Czechoslovakia split into the Czech Republic and Slovak Republic in the Velvet Revolution at the end of

1989. The classic book on the subject by Dr Abby Innes of LSE is called *Czechoslovakia: The Short Goodbye*.

WAR OF AGGRESSION

One might argue that the term 'War of Aggression' covers many, if not most wars, except those of self-defence. But here we get onto tricky legal and perhaps moral ground.

Insofar as international law was codified and adhered to, suzerainty over an area of land and its inhabitants, taken by military force, was recognised historically under the 'right of conquest' principle.

Waging aggressive war, as a criminal act, was first codified in the Nuremberg Principles and used to prosecute Nazi leaders at the end of World War II. Unsurprisingly, their defence was that there was no existing law at the time of their acts that criminalised what they had done and that, as a general legal principle, a law could not or should not be retrospective. The Nuremberg court did not accept this as a defence and several Nazis were convicted of that and 'crimes against humanity', and executed. Twelve were sentenced to death, seven received prison sentences (ranging from ten years to life) and three were acquitted. But the Court accepted that it was a firm principle of international law that countries could not be judged for what they did to its citizens in time of peace. The policy of *persecution, repression and murder of civilians* within Germany before the outbreak of war were *not* crimes against humanity because as revolting and horrible as many of these crimes were, it has not been satisfactorily proven that they were done in execution of, or in connection with, war crimes or crimes against peace. But this nicety, which allowed tyrants to murder without international interference, has changed over the years, culminating in the UN's 'Responsibility to Protect' (RTP), a global commitment which was agreed by all member states of the United Nations at the 2005 World Summit in order to discourage genocide, war crimes, ethnic cleansing and crimes against humanity. RTP has not been particularly successful, but at least it provides a moral and political anchor point for egregious human rights abuses in other states.

But back to Nuremberg: the idea of the 'right of conquest' abated slowly after the end of World War II, following the Nuremberg judgements.

However, it was not until 1974 that there was a recommendation from the United Nations General Assembly to the Security Council that the 'right of conquest' – hitherto practice rather than law – should be recognised as an international prosecutable crime (the non-binding United Nations General Assembly Resolution 3314).

The Russian invasion of Ukraine throws all this up in the air. In this case, Putin's defence would be that Ukraine is not another country, and always was a part of Mother Russia.

Conquest should not be confused with annexation. If Russia succeeds in conquering Ukraine and then subjugates its population, then that would be treated, under international law, as a conquest, and would be illegal. China took over Tibet in 1950/1951: described as the 'Peaceful Liberation of Tibet' by the Chinese government, or the 'Chinese invasion of Tibet' by the Tibetan Central Tibetan Administration. There were some casualties, though: some 300 Chinese and Tibetan troops were killed. China claimed this as annexation, with the co-operation of the Tibetan administration. One can immediately see that this would be open to debate.

COLD WAR

Most commentators refer to *The* Cold War as that between the United States and its Allies, and the Soviet Union and their allies between 1947 to 1991 when the Soviet Union collapsed. It is called 'cold' because there were no major armed conflicts between the protagonists. However, they each supported proxy wars, such as Soviet support for North Vietnam during the American war there and also various wars in the Middle East.

Casting around for other 'cold wars' might reveal 'The Great Game', fought between Britain and Russia from 1830 to 1895 or maybe Imperial Russia and the Ottoman Empire, but this actually turned 'hot' in the Crimea between 1853 and 1856 and again during the Russo-Turkish War (1877–1878). To all intents and purposes, though, when people refer to 'The Cold War' they are referring to that between the United States and Allies, NATO, and the Soviet Union and their allies, the Warsaw Pact.

EXISTENTIAL WARS

An existential war is one where the very existence of one of the protagonists is under threat of being destroyed. Losing the war would mean that their culture, their language and their way of life would be destroyed and their country occupied. This was a phenomenon of ancient wars, with Caesar's conquest of Gaul resulting in about one third of the three million population being killed, one third being sold into slavery and only one third surviving. Such wars still existed in the 20th century. Hitler's plans for the Slavic states were to destroy them as states.

Historically, there is one other classification which sits aside all others. Until the end of the Second World War, many wars were about European countries' imperial expansion. Although imperialism covers much of history, a representative example is the 18th century competition in North America and India between Great Britain and France. The 'Scramble for Africa' (also the title of a book by Thomas Pakenham (1992)), involved the invasion, annexation, and colonization of Africa by Western European powers. In the last 20 years of the 19th century and until the advent of the First World War, Belgium, Great Britain, France, Imperial Germany, Italy, Portugal and Spain all competed in this vast continent, largely through military means, but also by trade and the appropriation of natural resources. Imperialism was one of the factors that motivated Hitler's dreams.

Ultimately, by 1914, some 90% of the African was seen as a 'possession' of those European powers. Imperialism, its provenance and, and, consequences is a vast subject, and one that still stimulates much academic debate. One might imagine that international affairs has matured sufficiently and that countries compete on the basis of trade and financial strength. Alas, as the Russians annexation of Crimea, they wish to consume Ukraine and China's design on Taiwan have shown, imperialism is still a major factor.

CONCLUSIONS: CAN WE CLASSIFY WARS?

There were two main objectives in outlining the classifications in this chapter.

First, was to put into perspective the incidence of wars over the years whose motivation was reputedly religious. As can be seen, this is a small proportion of what is usually known as religious war. Mostly, 'religious wars' had other and largely overriding *political* goals.

The second aim was to describe the scope and depth of the differences between various types of war as a *political* act, rather than different types of *warfare*. Warfare as such would have dozens more headings with titles ranging from 'low intensity war', through 'jungle warfare' to 'total war' and many others. Military leaders are often accused of re-fighting the previous war, with methods and tactics which were then successful. It is an unfair jibe: military leaders do not invoke wars; that is the role of the politicians, albeit with the advice of the military.

There are several salient points. The first is that the next war will not be the war we were planning to fight, the war we are equipped to fight, the war we want to fight – or even the war we can fight; it will the war that the enemy is actually fighting

The second point is best explained in the famous interview in 1982 between Sir Robert Day and John Nott, the then Secretary of State for Defence. Day described Nott, who was announcing that he would not stand at the next election, as 'a transient, here-today-and-gone-tomorrow politician'. Day asked whether the public should believe the MP's statements on defence cuts. Nott promptly stood up, calling the interview 'ridiculous', removed his microphone and walked out of the studio. To be fair to Nott, he did have the self-deprecation to entitle his autobiography *Here Today, Gone Tomorrow*. The politicians who determine the armed forces' configuration, their equipment and, most importantly, budget, will not be the politicians who have to fight the next war. *Some consensus about the types of future war is essential.* It might be observed that some consensus about all politics could be useful, and this could certainly be applied to infrastructure, health and finance. However, war has such a long lead time that it must be a prime candidate for consensus and coalition working.

Identifying the broad category of any prospective war might also identify its likely success in achieving political objectives.

Let's not forget either, that the enemy has a vote: they will have their own political objectives that will influence their approach. Napoleon was a master of exploiting his enemy's tactical mistakes. ('Never interrupt your enemy when he is making a mistake, it is bad manners.') He was less assured at judging his enemy's political goals or considering what compromise he might accept, which proved fatal.

Whatever war is anticipated and whatever size, configuration and equipment is agreed, future war will always be novel, with its own character, political influences and constraints. It won't look exactly like any previous war, but it might and probably will fit into one or other broad classification. Realising this, might help with avoiding a war or prosecuting the war itself and ultimately improve its chances of success.

CLASSIFYING WAR: CONCLUSIONS

Wars are notoriously easy to get into but difficult to get out of. Some political scientists suggest, perhaps optimistically, that fewer than half of all wars achieve their original objectives for those that initiate it. Consider Korea, Suez or Vietnam or, more recently, Afghanistan, Iraq and Libya.

- How much of this can be put down to fighting the wrong sort of war?
- How much of this can be put down to insufficient political intelligence?
- How much to initiating the war too hastily?
- How much to weaknesses in strategic control?
- A great weakness for all governments is lack of retrospection about past wars.

In the United Kingdom, the historic constitutional right of the monarch to declare war has been usurped, or at least appropriated, by modern governments. With only a nod towards democracy, military involvement is voted on in the House of Commons, with (confidential? sensitive?) intelligence held back and the MPs 'whipped' to toe the party line.

Thus, it is largely the responsibility of the prime minister to decide whether the country goes to war or not. One wonders how seriously they consider the politics of the matter. Not their politics or those of putative allies, but the politics of the hapless target of the war. It may be a matter of respect: the population of Iraq is about thirty-eight million souls, the same as Canada, yet there was little regard for Iraqi citizens.

Categorising war, either in the configuring and equipping stage or in the immediate planning of a particular war, may seem over-obsessive, but success will go to parties who are quite clear about what sort of war they are fighting, and what the ultimate objective might be

War is not comprehensively understood, sometimes impatiently initiated and, because of weaknesses of strategic control, simply unsuccessful.

Regardless of faction, the war in Syria has been murderous, tragic and without purpose to the vast majority of the population.

8. TERRORISM

Everyone knows what terrorism is ...

It is people blowing up trains or concert venues; it is seemingly random attacks or assassinations with a knife; it is hijacking civilian aircraft and insisting they fly to – what to the terrorists – is a safe haven. Yet suppose you are a legislator whose task it is to draft suitable laws to prosecute terrorists. The first question you might ask is: how does blowing up, assassination or hijacking differ from ordinary crime? You might then ask whether you need terrorist legislation at all. What is the essential difference between crime and terrorism?

Consulting commentators such as academics or think tanks would not help: there is no universally accepted definition of terrorism. Indeed, some people, recognising that terroristic acts are, in any case, criminal, might just suggest that terrorism simply doesn't exist as a subject, and there is no need for specialist legislation.

Even international efforts have not succeeded in formulating a universal definition. After the 1972 Munich Olympics massacre, where eleven Israeli athletes and officials were killed by the Palestinian terrorist group, Black September, the United Nations Secretary General, Kurt Waldheim, suggested that the UN should 'take practical steps that might prevent such events happening again'. Most UN members agreed, but there was a small minority of Arab, African and Asian countries who complained that in their own liberation struggles, they were obliged to use what could be called terrorism to further their cause. This small minority also claimed that it was not violent acts themselves that needed focus, but the underlying causes of their grievances.

Legitimate states, whether democracies or dictatorships, will often describe liberation movements as terrorists, however bona fide they are to the external world, however just their cause and however much popular support they have. The current example of this is might be Belarus, where opposition protesters are labelled 'terrorists' by their dictatorial president, Lukashenko.

THE DIFFERENCE BETWEEN CRIME AND TERRORISM

The core difference between crime and terrorism is that for any action to be called terrorism, it must have a *political context.*

It is this political context, characterised by the often quoted 'one man's terrorist is another man's freedom fighter', that makes terrorism so difficult to fully understand and to counter. This aphorism about terrorist / freedom fighter might be thought of as morally dubious: after all, murder and destruction are both crimes under almost all legislative systems. Yet it is a tricky one. Nelson Mandela was branded a terrorist by Margaret Thatcher, but it is now accepted that to end the brutal iniquities of apartheid, it was a legitimate route to take, having failed to make any progress with the then government of South Africa. Some revolutionaries are branded as 'terrorists' by the established government, but they may be fighting against an oppressive and murderous regime.

Terrorism has a place in this book because it involves both violence and politics. Major terrorist organisations, such as Revolutionary Armed Forces of Colombia (the 'People's Army'), more popularly known as 'FARC', or the Naxalite–Maoist insurgency in India or al-Qaeda may need a full-scale military response. Also, as we shall see, terrorism is a tactical activity, whereas a strategic approach is required to counter it.

A precise definition matters because, however misconceived the cause and however brutal the attacks, there may well be some popular support for the terrorists themselves. During the 'Troubles' in Northern Ireland (1967 to 1999), it was difficult for the British Army to operate in Roman Catholic areas. During the Nazi occupation of France during the Second World War, 'La Résistance' could not have operated without the support of the general population, despite brutal reprisals. One can be sure that the Nazi occupiers branded them terrorists.

A HISTORICAL PERSPECTIVE OF TERRORISM, AND THE CHANGING MEANING OF THE TERM

Originally, 'terror' did not have such a pejorative meaning. During the French Revolutionary period, the 'Reign of Terror' (La Régime de la Terreur, 1793 to 1794) was focused on maintaining public order during a transitional period, monarchy to republic. Louis XVI had been guillotined in January 1793. For those familiar with that period, Robespierre was guillotined in July 1794, and The Terror mutated into a further period of executions and massacres. As the sage says, most revolutions consume their own children.

Retrospectively, the first 'terrorism' is often identified with the Jewish revolt against Roman rule in the 1st century AD. According to the Jewish-Roman historian, Josephus (not the most reliable witness), some Jewish collaborators with the Romans were assassinated by the Sicarii, a splinter group of the Jewish Zealots. Later, they directed their campaign against temple priests and other wealthy elites, who probably benefited from Roman rule. It had little effect on the Romans, who exacted cruel retribution. In fact, the main benefit accrued to Rome; the future Emperor Vespasian used the war booty to build the Colosseum; it's still there.

Between 1090 and 1275, the 'Order of Assassins', a sect of Shia Islam, lived in the area between Persia and Syria. They killed hundreds of leaders thought to be enemies of their state, including three Caliphs, a ruler of Jerusalem and several Muslim and Christian leaders. They did not seem to have much of a political agenda, other than their service to their state. They suffered during the Mongol invasions of the 13th century and eventually died out.

After the French Revolution and up to the 19th century, one can be sure that there were other different individuals or groups who carried out assassinations of the ruling elite, but evidence for this, and the appellation 'terrorist' does not appear very much in the historical record.

With the increased political consciousness during the 19th century, there were various revolutions, insurgencies and terrorist attacks. The Irish Fenians campaigned throughout the later 19th and early 20th century for an independent Irish republic. Between 1881 and 1885, a small group, some of whom were known as the dynamiters, carried out a bombing campaign against the British, targeted at infrastructure, government, military and police targets in Ireland and on the mainland, and particularly London.

During the 1960s, the Argentine Marxist revolutionary, Che Guevara, with his idea of 'foco' imagined that paramilitary groups could provide a focus for general antagonism against the existing government and so foment a general insurrection. This dynamic is unproven. Che Guevara was popular at the time, but his followers, more intellectual and romantic than practical, did not heed his advice that his foco was not sufficient to change government. His idea has an echo today in that one of the motivations for terrorist attacks is to gather support from non-followers or those uncertain of joining the cause.

Most of the currently relevant changes in terrorism happened during the 20th century, and there is little connection with the Sicarii Zealots, who are often quoted as the first protagonists. After the First World War, the concept of terrorism changed. Whereas the 19th century had seen revolutionary movements *against* governments, terrorism came to be used as the practice of totalitarian states oppressing their own citizens – such as Nazi Germany, Stalinist Russia and Fascist Italy.

AFTER THE SECOND WORLD WAR

After the Second World War, the concept of terrorism evolved again. Now, terrorism was associated with indigenous anti-colonialist groups who wanted an end to European rule. As early as 1946, the militant Zionist organisation 'Irgun' bombed the King David Hotel in Jerusalem, then the British Mandate Administrative Headquarters. Ninety-one people of various nationalities were killed and forty-six were injured. The British withdrew in 1948 but this was due to the lack of resources rather than the terrorists. The Israeli state was declared the same year.

EOKA in Cyprus and the Mau EKA in Kenya hold examples of anti-colonialist terrorism; the most active and long lasting being the PLO, the Palestine Liberation Organisation and the Basque ETA.

Although during the 1960s and 1970s, terrorism, with its counterpoint 'freedom fighter' was seen in a revolutionary context, it now came to be seen as an ideologically motivated theme of minority ethnic groups wanting independence from the overall state, ETA in the Basque country in Spain and Terra Lliure or Free Land in Catalonia being examples of this.

There was a brief panic in the 1980s that terrorism was part of a global conspiracy sponsored by the Soviet Kremlin, and then in the 1990s when various states such as Iran, Iraq, Libya and Syria became state sponsors of terrorism, largely against who they saw as the Great Satan: the United States of America.

During this time, there were many other terrorist groups, usually campaigning against their own government. For example, there was the Italian Red Brigade (1970 to 1988), a Marxist–Leninist group responsible for up to seventy-five murders and particularly the abduction and murder of former prime minister, Aldo Moro; and Action Directe, a French far-left group responsible for a number of assassinations and violent actions in France between 1979 and 1987 and who styled themselves 'libertarian communists'. In Spain, the 2004 Madrid train bombings caused a horrendous 193 fatalities and over two thousand injured casualties. Originally thought to be an al-Qaeda attack, it was later thought to be carried out by ETA, the Basque separatist group.

By way of illustration and contrast, see panels for the Provisional Irish Republican Army and the Red Army Faction.

THE PROVISIONAL IRISH REPUBLICAN ARMY

The relationship between the British state and Ireland has historically been troubled. Absent landlords, living in England, exploited the Irish people during the late 19th and early 20th century (and earlier) and there were many movements for an independent Ireland. Things came to a head in the Easter Rising, an armed insurrection during April 1916. The concept of an 'Irish Free State' was often debated in the British Parliament. After this Easter Rising, British heavy handedness, when sixteen of the leaders were executed, further encouraged the popularity of an independent Irish republic.

Irish partition in 1921 divided Ireland into two self-governing polities: Northern and Southern Ireland, with Northern Ireland remaining in the United Kingdom. In the south, political complications led to the Irish civil war; the Irish Free State supporters won. But the republic was not happy with the partition of Ireland, and neither were the Catholics in Northern Ireland. Since then, the pro-treaty (The 'Treaty' refers to the 1921 Anglo-Irish Treaty between the government of the United Kingdom of Great Britain and Ireland and representatives of the Irish Republic. It recognised the Irish Free State and concluded the Irish War of

Independence) force became the National Army (Ireland), and then the Irish Defence Forces.

The Provisional Irish Republican Army, popularly known as the 'Provos' became active in 1969, the year that the British state ordained 'direct rule' from Westminster, heralding 'the troubles'. The Provos were successor to the 'original' IRA but not organisationally related. The 'real IRA' now refers to another dissident paramilitary group. The Provisional IRA's political agenda came to end Westminster rule in Northern Ireland, push for Irish reunification and thus bring about an independent republic for the whole of Ireland. Overall, 'the troubles', cost over 3,500 lives.

Their political objective was clear. Did the terror tactics further their cause? The British Army, who assisted the police in Northern Ireland between 1970 and 1999 claimed that they had fought the Provos to a standstill. The Provos claimed that they had obliged the British state to negotiate openly with them, which produced the Good Friday Agreement in 1998. This debate continues, but is something of historic interest, as there is a general feeling in Ireland that they want to 'move on'. Until Brexit, peace and a degree of stability had reigned in both the Republic and Northern Ireland.

Part of the campaign for an independent Ireland was what the British saw as terrorism, and it may be that the British would still be interfering in Ireland had there not been an armed element.

Many commentators now think that the reunification of Ireland is inevitable.

THE RED ARMY FACTION: GERMAN TERRORISM IN THE SEVENTIES AND EIGHTIES

The Red Army Faction (German: Rote Armee Faktion - RAF) also known as the Baader–Meinhof Gang after its leaders Andreas Baader and Ulrike Meinhof, was a German left-wing terrorist organisation that espoused left-wing ideas based on readings of Gramsci and Marcuse and, eventually, Marxism–Leninism. They were also dissatisfied with the extent of the West German government's efforts of post-war de-Nazification, as former real and assumed Nazis held senior positions in the government and in industry.

They operated in West Germany (simply 'Germany' after reunification in 1990), France, the Netherlands and Sweden. They were one of the most violent of all European terrorist groups, being responsible for thirty-four deaths, including assassinations of industrialists and other business leaders.

The question is: can we believe and indeed could *they* believe that their murders, bomb attacks and hijacks might persuade politicians and the relevant authorities to consider a more left-wing or even socialist regime? Did they really believe that they could dismantle the international systems of what they saw as imperialism and capitalism and foment a Marxist–Leninist revolution? Set against the usual and historic state response of more security measures, interpreted by the terrorists as oppression, this must be seen as highly unlikely, and essentially counter-productive.

In an MA thesis from 2009, *West German Terror: The Lasting*

Legacy of The Red Army Faction by Christina L. Stefanik, Bowling Green State University, Idaho, she quotes from a 2002 *Spiegel* interview, with Astrid Proll, who was an early member of the RAF. When asked about the nature of the RAF, Proll said, 'I don't even know if the RAF was a political group. It was more like the self-pretentiousness of an entire generation.' Stefanik completes her thesis by suggesting that 'The RAF is a large piece of the German post-war puzzle. For some, Baader, Ensslin, Meinhof, Raspe, Meins and other deceased RAF members, will remain martyrs, or at least entrancing figures of German history. For others, the RAF was nothing more than a ruthless gang of selfish killers, victims of nothing who were treated better than they should have been.'

Perhaps the truth lies somewhere between these two extremes. She goes on to say: 'One person's accidental terrorist is another person's cold-blooded murderer. A new government in a new state, with its unique historical baggage, reacted the best way it knew how. The past obviously cannot be undone, but one must wonder how many more decades of young Germans will be fascinated by the actions of a long-gone terrorist group called the Red Army Faction.'

It is a clever and percipient comment, but *new government in a new state*? No, however one thinks about the state as an institution and however one traces the provenance of the *idea* of the state, its survival as itself is paramount to itself.

So, over the centuries, and up to the end of the 20th century, terrorism had changed from assassinating dissidents, to assassinating heads of state, to causing serious violence against colonial masters, to pretentious, self-referential, self-justifying but murderous dissidents. Imagining that they heralded a new world order, they spouted Marxist–Leninist dogma without a full understanding of the way states, international relations and politics work. Marx would have been horrified.

THE 7 JULY 2005 LONDON BOMBINGS (OFTEN REFERRED TO AS 7/7)

This attack provides a different perspective on terrorism. On 7 July 2005, Islamist terrorists carried out four separate suicide attacks on London's public transport system, using, it was thought, improvised explosive devices – home-made bombs.

The four bombers were killed instantly, together with fifty-two other people of eighteen different nationalities. Seven hundred were injured. This made it the worst terrorist incident on the UK mainland since a bomb on a Pan Am plane was brought down over Lockerbie in 1988 with the loss of the 207 people on board and three on the ground. It was the UK's first Islamist suicide attack.

While still a terrorist attack, it was different in many respects from the 9/11 attack. The terrorists were home-grown UK citizens, with no previous convictions. None of them had come to the attention of the intelligence community. Three of the bombers were British-born sons of Pakistani immigrants; one was a convert to Islam born in Jamaica.

Two of the bombers made videotapes, mentioning Islam: 'Democratically-elected governments continuously perpetuate atrocities against my (sic) people and, specifically, Palestine, Afghanistan, Iraq and Chechnya.'

As such, they echoed Osama bin Laden's 2002 'Letter to America', outlined in the next chapter.

The lexicon also changed, with words such as *freedom, liberation* and *workers* and even *self-defence* being used by the perpetrators to describe themselves. To the victims, they were still terrorists. Despite this, and despite an academic interest in defining terrorism more closely, it was still the deliberate use of organised violence against civilians, off-duty military personnel and infrastructure (essentially non-combatants), for the purpose of prompting, encouraging and reinforcing political change. A clear political purpose might be rebellion or secession, whereas attacks which appear not to have any particular purpose might prompt harsh and repressive measures from a government that may eventually cause that government to fail, a *political* objective.

DEFINING TERRORISM

Internationally, there seem to be as many definitions as there are legislatures. To ensure that they catch all the suspects, some legislatures define international terrorism separately. Most mention violence against civil society in one way or another; all mention the political aspect of terrorism. Given the lengthy history of terrorism, it is worth defining the term more closely. The quest for a conclusive definition of terrorism has been described as an 'academic dead-end', but that may be because the aspiration is for a pithy aphorism, shorn of qualifications and subclauses. Let us abandon that constraint in the interests of a more comprehensive definitional commentary. For this we can say that terrorism is:

The use or threat of violence against civic society, individuals, minority groups, or the state itself, or private infrastructure.

The targets are essentially non-combatants.

Its purpose is to instil fear and insecurity and force or prevent political change, which may be religious, racial or ideological.

It can be carried out by non-state actors or states themselves, who may target their own populations, minority groups or other states.

In some cases, the political objective of a terrorist attack is 'the propaganda of the deed', or to gain kudos with the terrorists' own constituency in order to aid recruitment and to raise funds.

It may be wordy and somewhat clumsy, but this definition covers all the aspects of terrorism. It is here that terrorism differs from crime. Crimes are committed for a whole range of reasons; there is always some tangible material gain, profit or gratification for an individual or a group, even to the extent of revenge or eliminating a rival. With terrorism, the motivations can be ideological, religious or political, the benefit being to many more and unknown people. Revenge might also be a factor. There is a degree of overlap: some terrorist groups practice robbery and deal in drugs to gain funds for their activities and some drug cartels (for example, FARC in Colombia) also have a political agenda, providing social services to the areas it controls. If you need a short, working definition of terrorism …

Violence against civic society for a political purpose
… will serve.

THE BRITISH TERRORISM ACT (2000)

Although there was some anti-terrorism legislation during the 20th century, the main milepost in dealing with terrorism was the British Terrorism Act (2000). Since then, some of the provisions have been enhanced or repealed and some other legislation has been passed, the latest being the Counter-Terrorism and Sentencing Act (2021).

The definition of terrorism has expanded, and certain actions either before or after a terrorism outrage are now illegal. There is much concern from human rights groups about some of the restrictions, for example holding papers or downloading information about terrorism, expressing support for a terrorist group or glorifying it.

THE ROOTS OF TERRORISM

Terrorism is a tactical activity with, in most cases, a largely indeterminate and unachievable strategic objective: a Marxist–Leninist state; a World Caliphate; sorting all the problems of the world while you're at it, etc. Yet Counter-Terrorism must involve a strategic approach, not just a collection of tactical actions. A strategic approach might start with a clear analysis of the roots of terrorism, which often follow conventional wisdoms or prejudices.

Commentaries often cite poverty, lack of education, state collapse, with failed states providing havens for terrorists and general low economic activity. Yet a detailed examination of any clusters of the provenance, progress and cessation of terrorist activity would suggest that all terrorisms, indeed, like all wars, have their own particular causes and courses and also, interestingly, at some point, end.

Nevertheless, there are some pointers. Poverty and ignorance are often quoted as motivations for terrorism and there is no doubt that these contribute. In a book entitled *Bombing to Win*, Richard A Pape, an American political scientist at the University of Chicago, suggests that terror bombing, carried out by states, far from turning a population against its political masters, actually hardens their reaction to the enemy and their allegiance to their political leaders. Such was the case in Hitler's Germany: some 300,000 civilians died as a result of Allied bombing, but this had the paradoxical result of increasing support for Hitler and his regime. Recall that the extensive bombing of Afghanistan,

Iraq and, later, Libya, did not endear those populations to the countries bombing them. Pape translates this into a suggestion that an important motivation for terrorism is oppression, real or perceived, which will boil over eventually, as in Palestine. In Peru too, the Shining Path group (Sendero Luminoso) exploited people's feelings of oppression.

Foreign occupation contributes to sometimes perceived, sometimes actual, injustices and humiliation. Far from blaming their own government, populations tend to project their problems onto their occupiers. The ruling party of Palestine's West Bank, Fatah, are quiescent in the face of Israeli occupation, yet it is the Israelis who get the opprobrium.

ISLAMIC TERRORISM: A PARTICULAR THREAT?

Islamic terrorism was a movement before 9/11 and became very prominent thereafter. But what exactly is 'Islamic terrorism'? One might imagine that it is easy to define: terrorist acts carried out by Islamicists motivated by religious fervour. But in a similar way to almost everything one can say about terrorism, one can also respond with a 'yes but'. Even the expression 'Islamic terrorism' is disputed, being called variously 'counter-productive', 'too politicised' and 'damaging to community relations'.

To take a more objective view, the problem with the term, and the definition, is that there is an ulterior suspicion that Muslims in general are sympathetic to the cause, and that the target of the terrorism is aimed at the Christian, Jewish or even secular West. These assumptions are simply wrong: the vast majority of Muslims are horrified by the idea of Islamicist terrorism. The vast majority of Muslims practice their faith peacefully, and some three quarters of victims of Islamic terrorism are Muslims themselves. Terrorists from a western, supposedly Christian background are not called 'Christian terrorists', and neither should terrorists who happen to be Muslims be identified as Islamic terrorists.

Fortunately, definitions have moved on, and the term now most favoured is 'Islamist', thus 'Islamist terrorism'. It's a fine lexical difference, but important.

Yet self-avowed Islamicist extremist groups such as ISIS, the Islamic State of Iraq and the Levant, Boko Haram in Nigeria, the Taliban in Afghanistan, Al-Shabaab in East Africa and Yemen and the remains of al-Qaeda are still potent and need to be handled. The problem for the British and other states – particularly the French – is that the focus sometimes moves to all young Muslim men, to the detriment of both the state and the subjects themselves.

'MUSLIM YOUTH'

For complete coverage though, and in addition to the Baader–Meinhof gang and al-Qaeda, we also need to think about radicalised youth, mainly young Muslim men, seeing media coverage of the horrors inflicted on what they would see as fellow Muslims by occupying forces in Muslim countries. They then might carry out further research on the internet and find appeals to their youthful idealism. They may then feel part of some broader movement. Such young men often talk about their 'brothers': similarly influenced young Muslim men fighting a secular or apostate world. They seem not to realise that the vast majority of Muslim men and women do not seek a worldwide caliphate and are largely committed to some form of democratic liberalism.

In 2008, *The Guardian* newspaper published a report from MI5 that challenges the conventional views on who might be a potential terrorist in Britain. They concluded that there is no easy way to identify those who might become involved in terrorism. Having examined hundreds of case studies, they concluded that there is no single pathway to violent extremism. And far from being Islamist fundamentalists, most are religious novices. One young man who was arrested on his return from working with ISIS in Iraq was found to have a volume called *Islam for Dummies* in his luggage! So, assumptions cannot be made about people based on skin colour, ethnic heritage or nationality. In other studies, most terrorists were found to be college educated, not the poor and desperate.

Despite the terrible costs of joining a terrorist group, this young man might see rewards, such as affirmation of his own disparate views, working with like-minded individuals and ultimately, maybe, the apotheosis of martyrdom.

HOW THEN DOES TERRORISM END?

Intuitively, we know that all terrorism campaigns end, or the group becomes quiescent. In principle, the PLO in Palestine still exists and is a focus for anti-Israeli actions but no longer mounts 'spectaculars', such as hijackings, and its Intifadas have not achieved their objectives. FARC in Colombia has been seriously reduced in strength. The political wing of the Provisional IRA is now power-sharing in Northern Ireland. ETA have achieved concessions form the Spanish government and, in 2018, published a letter saying it had completely dissolved all its structures and ended its political initiative. The horrific Red Army Faction, Action Directe, and Italian Red Brigade are no more. Al-Qaeda may be a shadow of its former self, and other groups claiming to be al-Qaeda affiliates are actually more distant franchise operations than successors. Notwithstanding, al-Qaeda remains a threat and is likely to rise again. But terrorisms do end.

In 2011, an American academic, Dr Audrey Kurth Cronin published a book entitled *How Terrorism Ends*. After a considerable and exhaustive research effort, she suggests that, when coping with terrorism, it may be more pertinent to consider how it ends than how it begins. She advances six main headings for considering this:

DECAPITATION

The group's leader, and maybe inspiration, is either captured or killed. Where the leader has built up a committed following with many lieutenants, decapitation will not work, but where the leader is the main inspiration for the group, then decapitation can leave their followers disoriented and thereby impotent. In these cases, the group will simply die out.

GROUP ENTERS A LEGITIMATE POLITICAL PROCESS

Most governments claim that they 'never negotiate with terrorists', but of course some back door negotiation, almost always deniable, takes place. Notwithstanding resistance from those who are more committed to a peaceful campaign, this is comparatively rare, although the Provisional IRA are now power-sharing in Northern Ireland, through their political wing, Sinn Féin.

GROUP ACHIEVES ITS POLITICAL AIMS

Which were, exactly? Most groups' objectives are hyperbolic, and a typical example of this would be ETA in the Basque region of Spain and, to a lesser degree Catalonia. Terrorist campaigns in both these communities sought complete independence from Spain, but they have settled for devolved powers.

GROUP LOSES POPULAR SUPPORT

As Mao Zedong warned, insurgencies cannot survive without the support of the local population. This might also apply to terrorist groups, and although most people will express horror at the thought of terror attacks, there has to be a small amount support from sections of the general population. For example, when the Provisional IRA was active in London, they relied on safe houses owned by Irish Republicans for havens.

GROUP IS ELIMINATED BY BRUTE FORCE

Several terrorist groups have been eliminated or considerably reduced, by military action, particularly where they occupy a geographic area or an area where there is much support in the general population. Examples of this are FARC and the Tamil Tigers in Sri Lanka, the latter brutally suppressed and eliminated by the Sri Lankan army who killed the top leadership in the process.

THE GROUP TRANSITIONS TO OTHER FORMS OF VIOLENCE

Some terrorist groups fund their operations – and their livings – with petty crime or larger-scale, organised crime. *Some* terrorist groups drop the political aspects of their activity *and sometimes* transition to petty or organised crime, as happened with some sections of the Provisional IRA after the Good Friday Agreement.

Dr Cronin implies that instead of thinking about how well we are succeeding against terrorism, we should focus on the question: *How will this particular terrorism end?*

DOES TERRORISM WORK?

In 2016, Richard English, a professor at Queen's University Belfast posted a piece on *Timeline* (a blog) entitled 'The Question No one is Really Asking: Does Terrorism Work?' He opens the article with the suggestion that 'to even pose this question today is beyond the pale'. There is a good deal of political correctness about answering this conundrum. Most people would immediately respond to the question with 'Of course it doesn't. We can't be seen to be giving in to murderous thugs …' Challenged to comment on extrajudicial drone killings, the same people might respond that 'This is an entirely different affair.' Moral, political and strategic questions arise, sometimes to the confusion of all.

Most politicians will assert that, 'We don't negotiate with terrorists …'

when they probably do. This is handy rebuttal to avoid owning up to possible concessions, previously denied. To be fair to the politicians, the problem is that if the media gets hold of even the whiff of a concession, it will parade the latest victim and claim that the government 'ought to do something', while at the same time eschewing engagement with the political side of terrorist demands.

Yet we must engage with every aspect of terrorism, including the question of whether it works, if we are to understand it, counter it and eventually, we might hope, eliminate or reduce it considerably.

To counter or at least deal with terrorism, we must understand the effectiveness or otherwise of terrorist campaigns. But how do we do this?

Questions crowd in: how to define effectiveness; are we considering tactical or strategic effectiveness; and, having defined success, how do we define failure and can we attribute the elimination of a particular terrorist group to our own efforts or to the terrorists? It is therefore an uncomfortable political judgement as to whether there is any real political motivation behind terrorist demands.

EFFECTIVE TERRORISM

Right-wing state terrorism in Hitler's Germany, Stalin's Russia and Mussolini's Italy resulted in success in terms of taking power and the establishment of authoritarian regimes.

Though the notion should be accompanied by a big 'but', Osama bin Laden may have had a vision, if not of a worldwide caliphate, of at least a dilution of American influence. And although it's taken twenty years, via Obama being hobbled by the Republicans, Trump ('nuf said) and Joe Biden's Afghanistan withdrawal, he may have achieved just that. We examine American foreign policy since 9/11 in the next chapter.

The Irgun bombing of the King David Hotel in Jerusalem in 1945 may be seen as an example of terrorism that hastened the formation of the

Israeli state. But the independent Jewish state was bound to come about at some stage, after the Balfour Declaration (1926), some twenty years earlier and pressure, often violent, from Zionists. There was also pressure on the British administration and also from the United States too.

Cypriot terrorism against the occupying British forces is often held up as an example of successful terrorism, but this must be seen against the background of decolonisation. In fact, and although Cyprus is now an independent republic, the RAF still has a large base there on the Akrotiri Peninsula.

Some terrorist groups, while not actually achieving their overall objective of independence, have wrung important concessions out of the state. ETA, the Basque separatist group, whose toll of casualties amounted to about 850 dead and also the assassination of the Spanish prime minister, Luis Carrero Blanco, in Madrid in 1973, did not achieve an independent Basque state, but their tactical success wrung many concessions out of the Spanish state. The Catalonian separatist group, Terra Lliure ('Free Land') were less active and less brutal than ETA, but manged to wring some milder concessions from Madrid. The Provisional IRA would claim that they have managed to end the occupation of Northern Ireland by the British Army, and are well on the way to a united and independent Ireland. There are then many terrorist groups where they have achieved nothing like their stated objectives, but would claim success in one sense or another. For example, the PLO still exists and is still trying to achieve an independent Palestine. Many of the anti-colonial movements, EOKA in Cyprus and the Mau Mau in Kenya would claim success, whatever their colonial masters might say; this must be seen in the context of a general anti-colonial movement.

Some terrorist actions are not only ineffective, but detract from the terrorists' objectives. In the seventies, the Baader–Meinhof Group, the Italian Red Brigade and the French Action Directe, preaching a left-wing future, were failures, both tactically and strategically. The Peruvian Sendero Luminoso (Shining Path) was not successful, despite causing between 35,000 and nearly 70,000 deaths.

One of the themes of the first book in this series, *About War*, was the utility of force: how does one convert military action into political gain? The Palestinians offer a good negative insight here. Various Palestinian Intifadas over the years – 1987 to 1993, 2000 to 2005, and maybe in the present day – have not advanced the Palestinian cause in any material way. By way of contrast, the violence visited on the Palestinians by the Israeli Defence Force has not advanced *their* political objectives at all, in the sense of security and peace.

Overall, there are hundreds of designated terrorist groups in the world. The CIA identifies some sixty-five plus FTOs (Foreign Terrorist Organisations) and the British Home Office some seventy-eight PITGs (Proscribed International Terrorist Groups). Obviously, there is double counting but this gives an idea of the scale of aspiring terrorists. Only a few of these seem to be active.

How do we qualify 'effective'? What we can say is that *some* terrorist acts are effective *some* of the time. There are very few who actually reach their stated goals or even those they might settle for. Those that are effective and claim success, usually have other contributing factors, like decolonisation or vigorous attempts by the state and the aggrieved polity to resolve their differences.

Terrorism will remain a world threat and we should brace ourselves for more, seemingly senseless attacks. But political change does not generally come about by acts of terrorism and the sooner potential terrorists learn that, the safer the world will be. This does not mean that in any way we should let up on intelligence gathering, anti-radicalisation strategies or putting adequate resources into counter-terrorism. As long as there is a danger from terrorism, these must continue.

COUNTER-TERRORISM STRATEGY

First, a little theory: terrorism is essentially a tactic. The idea of a 'war on terror', as adumbrated by George W Bush, has always been disparaged, on the basis that you cannot wage war on a tactic. Tactics are what happens at the front line: increased security, better intelligence and the engagement of local police and community leaders with people who might be potential terrorists: indeed, some of what the British government has been doing.

Strategy is about the longer term, a vision of the future where we might address some of the terrorists' legitimate concerns, instead of dismissing them out of hand. This might include a lasting peace in the Middle East or a resolution of the Palestinian problem. Strategy might also include, for example, teaching Civics in schools, and refining the processes with which we deal with terrorism. Strategy is fully defined in *About War* and replicated in Appendix 1 of this volume. In the UK, the government's *Prevent* strategy (part of CONTEST, the overall counter-terrorism strategy) is probably the only and best solution to this domestic terrorism. The other aspects of CONTEST are *Pursue*, *Protect* and *Prepare*.

One problem here is that what passes for counter-terror strategy is often not much more than a collection of various tactical actions. Fair enough in terms of keeping the population safe, or at least satisfied, but does it reflect the broader, longer-term problems which might invoke feelings of alienation or oppression? Most commentaries on terrorism – particularly true of American writing – are wholly unreflective: there seems to be little consideration that the root causes of terrorism might be policies pursued by the targeted people, or their leaders, in the past.

In terms of the progress of any particular terrorist group, liberal, democratic free-market Western economies (if such exist; many fall short in some ways) bemoan the absence of those values and imagine that countries lacking these are partly dysfunctional and will thus harbour and even promote terrorism.

CONCLUSIONS

Terrorism is a broad subject, perhaps too broad to consider as a distinct topic on its own. At the social psychological level, it concerns the effect of terror tactics, which really do make people feel terrified out of proportion to their own risk. At the tactical level, it concerns impressionable young men and some young women sitting at their computers in their bedrooms imagining that they are part of a worldwide group intent on righting all the world's wrongs. Young people imagining that they can change the world is hardly a new phenomenon.

The study of terrorism, like the study of other war-related subjects, depends to a large extent on the perceived current need, or the threat, of any particular activity. It is not so long ago that there were endless conferences, papers and books on Peace Support Operations, counterinsurgency (COIN) and nation building. Has the need disappeared or have people tired of the lack of success, or just got bored? After 9/11, the focus shifted to terrorism and counter-terrorism. There have been fewer terrorist attacks over the past few years, though it's difficult to know to what extent this is the result of counter-terrorism efforts.

Now the focus is shifting to great power competition, cyber security and the threats posed by mass migration. The problem is that the terrorist movements in general might be taking a longer-term view of the world than the comfortable, prosperous and peaceful West. It doesn't matter that the solutions to whatever problems the terrorists imagine may lie in their own hands and that there may be many agencies ready and willing to help. Slaughtering thousands of people is not going to answer the question of whether the West has stolen Islam's wealth ...

Studying, analysing and coping with terrorism is challenging. Unlike say international relations in general, there is little contemporary data, the motivations are difficult to understand and protection against terrorist attack is expensive and intrusive. And we have to recognise that there is another, somewhat more romantic dimension. Che Guevara, the revolutionary leader, 1928 to 1967, dubbed 'Poster Boy of The Revolution' by the *Washington Post* in October 1997, was actually feared for his brutality and ruthlessness. Yet, given his charisma, his famous portrait can be found in many bedrooms and on many T-shirts. He, or at least his image, is as famous as any consumer brand. The Baader–Meinhof Gang were brutal killers, but recall Astrid Proll's comment about it being more like the 'self-pretentiousness of an entire generation'. You can still buy Red Army Faction posters, shopping bags and T-shirts emblazoned with the Baader–Meinhof logo.

To counter terrorism, we can carry on as we have in the past, doing our best to mitigate its effects: a tactical approach. A strategic approach might be, as part of diplomacy in general, to address the broader issues that incite terrorism. In his contribution to the publication *Superterrorism: Policy Responses*, Professor Sir Lawrence Freedman made some observations about liberal or humanitarian interventions, now out of fashion. He suggested that the causes of many contemporary problems, and thus terrorism, were weak states, 'unable to manage their own affairs and thus descending into the old apocalyptic scourges of persecution, war, famine and disease.'

One of the tragedies of America's reaction to the 9/11 attacks is the retreat of Liberal Internationalism. Freedman warns that any weak state is likely to produce or harbour terrorists and that it is in the interests of the West to treat these weak states as a strategic problem, if not an exigent threat. There is also the moral issue: should we, in the peaceful and prosperous West, care at all for impoverished and war-torn countries and their wretched populations? This concerns who we are and what we are, our moral outlook and what we see as our responsibility for the global community. Many people would suggest that, since the West was founded on Christian ideals, this was the very least we could do. Also, given the phenomenal amount of money spent on arms, only a small proportion of this need be diverted to peaceful purposes. Thus, a strategic approach might address, inter alia, the idea of a lasting peace in the Near and Middle East. There would be plenty of other opportunities. Of all the states in that region, we could identify many as having a security and thus terrorist concern:

The Balkans (largely through crime and corruption); Lebanon (simply a broken state); Syria (still experiencing a civil war); Yemen (ditto); a putative Kurdistan (still aspiring to independence); Armenia / Azerbaijan / Nagorno-Karabakh (only held together with a Russian peacekeeping force); Libya (only emerging slowly, if at all, from warlordism caused by the removal of Muammar al-Gaddafi); and, of course, the Palestine/ Israeli problem. There may be many others.

Suggestions for a strategic approach would elicit a weary nod from political leaders, implying that it is exactly what they were about. But when you consider the strategic aspects of the Afghanistan debacle, the Iraq debacle and even Libya, this has to be questioned. It doesn't help that the U.S. may be retreating into semi-isolationism and focusing on domestic, right-wing terrorism, and thus not providing the leadership needed to focus and maintain a credible strategic response. Given an increasing partisanship within the U.S., which, in pitting left, right, Democrat Republican, MAGAs (Make America Great Again), religious fundamentals, white supremacists and heaven knows (though I doubt heaven has an opinion) how many others, the United States may find it difficult to achieve any consensus in its strategic outlook.

Defining and implementing strategy, a theme of this series, is not difficult. There are plenty of intellectual and informational resources available and, properly briefed, teams of politicians, diplomats, military people, academics and think tankers can be assembled. The constraint is largely one of timescale. Politicians want quick cheap solutions which are approved of by voters. The problems themselves require long-term thinking and investment.

It is a conundrum that has been around for a long time and looks likely to remain.

9. THE STRATEGIC CONSEQUENCES OF THE AMERICAN RESPONSE TO 9/11

On the morning of Tuesday, 11 September 2001, the world changed dramatically ...

Four aircraft, which had taken off from airports across the north-eastern United States, were hijacked by what were suspected to be al-Qaeda terrorists, though their true provenance was not known at the time. In fact, al-Qaeda's involvement was denied by Osama bin Laden, the group's leader, and it was not until 2004 that he admitted responsibility.

Two of the aircraft crashed into the North and South towers of the World Trade Center in New York City, one aircraft crashed into the Pentagon and the third, where the passengers had struggled with hijackers, crashed into a field in Pennsylvania. It was thought that this aircraft was intended to fly into the White House or the Capitol building in Washington.

The total casualties of nearly 3,000 comprised the passengers and crew of the four planes, the occupants of the Twin Towers and the rescue workers who were killed or died in the aftermath.

Hitherto, terrorist attacks were thought of as demonstrations to gain attention for terrorist aims, even though they might cause dozens or scores of deaths. It was sometimes said that terrorists wanted 'a lot of media attention, but not many dead'. This attack, the deadliest and most costly in human history, became known as 9/11, the U.S. code for emergency services as well as the date in American format (the European version would have been 11/9). The attacks changed terrorism, security arrangements and, when the consequent actions by the United States are taken into account, the world forever.

THE 11 SEPTEMBER ATTACKS: A PERSONAL TESTIMONY

My friend and colleague, Jack, took a flight from Boston Logan at
8 am on that Tuesday …

I was on an 8 am flight out of Boston Logan airport. Yes, the
same airport that the terrorists left from on other flights around
the same time. I flew to Washington Reagan airport arriving at
about 9.15.

I disembarked and was walking through the terminal to find
the car that had been sent to pick me up. People were clustered
around any TV and, while I was watching, I witnessed a plane fly
into the Pentagon.

I then ran downstairs and went outside to find the car. I saw a
pall of smoke going up right in front of me and a crowd of people
run up an embankment opposite the terminal. It was the attack
on the Pentagon.

Almost immediately, I saw the car with my name in the
window and got in – I was going to a hotel downtown for a board
meeting. As we left the airport to go over the bridge into DC,
the traffic started to jam. Behind me I could see the Pentagon
and a big cloud of black smoke. I remember vividly seeing a car,
a Porsche, driving towards the Pentagon at high speed – there
was no other traffic going in that direction. The driver was a
military officer who had not had time to put his tie on and he had
a panicked expression on his face; I remember that so clearly.

My car got about another quarter mile and then the traffic
stopped. I learned later that the police had closed all roads into
DC. I got out and walked. I tried calling my wife on my cell

phone but I could not get a call through – the cellular system had collapsed under the weight of all the calls.

I eventually found a payphone and called my assistant. It was now about 60 to 90 minutes after I landed. She told me the news of the attack and said that DC was locked down and all flights in the U.S. were grounded. I asked her to let my wife know I was OK. Rachel, of course, had heard on the news that flights from Boston leaving at the same time as my flight had been used in the attacks. So, she spent a very bad couple of hours before hearing that I was safe.

I found the address of a car rental place and walked over to it – about thirty minutes. They did not have any one-way rentals, so I took whatever they had figuring I would get it back to them somehow. Then I drove out of DC, stopping at another payphone to call my wife. She told me to come straight home, which I did. It's about a six-hour drive. The route took me right past New York on the other side of the river, where I saw the pall of black smoke from the remains of the Twin Towers and a haze over the city. It was such a bright, clear day.

Once I got over the FDR bridge it was past 4 pm and I had not had anything to eat or drink since breakfast, so I called a friend who lived in Rye and he said to stop by his house. He worked on Wall St and had earlier walked out of Manhattan amid the smoke and dust until he could get a ride home. I had a sandwich with him. It was pretty sombre. He had seen some ugly sights.

I got home about three hours later, in time to see the children before bed. My poor wife had been so panicked for over two hours.

I will always remember every detail of that day.

AL-QAEDA'S PERSPECTIVE ON 9/11

Osama bin Laden's feud with the United States had started in 1996 with a thirty-page, rambling 'Declaration of War Against the Americans Occupying the Land of the Two Holy Places', supplemented by various other diatribes, which included a post-9/11 'Letter to America' in 2002, in which he cited many grievances, such as Jewish appropriation of Palestinian land, general repression of Muslims in Somalia and Chechnya, the starved Muslims of Iraq, pro-American governments in the Middle East, 'who act as your agents', with the Philippines and Kashmir thrown in for full measure. There was also a general allegation that the United States was 'denying opportunities' for the Muslim world, having 'stolen our wealth'. Industrial enterprise and innovation do not seem to have occurred to him. Part of his manifesto was the removal of all foreign influences from Muslim countries.

Implicit was the notion of revenge, with the United States being 'responsible for many Muslims' deaths'. The idea seemed to be that hitting the United States hard enough would cause their withdrawal. This was based on Hezbollah's bombings of American Marine barracks in Beirut in 1983, which did just that. There was also the now famous 'Black Hawk Down' incident in Somalia 1993 (made into a film in 2001), after which the Americans withdrew. Both missions were contributions to Peace Support Operations.

It was an if-you-hit-Americans-hard-they'll-run philosophy.

Al-Qaeda's first attack was on the World Trade Center in February 1993. A truck containing explosives was driven into the underground garage and detonated. The blast killed six people and injured 1,500 others. It was not an official al-Qaeda operation, although Ramzi Yousef, the operative, had trained in al-Qaeda camps.

Al-Qaeda also attacked American embassies in Kenya and Tanzania in 1998, killing 224 people, twelve of them American. Then, in 2000, al-Qaeda suicide bombers rammed a small boat filled with explosives into the side of the U.S.S Cole (an American navy destroyer) while it was refuelling in a Yemeni port. Seventeen sailors were killed and thirty-nine injured. Although these attacks were taken seriously, the United States did not see them as a major assault on American hegemony, nor of course were they on American soil.

9/11 was a triumph of planning and organisation for al-Qaeda and was intended to ignite demands from the American public that the U.S. government pull out of the Middle East, resolve the Palestine problem and allow the Muslim world to re-establish their mediaeval wealth via a worldwide caliphate. This caliphate would ignite a global Muslim uprising against nominally secular but Muslim majority states and Islamic states who were not true to the teachings of the prophet. And then, in the afternoon …

How wrong could they be? Had Osama bin Laden not read any history? Had he not seen the *Popeye the Sailor* cartoons, with Popeye eventually rolling up his sleeves and declaring 'That's all I can stands, I can't stands no more.' Although it was sixty years earlier, the Japanese attack on Pearl Harbor surely demonstrated that, with enough provocation, the Americans, far from running, would exact terrible retribution. And Pearl Harbor suffered fewer casualties than 9/11. Over 2 million Japanese perished in the subsequent war.

After Pearl Harbor, Japanese Admiral Isoroku Yamamoto, who planned the attack would reportedly write in his diary, 'I fear all we have done is to awaken a sleeping giant and fill him with a terrible resolve.' He was right: Yamamoto's plane was shot down by American fighter planes after American code breakers discovered his flight plans in April 1943. Japanese military morale suffered as a result. Osama bin Laden was never ignorant of this, or considered himself immune.

On 7 October 2001, and after the Taliban government in Afghanistan had refused to hand over Osama bin Laden and expel al-Qaeda (even if they could have done), the Americans, with close allies, including the UK, invaded Afghanistan and Osama bin Laden was obliged to flee. He spent several years hiding or on the run. Al-Qaeda was never the same again – at least so far. In terms of resolving all his grievances, it looked as if Osama bin Laden had failed. But al-Qaeda was still potent: it inspired various other Islamic terrorist groups such as ISIS, the Islamic State of Iraq and the Levant, an apocalyptic movement with aspirations to establish a caliphate in Iraq and Syria. In this, they did have some short-term success until defeated by American and Allied bombing, with some help from the Kurds. ISIS emerged from the remnants of al-Qaeda in Iraq, but the two organisations grew apart. They are significantly different: apart from sharing the same Salafi jihadist doctrine, ISIS actively sought to conquer and rule territory. On the other hand, al-Qaeda's leader, bin Laden, claimed that if they created a territorial state, then the West would easily defeat them.

He was right: ISIS was eliminated in Iraq and Syria. However, this was not the end of ISIS and now they are thought to operate in as many as eighteen countries, including Jordan, Saudi Arabia, Turkey and Uzbekistan, together with several east, north and west African countries.

Several groups then evolved, claiming to be subsidiaries and part of al-Qaeda, such as al-Shabaab in Somalia and Boko Haram in north-east Nigeria, but these were more of a branding exercise than real affiliates. Nevertheless, calling themselves 'al-Qaeda' probably increased the fear they instilled in the general population, the relevant government, and possibly the American intelligence services.

AMERICA'S PERSPECTIVE ON 9/11

Although in the fullness of time, egregious intelligence failures were discovered, the United States acted swiftly. At 7 pm on the evening of

9/11, President George W. Bush defiantly announced that '... they (the terrorists) cannot dent the steel of American resolve ...'. Shortly after, Operation Enduring Freedom was conceived and launched. New security operations, the most well-known being Homeland Security, were instituted, some of which were successful, some, according to *The Atlantic* magazine, 'a carnival of waste, endless turf wars between bloated federal agencies – and, in many cases, remarkably little additional security'.

Nevertheless, as part of Operation Enduring Freedom, part of the 'War on Terror', sometimes called the 'Global War on Terrorism' or GWOT, the U.S. invaded Afghanistan. As well as chasing al-Qaeda out of Afghanistan, the Taliban were removed from operational power, but the occupation of Afghanistan continued for another twenty more years, with operations against a reactive Taliban insurgency.

9/11 was a particularly American affair, and the rest of the West welcomed American leadership. Tony Blair, the then prime minister of the United Kingdom, promised to stand 'shoulder to shoulder' with the Americans, and the French newspaper *Le Monde* suggested that 'we are all Americans now'. Interestingly, *Le Monde* rode back on this in the days that followed, and eventually thoroughly disapproved of America's subsequent actions. It is also worth mentioning that although it was an attack on American soil, sixty-seven Britons lost their lives. Also four French nationals. There was certainly at the time a sense of outrage – certainly in Europe, not merely based on sympathy but on fellowship with the Americans. It also remains the biggest loss of life due to a terrorist attack.

Article 5 of the Atlantic Charter was invoked, the only time in the history of NATO that this has been invoked. NATO became involved after August 2003, taking operational control of the International Security Assistance Force, ISAF. The Americans retained control of some of the operations in Afghanistan.

Yet the American response was crass. Announcing that any state that harboured terrorists would be the target of American wrath might have been fair enough, but invocations of 'good and evil' and '... if you are not with us, you're against us ...' were over the top, and fed the idea – which the Americans wanted to avoid – of a 'clash of civilisations' between the West and Islam. *The Clash of Civilisations* is a thesis that political, cultural and religious identities would be the main source of conflict in the post-Cold War world. Originally published as an article in the journal *Foreign Affairs* in 1993, the author, the American political scientist Samuel P. Huntington, later published it as a book.

And calling operations against terror a 'war', involved two errors. First, one cannot wage a war against a *tactic*, which terrorism is. Second, if it's a war, then surely the fighters, the terrorists, are warriors who they would claim should be treated as prisoners of war if captured. In fact, the United States called them 'unlawful combatants' but, having given them such a term, they weren't quite sure what to do with them, so they banged them up in a prison in Guantánamo Bay, which continues to exist.

At the time of writing, the current U.S. President Joe Biden has withdrawn American troops from Afghanistan. This has obliged other NATO troops to withdraw their troops as well. The American-trained Afghan army crumbled at the sight of the Taliban, and Kabul was taken very swiftly.

Despite assurances from the Taliban that their new government would be benign, thousands of Afghans are attempting to leave the country. There is general international condemnation of President Joe Biden's decision: the lack of communication with other NATO members; the lack of planning for the complex withdrawal; and the disastrous aftermath. However, it has to be mentioned that other NATO members, particularly the UK, did not seem to have a contingency plan in place. In general, when considering contingency plans, it's no good saying afterwards that it all happened too quickly for us to keep up with. Even the UK Foreign Secretary had to be encouraged to come back from his holiday to take control of the evacuation.

Joe Biden does not need any sympathy for this, but to be fair to him, and as he said in his address, were the American public going to tolerate further lives lost in pursuit of a hopeless cause? In all, some 200,000 people had been killed; over 60,000 from the Afghan security forces, over 2,400 United States troops and, for reference, 456 United Kingdom service personnel. Unfortunately, the condemnation of the way that the final evacuation of Kabul and Afghanistan was handled has clouded larger issues of the success or otherwise of the intervention in Afghanistan. To some extent there was a clear rationale for this invasion. The Taliban government had refused to hand over Osama bin Laden, and with its brutal treatment of the population, risks alienating both that population and the wider world. This leads to the question as to whether we have done with al-Qaeda, and, by implication, whether we have done with terrorism. Given the long history of terrorism, this is unlikely, but we might anticipate it taking a different form.

THE INVASION OF IRAQ

In March 2003 the Americans, together with other allies, a 'coalition of the willing', invaded Iraq. Retrospectively, it was one of the most controversial military operations in the early 21st century. Although combat operations were over in short order, the subsequent casualties, the various insurgencies, the Civil War, the rise of ISIS, the Islamic State, and various other problems, damaged the reputation of the United States and its allies and called into question the whole idea of military intervention, liberal or otherwise, in other states.

There was some rationale for the invasion of Afghanistan, but some commentators thought the main rationale for the invasion of Iraq was that it 'could be done', and perhaps a sense of unfinished business after Bush senior's refusal to 'carry on the Baghdad' after liberating Kuwait in 1993. It is unfortunate that Afghanistan and Iraq are thought of in the same way. The same might be said for the bombing of Libya in 2011, as detailed elsewhere.

The stated rationale for the invasion was that Saddam Hussein, the then president of Iraq, was developing WMD, Weapons of Mass Destruction. Although WMD covers chemical, biological and radiological weapons, it is generally thought of as nuclear weapons. The story of nuclear weapons inspectors, the refusal of Iraqis to cooperate with inspections, and the demands that the Americans made on Saddam Hussein to resign and remove himself from Iraq, are long and involved and do not concern us here. What the invasion of Iraq proved was that in any conventional war, the Americans were militarily peerless and, given sufficient motivation, could easily triumph over any other states' armed forces. Yet the U.S. established a Coalition Provisional Authority within Iraq. Was this effective?

In 2009, RAND Corporation, an American non-for-profit global policy think tank, published a report entitled *Occupying Iraq: A History of the Coalition Provisional Authority, the CPA*. It attempted to 'recount and evaluate the efforts of the United States and its coalition partners to restore public services; reform the judicial and penal systems; fight corruption; reduce inflation; expand the economy; and create the basis for a democratic constitution, free elections, and representative government'. (And in the afternoon …). It also addressed the occupation's most outstanding failure: *the inability of the United States and its coalition partners to protect the Iraqi people from the criminals and extremists in their midst.*

Much of the culpability for failure is centred on L. Paul Bremer, an experienced diplomat who had at one stage been an assistant to Henry Kissinger. His title varies from report to report, from 'Administrator of the Coalition Provisional' to 'Presidential Envoy to Iraq', and incidentally having plenipotentiary powers, to 'Head of the Civilian Administration'. Allegedly modelling his plan on the de-Nazification of Germany after the Second World War, Bremer was intent on the de-Baathification of the Iraqi state. In fact, he wholly misunderstood the reality of the de-Nazification programme. It had a divide. Although POWs were scrupulously vetted before they could return home (die-hard Nazis remaining for 're-education'), the reality of government, particularly at local level in West Germany, meant that ex-Party members either stayed in place or were appointed because they were the only ones with experience. To the Shi'ite and Kurdish majority, this may have been the most popular step but it further antagonized the Sunni community, from whence an insurgency soon arose. About forty-two per cent of Iraqis are Sunni, fifty-one per cent Shia, the balance being Kurds and Turkmen.

The second mistake was to disband the Iraqi army, the single biggest condemnation of the CPA's fourteen-month reign. This abolition of this respected national symbol, recently defeated, had a traumatic effect on both the Shi'ite and Sunni communities. The army was unlike the Ba'ath party, where membership was necessary to getting a job and promotion. Eventually, Iraqi army personnel were put on inactive status, paid, and individuals recalled incrementally and selectively. But at that stage, it was too late: the Sunni insurgency had started.

RAND reports that 'Bremer's powers were much more limited than they appeared. He had no direct authority over 98 per cent of official American personnel in Iraq. They were under military command.' But it wasn't all Bremer's fault: 'Even more debilitating was Washington's persistent inability to fill more than half the mid-level and junior positions in the CPA and these seldom for more than three to six months at a time. As a result, while intended to be a dominantly civilian organization, the CPA remained heavily military.' In brief, there was a chronic shortage of experienced middle-level managers. In particular, there was a shortage of Arabic-speaking regional experts and officials who had worked in previous post conflict stabilisation efforts. Not only that, but there was also a shortage of experienced diplomats and civic managers who understood Iraqi culture.

So, what was the plan? RAND reports that 'Prior to Bremer's appointment, American planning for post-Saddam Iraq had proceeded along two ill-defined but divergent tracks, one moving toward the extended occupation, as finally happened, the other toward a swift handoff to a nonelected Iraqi successor regime.'

PLAN? STRATEGY? THE 'ENEMY' HAS A VOTE TOO!

In Volume One of this trilogy About War, we defined war as:

a hostile act of coercion or the threat or use of organised violence designed to change the political balance between polities.

And we define strategy as:

about planning for the future, about how any polity uses its incumbent resources (people, process and hardware and those they can develop) to achieve their long-term goals.

It is about reconciling internal and with outside actors' ends, ways and means.

Any strategic approach must incorporate political imagination and an anticipation of competitive moves. It is therefore dynamic and contingent.

Strategy is manifest in plans and processes, but the crucial dimension is that those involved think strategically.

Implicit in these definitions are two principles. The first is that war – organised violence – should only be used to establish a better political balance between polities. The second is that strategy must address the ends, ways and means conundrum, which involves having a clear vision of the future and the means of getting there. Leaving aside the issue of the questionable rationale for the invasion, it is difficult to disagree with the United States' aspirational objectives outlined above. RAND reports that: 'There was a good deal of planning in the State and Defense Departments and in several military commands. But these disparate activities were never fully integrated into a national plan...'. Thus, not only was the CPA chronically understaffed, but they had to create a strategic plan 'on the fly'.

But it seems that whereas there was lengthy and detailed planning for the military side of the operation, not only was the planning of the civilian side very weak, but most of it seems to have been missing.

It is often assumed, and proclaimed, that the invasion of Iraq was a disaster, but this obscures the compelling lessons that could be learned from the invasion. Setting aside the WMD rationale, it is clear that many other mistakes and misconceptions led to the final tragedy. Pulling all this together, we can identify several lessons:

First, the United States military is a powerful, well-equipped force who can clearly cope with almost any other army in a conventional war. They clearly take military planning, largely logistical, very seriously and this is successful in facilitating military victories. But were other realistic alternatives considered other than 'shock and awe'? Many of the troops in the Iraqi army deserted in the face of the American and British assault. It is known that some of the 'kills' of tanks reported by the Allied forces were in fact on abandoned tanks, the crews having fled in the face of the counterforce. If 'shock and awe' was the key to frightening and cowering the Iraqi army, could that not have happened in just one sector? Was it really necessary to destroy so much infrastructure and cause so many casualties? Estimates of the casualties from the invasion were, on the Iraqi side, a minimum of 7,000, and up to 45,000. More than two hundred American troops were killed. Could the allies not have established a perimeter and invited the Iraqi troops to desert?

Second, it's tempting to claim that the Americans do not have the depth of understanding of other cultures, of the idea of political balance, or the problems of Shi'ite / Sunni antipathy. But – and here is a challenge for anybody looking at a military/political (what else?) engagement – didn't the U.S. have access to any amount of exhaustive and accurate information about other cultures, politics and religious differences? Indeed, about Iraq? Strategy, as detailed above, is about anticipation of competitive and other moves. It is essentially contingent. What were the plans for dealing with those aspects? Where were the cultural experts on Iraq?

It comes down to what we call, in *About War,* '*the dreary but vital subject of governance*'. We assert that Governance is the key, and of fundamental importance, when considering military action. Who was in charge of the invasion and subsequent occupation?

One candidate was within the country, or 'theatre' as the military would call it. American forces came under Lieutenant General Ricardo Sanchez. Bremer of the CPA and Sanchez maintained cordial relations. Sanchez was under formal orders from Donald Rumsfeld, the U.S. Secretary of Defense, to support Bremer, which he did. Yet Sanchez's view was that he was not thereby obliged to give Bremer any indication of military operations at the tactical level.

An example from Washington, according to the RAND report: 'The CPA's relationship with Washington was also improvised and unclear, as was Bremer's with his bosses. The CPA was, at one and the same time, an element of the Defense Department, a multinational organization, and a foreign government.' Furthermore, Rumsfeld had never established within the Defense Department an adequate mechanism to monitor, support, and guide the CPA's activities and to keep the White House and other relevant agencies informed on what was going on in Baghdad. Moreover, it is quite clear that the United States simply cannot not do nation building. Foreign entanglements have been anathema for the U.S.. A key theme of American foreign policy from George Washington: '... *careful foreign policy of friendly neutrality that would avoid creating implacable enemies or international friendships of dubious value, nor entangle the United States in foreign alliances ...*' through Condoleezza Rice to Donald Trump ...

Finally, one rarely asked and certainly unanswered question, given that the United Kingdom was part of the coalition invading Iraq: what was their role in the sorry tale? Answers come there none.

POLITICAL CONSEQUENCES OF THE AMERICAN RESPONSE TO 9/11

The consequences of 9/11 were profound and far-reaching for both the perpetrators and victims of the war on Afghanistan and Iraq. It would be gross hyperbole to lay all the changes and current problems of the world at the feet of the American reaction to 9/11, or to al-Qaeda itself, but it is useful to flag some current international issues and imagine those that have some provenance in the American response.

- President George W Bush's 'Global War on Terror' displaced al-Qaeda from Afghanistan and severely restricted their activities. Several other Jihadi groups set themselves up as new al Qaedas (for example, Boko Haram and al Shabab), but these were distant franchisees rather than subsidiaries.
- Together with al-Qaeda itself, these are still potent but constrained.
- The political vacuum in Iraq after the invasion saw the rise and expansion of ISIS, the Islamic State of Iraq and Syria, an

apocalyptic and murderous cult intent on establishing a local and then international caliphate.

- It is now generally accepted that George W Bush should have declared a war on terrorist groups, not necessarily named, but certainly including al-Qaeda. The 'Global War on Terrorism' made every potential terrorist consider themselves a warrior, following a noble cause, rather than a misguided criminal.
- Although Osama bin Laden's hopes were expressed in his 2002 'Letter to America' (see main text), might he not have settled for a constructive American approach to the Middle East. Some efforts have been made: the U.S. withdrew active troops from Saudi Arabia in 2003. This does not seem to have satisfied OBL.
- Let us posit that the invasion of Afghanistan was legitimate in terms of chasing al-Qaeda out. It was the way that the subsequent occupation was managed that represents the problem: corruption left rampant, the lack of any clear strategy, or even political objective, the horrendous casualties and the reference group being the urban elite rather than the rural poor – the bulk of the population.
- There was bungled withdrawal, decided unilaterally by the U.S., without consultation with its NATO partners.
- The complex relationship between United States and Pakistan is laid bare. Pakistan's complicity with the Taliban and U.S. support for Pakistan is one of the great mysteries of our time.
- The civil war in Syria, where Russia labelled all anti-Assad fighters terrorists.
- The civil war in Yemen, where U.S.-backed Saudi and United Arab Emirates' forces took on Houthi rebels, whom they deemed terrorists in pursuit of a wider struggle with Iran.

- The realisation, or simply confirmation, that the Americans have very little idea of other countries' social and political cultures, those that are not based on, and what the Americans see as, 'freedom and democracy'. Not everyone wants to live in a consumer goods paradise.
- At the very least, the United States could have refuted some of Osama bin Laden's claims, where, in his 2002 'Letter to America' he called for: '... sincerity, the best of manners, righteousness, mercy, honour, purity, and piety ... also to be a people of manners, principles, honour, and purity ...'.
- It is not clear how OBL thinks that slaughtering thousands of people squares with these nostrums ...
- Trump's right-wing nationalism which, in consequence, gave rise to the repudiation of the Iran deal, now being renegotiated.
- Many drone strikes and extrajudicial killings sullied America's reputation for moral leadership.
- As did the United States' attitude to the ethics of war: 'enhanced interrogation', Abu Ghraib, etc.
- NATO's disaster in Afghanistan highlighted a general failure of role, purpose and capability and, given French President Macron's 'brain dead' jibe, its very future.
- With such political capital spent on the Global 'War on Terror', insufficient attention given was to diplomacy and peace stabilisation in the Middle East (throw in climate change for good measure).
- As part of that, tension increased between Iran and Israel and between Iran and Saudi Arabia.
- There was a general monstering of Iran, conveniently forgetting U.S. and British complicity in the overthrow of

Mossadegh and also the support the Americans gave to Iraq when Saddam Hussein fancied a bit of Iran's oil. The Iran-Iraq war lasted from 1980 to 1988 and ended in stalemate, with between 400,000 and 1.2 million casualties, military and civilian, on both sides.

- Radicalised young men and women imagining they are part of a global movement against the West, and setting off bomb and suicide attacks in London, Manchester, Paris and other European cities incited Islamophobia and anti-migrant, anti-foreigner sentiment.

- There was potentially the serious decline, perhaps terminal, of Liberal Internationalism and its coeval, liberal interventionism.

We are left with a critical quandary: what place is there for counterinsurgency and Peace Support Operations now? The world now looks very different to how it did in the year 2000.

COMMENTARY

There are literally hundreds of Think Tanks in the United States; the University of Pennsylvania estimates 2,203 in total. Of course, not all of these are concerned with defence and security matters but the ones that are, and American War Colleges, frequently have articles on Clausewitz who, as we explain at several points in this book, and in *About War* asserts, rather obviously, that war is a political act. If no international politics is concerned, military action is simply gratuitous violence.

It is therefore staggering that a well-respected American journal such as *Foreign Affairs* could publish an article in May 2020 entitled: 'America's Opportunity in the Middle East: Diplomacy could succeed where military force has failed.' Who knew? It is equivalent to the old corporate mantra of 'beatings will continue until morale improves'.

Military action must have some political angle, and be dedicated to a better political relationship between polities. Those polities could be internal to a nation state, or a third-party external polity, such as the United States.

The flagrant and deliberate lack of any overall policy or vision and the consequential lack of any overall strategy for the Middle East, from either the United States or Europe, debilitates international relations, causes an untold number of deaths, misery and economic ruin, and, for those countries with a Muslim majority population, reinforces the view that 'The West' is not only against Islam, but is out to exploit those countries.

There is the very real danger that, with America's drift into semi-isolationism, worries about climate change, China (and Russia? and North Korea?) and an increased American political bi-partisanship crippling political initiatives, the Middle East might move down America's agenda. Taken together with the death of Liberal Internationalism and thus liberal interventionism, it is a bleak and miserable scenario. We cannot lay all this at the door of Osama bin Laden, al-Qaeda or the 9/11 attack, but, in retrospect, historians may see this as a stimulus and watershed moment. Whatever, the executor of this tragedy was the United States of America.

10. DETERRENCE, NUCLEAR DETERRENCE AND NUCLEAR WAR

Societal attitudes to war fluctuate between several extremes.

Social norms discourage talking about war as distasteful, unpleasant and dangerous, something of being wary of the old adage 'talk of the devil and he's bound to appear'. Suggesting that you are writing a book about war will usually result in a stunned silence around the dinner table. Pointing out that the putative book is about war as a *political* act only raises more embarrassment. *Yes, well what would you expect from that lot ...*

It is not surprising when the images that people see on the TV news is of death, destruction and misery and what look like civilians, usually called 'fighters', firing wildly into the distance. (A professional soldier would rebuke any of his charges who fired in such a way as a waste of ammunition). Comments such as war is: unnecessary *(a failure of communication; can't they negotiate?)*; irrelevant *(what interests are they trying to protect)* or simply too awful and horrible to contemplate *(how can they do that to their own people?)* show not only their distress, but also a lack of engagement with the whole issue of war. You may wish to press your point that war is something that we all need to think about, and even when recognising that responsibility for invoking war is that of politicians, some will subconsciously blame soldiers (sailors, airmen) for the exigencies of war and the death and destruction that military action causes. This is particularly the case if any war is not going well.

All this changes dramatically if the integrity of British territory is compromised. The mood in the country transformed overnight when the Argentinians invaded the Falkland Islands in 1982 (*Go get 'em!*). The mood also changes dramatically if British troops are seen to be losing

(*Get our troops out asap!*) or winning (*What great armed forces we have!*).

All the above sentiments are greatly enhanced when talking about nuclear war. Since there are no examples on the TV, the progress of nuclear war is left to the imagination, recalling such words as Armageddon, nuclear winter, or mutual assured destruction (usually referred to as 'MAD'). Your dinner guest who speaks of such things would probably not reach the cheese course.

Nuclear weapons exist, and even in the event of a complete nuclear disarmament (discussed later in the chapter) and with the suspicion that a few such weapons might exist thereafter, we have to deal with them, and have a clear strategy for doing this. The discourse is enormous, much of it dating back to the sixties or even fifties, the vocabulary dedicated and arcane.

This chapter throws some light on what is, for many people, an obscure subject. We look at deterrence and what it really means, what nuclear weapons are, nuclear treaties and arms control, and a subject little known outside military circles: Tactical Nuclear Weapons. We look at the UK's CND (Campaign for Nuclear Disarmament) as a model of campaigns to reduce and eventually eliminate nuclear weapons.

THE ORIGINS OF NUCLEAR STRATEGY

Attitudes to nuclear weapons changed dramatically during the twenty years after the Second World War, the time at which Soviet Russia achieved parity with the United States in terms of their nuclear arsenal and delivery methods. Although this was more than sixty years ago, much of the thinking of the time persists to this day, in terms of perceptions, expectations and levels of trust. Were we considering trade deals here, we might think that the issues concerned were not exactly trivial, but not life-threatening. With regard to nuclear weapons, the results of getting things wrong could be calamitous. It's therefore worthwhile to study the roots of nuclear thinking, deterrence and relationships with other nuclear-armed countries.

The Americans exploded the first atom bomb near Alamogordo in the New Mexico desert in July 1945. This was followed in August by atom bombs being dropped on Hiroshima and Nagasaki on the principal Japanese island of Honshu in August. Various people had asked President Truman to drop the bomb on an unpopulated area (for example, in a mountain valley) as a demonstration, but he rejected this. Later, he commented that he 'never lost a moment's sleep over this decision'. It was the start of the nuclear age. The Americans, together with the British and Canadians, briefly had the idea of turning over the nuclear weapons to the United Nations (an extension of the war-time Baruch plan), but the Soviet Union did not agree.

Having listened to a speech by Joseph Stalin on Soviet Russia's foreign policy in 1946, diplomat George Kennan wrote his now famous 'long telegram', explaining Stalin's view that the rest of the world was hostile to Marxist-Leninism – thoroughly justifiable by American standards – and that it may have implied, and the Americans certainly inferred, that the Soviet Union was intent on a geographic expansion and even global dominance. Kennan's telegram was strongly anti-Communist and he concluded that Soviet Russia should be 'contained'. This became the main theme of what became known as the 'Truman Doctrine', adumbrated in 1947, which called for this 'containment' to be part of American foreign policy.

Harry S Truman had become president of the United States after Roosevelt's death in April 1945 and served until 1953 when Eisenhower was elected. The Marshall Plan, which contributed $13 billion of foreign aid to Western Europe (equivalent to about $114 billion in 2020), was partly to revitalise the European economy and partly to act as a bulwark against communism. Soviet Russia rejected the idea of participating in the Marshall Plan. Stalin believed that it would encourage Eastern Bloc countries to escape from Soviet control. In response, the Soviet Union created the Molotov Plan, later COMECON, a trading and finance system within Soviet satellite countries.

Soviet nuclear scientists had considered the possibility of an atomic bomb at some stage during the 1930s and gathered intelligence from British and American sources during the war period up to 1945. Klaus Fuchs is one of the famous British/German spies. When, at the Potsdam conference, news was brought to Churchill about the nuclear test at the Alamogordo test site, he was naturally surprised – Stalin less so, as he knew all about it already. After the Hiroshima bomb, the Soviet nuclear programme went into a higher gear, and, using some captured German scientists, they produced their first atomic bomb, called 'First Lightning', which was based on the American Hiroshima bomb. The first successful test was in August 1949 in Kazakhstan, but it was not until the early 1960s that the Soviet Union achieved nuclear parity with the United States. When Truman was told about the Kazakhstan test, he was somewhat dubious but was later convinced. He announced it to the American public in September. America's nuclear monopoly was over.

From then on, American foreign policy had to take into account the existence of nuclear weapons held by other states. The focus was a war with the Soviet Union, and to some extent this remains the focus, though now with the Russian Federation. The United States decided to increase both the quantity and quality of their nuclear atomic arsenal. But the main concern was how to formulate a strategy to counter a nuclear-armed, expansionist Soviet Union.

AND SO THE COLD WAR WAS BORN.
Dwight D Eisenhower was elected president of the United States for a term of office starting in January 1953. In the summer of that year, he

convened 'Project Solarium', a national-level exercise in foreign policy. The idea was to produce a policy consensus among senior officials in the national security community and the most appropriate strategy for dealing with the threat of Soviet expansionism. Both Secretary of State John Foster Dulles and George F. Kennan were involved. Eisenhower briefed three teams: one to take a mainly political approach; one for a more muscular approach; and finally one to look at how to enable a roll-back of Soviet space, *to diminish Soviet power – and Soviet-controlled territory – everywhere and by any means available.* The conclusions were undramatic and possibly the reason Project Solarium is not better known. In summary, they were:

- The Soviet Union was a long term, immanent, rather than imminent, threat.
- The threat was from the increasing number of nuclear weapons in their possession, as well as Red Army troop strength.
- The United States needed to both avoid public alarm and should maintain a system of alliances circumscribing the Soviet Bloc and maintain both conventional and nuclear military readiness.
- Once it had established its deterrent capacity, the United States should convey the truth about capitalism, democracy and human rights by various means to the oppressed populations.

All in all, it confirmed the Truman Doctrine of containment. However, and as a much tougher approach than Project Solarium might suggest, in a speech in 1954, Eisenhower's Secretary of State John Foster Dulles stated (shortened version):

'We need allies and collective security ... this can be done by placing more reliance on deterrent power and less dependence on local defensive power ... local defense will always be important, but no local defense will contain the mighty land power of the Communist world. Local defenses must be reinforced by the further deterrent of massive retaliatory power …'.

While he did not use the term 'massive retaliation', this was how it was represented and discussed. There were some detractors: the RAND Corporation thought it too aggressive and identical to a 'first strike' strategy, where a massive American nuclear strike would take out all Soviet nuclear capabilities. But, whatever it did to the Russian psyche, it was successful during the 1950s. This was largely because the Soviet Union lacked a 'second-strike' capability until the early 1960s. A 'second-strike capability' is where, however much devastation the enemies 'first strike' has caused, you still retain the possibility of launching a counter strike.

AND SO, THE CHARACTER OF DETERRENCE CHANGED

It was an unrealistic fear of Yuri Andropov, Soviet General Secretary 1982 to 1984 (see panel on Able Archer 83) that an American 'first strike' would destroy the entire capability of the defending side to launch any missile. Nuclear deterrence is based on the defender having a 'second-strike' capability – the capability of delivering as devastating an attack as the other side's first strike. Mutual Assured Destruction – MAD – would follow.

This is further reinforced by the 'triad' system, whereby the United States and Russia, and now China and India, maintain three different methods of delivering nuclear weapons: Intercontinental Ballistic Missiles (ICBMs); a Continuous At Sea Deterrent (CASD), and aircraft capable of carrying a nuclear weapon, be that free-fall or cruise. Land-based ICBMs are housed either in permanent silos or carried on road vehicles. One might imagine that such vehicles could be spotted by satellites, but a favourite ploy is to disguise them as watchtowers in the middle of forests. Although there is much commentary on resisting ICBMs, there is no absolutely proven method for doing this. Bombers can, of course, be spotted and possibly shot down. Britain and France use only the CASD, which is just as effective and will continue to be so until an enemy can identify and destroy a submarine carrying nuclear missiles. Even then (one of the ironies of nuclear weapons), should that submarine be anywhere near the attacker's coast, vast areas would become radioactive.

ABLE ARCHER 83

If the Americans were wary of the Soviet Union, Moscow was paranoid. 1983 was a bad year for world peace. Soviet fighter planes had shot down a Korean Airlines flight. President Ronald had called the Soviet Union an 'evil empire'. An ailing sixty-nine-year-old Yuri Andropov (Reagan was seventy-two) was running the Soviet Union from his Moscow hospital bed and had demanded intelligence to confirm his obsession that the U.S. was planning a surprise nuclear attack to decapitate the Soviet leadership. Meanwhile, Soviet armed forces were slowly getting bogged down in Afghanistan.

The annual NATO exercise, 'Autumn Forge', involved more troops than the Soviets had been expecting, although large troop movements were always notified to the other side before manoeuvres took place. Some 40,000 American and NATO troops were moved across Western Europe, including 16,000 American troops airlifted under radio silence.

After 'Autumn Forge', NATO decided to launch 'Able Archer 83'. This was an exercise to test the command and control systems of

NATO and the imagined scenario was that the Soviets had attacked Yugoslavia and Scandinavia and the Soviet Army had started to deploy into Western Europe. As expected, NATO forces were forced to retreat. Within a few months of the start of the game, NATO commanders asked the politicians permission to 'go nuclear'.

The problem was that, given the intelligence that Andropov had demanded, the troop movements, although benign, looked to the Soviets very much like preparations for a 'first strike'. According to Malcolm Chalmers of RUSI, there was great paranoia, certainly on the Soviet side, but maybe some out on the western side as well. He suggests that the Soviet leadership 'could remember the trauma of Hitler's surprise attack in 1941 that almost destroyed the Soviet Union and that this was the lens through which the Soviets viewed US policy.

Much of this was kept secret for many years, and has only been fully released recently. The final testimony might usefully come from Ronald Reagan himself. He wrote in his diary that: 'I feel the Soviets are so defence minded, so paranoid about being attacked that, without being anyway soft on them we ought to tell them that no one here has any intention of doing anything like that. What the hell have they got that anybody would want?'

What relevance might this have for today?

There was a failure of intelligence – both military and political – on both sides: the United States did not fully appreciate how paranoid the Soviet Union was about being attacked. For their part, the Soviets had been gathering intelligence selectively.

The Soviet Union remembered Hitler's attack, but unfortunately seem to have forgotten the enormous amount of help the Americans gave them during the Second World War; over 16 million tons of vehicles, aeroplanes, tractors and tanks, as well as petroleum products and food.

It all underlines the importance of frequent contact and communication between countries. The media are fond of saying that any particular summit meeting did not yield anything other than the usual bland communiqué, but some contact is always better than none.

Intelligence, legacy and communication, all well-known lessons; best not to forget the basics!

DETERRENCE THEORY

Although the United States and Soviet Russia had cooperated in defeating Nazi Germany during the Second World War, it became apparent during the 1950s that they would now be facing off against each other. The Americans assumed that Soviet Russia was intent on spreading Marxist-Leninism and taking over the world. A more realistic analysis might have revealed that this was somewhat hyperbolic, even if Soviet Russia had the resources to do so. In response, the United States would aid freedom to all peoples – a reflection of Woodrow Wilson's Fourteen Points in 1919, and set the stage for many later interventions, that led to global commitments. This can be seen again in JFK's 1961 pronouncement:

'Let every nation know, whether it wishes us well or ill, that we shall pay any price, bear any burden, meet any hardship, support any friend, oppose any foe to assure the survival and the success of liberty. This much we pledge – and more.'

THE SOVIET BLOC

During the Cold War, many academics, journalists and think tankers used alternately the expression 'the Soviets' or 'Russia' to describe several different bodies.

At its height, the pre-revolution (Tsarist) Russian Empire, comprised modern Russia, Ukraine, Belarus, Moldova, Finland, Armenia, Azerbaijan, Georgia, Kazakhstan, Kyrgyzstan, Tajikistan, Turkmenistan, Uzbekistan, Lithuania, Estonia, Latvia and Poland.

The USSR was the Union of Soviet Socialist Republics, encompassing most of the above republics (Finland became independent in 1917), plus Red Army conquests in the Second World War, namely East Germany, Czechoslovakia, Hungary, Romania, Bulgaria and Albania.

It was often called the 'Soviet Union', the 'Eastern Bloc' or the 'Communist Bloc' and, because of strong control and the threat of military intervention from Moscow (Hungary in 1956; Czechoslovakia in 1968), always followed the same policies, particularly foreign policy.

The Warsaw Pact, whose official (though ironic) name was the 'Treaty of Friendship, Cooperation and Mutual Assistance' was a collective defence treaty signed in Warsaw, Poland, in 1955, between the Soviet Union and seven other Eastern Bloc socialist republics of Central and Eastern Europe. It was thought of as a reaction to NATO.

There were also, from time to time, 'aligned states', such as Afghanistan and North Korea, and also non-aligned states.

Relevant to our argument here is that troops, weaponry and air power facing NATO were stationed 'forward' in East Germany and Czechoslovakia, etc.

This was then a second leg to the United States foreign policy, summarised as protecting a rules-based international order from deterring the Soviet Union from starting a nuclear war and providing resources for the success of liberty, loosely defined. The concept of deterrence, previously known as a strategy for war in general, was applied – and is still applied – to the nuclear question. Since it is pretty serious stuff, it is generally known as 'strategic deterrence'. What exactly does deterrence mean?

The *Oxford English Dictionary* defines the verb 'deter' as 'to discourage or turn aside or restrain by fear; to frighten from anything; to restrain or keep back from acting or proceeding by any consideration of danger or trouble'. Google dictionary suggests: 'to discourage (someone) from doing something by instilling doubt or fear of the consequences'.

This may seem rather pedantic, but fear, doubt, danger and trouble may seem rather too belligerent to apply to nuclear war. In his 2004 book, *Deterrence*, Professor Sir Lawrence Freedman, an experienced nuclear commentator, suggests that: 'Deterrence can be a technique, doctrine and a state of mind. In all cases it is about setting boundaries for actions and establishing risks associated with crossing these boundaries.'

Here, there is less about fear, doubt, danger and trouble, and more about boundaries, risks and, by implication, communication. Freedman goes on to describe that deterrence involves the adjustment of strategic choices with another, using force or threat of force as the agent. There is, implicitly, a rational opponent. The problem is that although they may not be stupid, they may not be what we would consider rational. Recall the American aphorism 'better to die on your feet then to live on your knees' or 'better dead than red'.

Where is the theory? We think of a theory as a method to provide understanding. Theories are generally based on empirical evidence, checked and verified, and then formalised. A theory should be capable of being replicated. The main problem with the theory of nuclear deterrence is that it cannot be tested or verified. Was it a successful theory? Well, we haven't had a major war, either nuclear or conventional, between the great powers, say the United States, Russia and China, but that only raises a number of consequential questions. Perhaps nobody's security was compromised; perhaps whatever else, they didn't think they would win; perhaps they were desperate to avoid war at any price. It's extraordinarily difficult to know which is the case, and yet billions, maybe trillions, have been spent on nuclear arsenals and delivery capabilities.

THE NUCLEAR TABOO

Since August 1945, when the United States dropped atomic bombs on Hiroshima and Nagasaki, no nation has employed nuclear weapons during any war or conflict. The non-use of nuclear weapons is one of the key characteristics of the nuclear age. Looking back through history, every new non-nuclear weapons system has been deployed, tested and used to gain a competitive advantage just as soon as was possible.

There may have been instances where American leaders considered using nuclear weapons: the Korean War, the Vietnam War, and the Gulf War 1991, but refrained from doing so. There is little evidence that Soviet Russia ever seriously considered using nuclear weapons – even tactical nuclear weapons – in Afghanistan, nor has the Russian Federation considered using nuclear weapons in Chechnya, Georgia or, horrific though it might be, in Syria.

This is not to say that their doctrine does not call for the use of nuclear weapons, simply that they have not actually used them.

Many people of the baby boomer generation assumed that at some point in their lives they would have to go off to war, and a proportion of those assumed that that war would be nuclear, between the United States and Soviet Russia, with United Kingdom involved as well. Fears abated when the Soviet system collapsed, and the Russian Federation inaugurated.

As we now know, nuclear war has not occurred for the last 77 odd years, and this is conventionally put down to a strategy of deterrence, mutually assured destruction – MAD – and second-strike capability. Though at the same time everybody feared that a nuclear war would result in a nuclear winter, and ultimately the end of civilisation as we knew it.

An enormous amount of intelligence gathering, research and analysis has been carried out into game theory, and into managing the escalation from a single nuclear weapon exchange up to all-out nuclear war. And yet, given the horror that most people would feel about nuclear war, we have, thankfully, managed to avoid it.

So it is worth asking the question as to whether the realist view of deterrence, MAD and second-strike-capability is sufficient to explain nuclear non-use. In fact, and not unexpectedly, there has been substantial revulsion against the use of nuclear weapons not just from populations at large, but from policymakers within the nuclear-armed countries' administrations.

For example, in President Reagan's 1984 State of the Union speech, addressing the Soviet Union, he asserted that, '... there is only one sane policy, for your country and mine, to preserve our civilization in this modern age: a nuclear war cannot be won and must never be fought. The only value in our two nations possessing nuclear weapons is to make sure they will never be used. But then, would it not be better to do away with them entirely?...'This was not popular with the security establishment at the time but in 1985, President Reagan met Mikhail Gorbachev, the General Secretary of the Communist Party of the Soviet Union (this was the 1985 Geneva meeting), and they issued a statement saying exactly this: '... a nuclear war cannot be won and must never be fought ...'.

This might seem a statement of what everybody was thinking anyway, but it was an important milestone in the relationship between Soviet Russia and the United States, as well as in the history of nuclear weapons. Also, the two men got on well.

These policy choices, coupled with both politicians' and populations' view on the use of nuclear weapons adds up to 'The Nuclear Taboo'. This is an injunction against not only the actual use of nuclear weapons but also issuing threats that they might be used. The Nuclear Taboo is a collation of the thought that nuclear weapons are immoral, that the country's international reputation would be impaired, that trust in their pronouncements damaged, concerns about nuclear pollution, and the dangers of escalation. The Nuclear Taboo has been a subject of a 2007 book by Nina Tannenwald at the Watson Institute for International studies at Brown University.

The Reagan Gorbachev statement was the turning point both in terms of the relationship between the United States and Soviet Russia, but also in the history of nuclear weapons. By Putin's invasion of Ukraine, and the threat to use nuclear weapons, he has broken the Nuclear Taboo causing immeasurable damage to international security, the Russian Federation's reputation and what was left of his own personal credibility.

The problem with the theory behind nuclear and even non-nuclear deterrence is that it can be said to have worked when nothing happens. It is difficult to identify the main contribution. Was it very smart diplomats ensuring that any potential enemy was convinced about the folly of going to war with us? Was it our superb conventional armed forces who could easily be deployed to wherever and would surely triumph over any enemies? Or was it indeed the threat of nuclear retribution? Nuclear deterrence (you nuke us, we'll nuke you) sounds straightforward but perhaps it cannot be tested as a theory. Commentators have devised several subcategories. We do not need to cover all aspects, but for example:

General deterrence is continuing efforts to avert unwelcome actions from opponents as a general feature of non-crisis situations. It is generally thought to be more effective than…

Immediate deterrence, which involves more short-term actions – such as sending in the troops or bombing – to avert an imminent or immanent attack probably during some crisis.

Direct deterrence is action by a state to avert attacks on its own territory, whereas…

Extended deterrence would be to avert attacks on other (maybe allied) countries.

Extended deterrence is important because it is the basis for Article 5 of the North Atlantic Treaty, which is an explicit American (well, NATO) commitment to a wider deterrence. Article 5 calls on member states to take 'forthwith, individually and in concert with the other member states, such action as it deems necessary, including the use of armed force, to restore and maintain the security of the North Atlantic area'. Contrary to common understanding, Article 5 does not oblige member states to respond *automatically* to aggression against any other member or with military action. There is no mention of nuclear weapons, so, if the integrity of the United States was not compromised, and in the event of a nuclear attack on Western Europe, would the Americans intervene with a nuclear strike of their own? It's not clear. This has provenance in the Cold War, in that nuclear deterrence involved preventing a Soviet *nuclear* attack on the United States, whereas extended deterrence involved discouraging a Soviet *conventional* attack on NATO members. Despite much debate at the time, the U.S. would never sacrifice New York for Paris.

NO FIRST USE: REALITY OR POSTURING?

'No First Use' is an undertaking, or at least an understanding, by a nuclear power not to use nuclear weapons against another nuclear-armed state unless first attacked *by that state* with nuclear weapons. Theoretically then, if every nuclear state stuck by their promise, there could be no nuclear war. Many people might expect that their country would adopt a 'No First Use' promise and also, a parallel undertaking not to use nuclear weapons against a non-nuclear-armed state. However ...

Most nuclear-armed states have not made this promise, and neither the United States and Russia have such a policy.

Possibly 'led' by the United States or in fear of Russia, the United Kingdom and France (and, incidentally, Pakistan) commit to a possibility or threat of using nuclear weapons against a nuclear or non-nuclear state in the event of an invasion. Much of American thinking about Russia is based on its historical perception of the Soviet Union. Indeed, on occasions, American Secretaries of State have sometimes slipped into talking about 'the Soviets' rather than the Russian Federation.

And here is an insight into nuclear strategy and deterrence:

Given what was the greater strength of the Warsaw Pact conventional forces, NATO's policy was to use (tactical?) nuclear weapons to stop a Soviet invasion. This has carried over into thinking about the Russian Federation. The NATO Summit in 1999 considered a proposal by Germany (non-nuclear-armed) to adopt a 'No First Use' policy. After all, in the event of even a tactical nuclear weapon being used to hold a Soviet, sorry, *Russian* advance, it would be their country that was irradiated. The idea was rejected.

India has a 'No First Use' policy, but has also declared that this 'might change depending upon the circumstances', which pretty much negates the whole concept.

Israel, in a fit of nice obfuscation, does not 'confirm or deny having nuclear weapons' – diplomatic talk for 'we've got them but we're not going to say how many'. This ambiguity fools no one, and it is thought that Israel has several hundred warheads with the capability of delivering them by air, missile or submarine. It cannot then subscribe to the 'No First Use' policy because it does not want to admit to having nuclear weapons at all. However, it has said that it 'would not be the first country in the Middle East to formally introduce nuclear weapons into the region'. They would most likely come clean if Iran ever acquired nuclear weapons.

China became a nuclear-armed state in 1964 and immediately

subscribed to the 'No First Use' policy. China has maintained only a relatively small nuclear arsenal, instead of competing in an arms race. Chinese calls to agree a 'No First Use' treaty bilaterally with the U.S. or on a multinational basis has fallen on deaf ears. Currently, China is thought to have some 350 nuclear warheads, and have ballistic, cruise missiles and submarine-launched ballistic missile capability. That just leaves North Korea, thought to have about thirty to forty nuclear weapons. It withdrew from the NPT (the Non-Proliferation Treaty) in 2003. They do not have a 'No First Use' policy.

TACTICAL NUCLEAR WEAPONS

So far, and implicit in this commentary, we have addressed what are known as 'strategic nuclear weapons'. It's something of an abuse of the word 'strategic' as a full-scale (strategic) attack or 'exchange', as the experts would call it, might signal the end of civilisation as we know it. At the other end of the nuclear scale, there are much smaller nuclear weapons of much lower yield and designed to be used in battlefield situations.

It is possible to build a nuclear bomb that will fit inside an ordinary artillery shell or small missile. There is no agreed definition of a tactical or battlefield nuclear weapon. They can range in power from tens of kilotons to hundreds of kilotons; the Hiroshima bomb, 'Little Boy', was about 15 kilotons, and the Nagasaki bomb, 'Fat Man', was about 21 kilotons.

Known as a 'tactical nuclear weapon', or non-strategic nuclear weapon, they were intended for use on a battlefield or in a naval encounter. They include free-fall bombs, short-range missiles, artillery shells, land mines, depth charges, and torpedoes. There is no exact definition relevant to yield or delivery system, which incidentally make nuclear arms reduction talks more challenging.

As suggested earlier, in NATO war games where the Soviet forces could not be stopped by conventional means, military commanders would request that they 'go nuclear'. The assumption here is that this would either be a massive attack on targets within enemy territory or the use of tactical nuclear weapons on the battlefield. This sounds plausible, until we think through the implications. There are three problems.

The first is how far the enemy might have advanced. Take, for example, a conventional attack by North Korea on the south, bearing in mind that the border is only about 50 km from Seoul. The use of such weapons, if they were available (at the moment they are not), would irradiate South Korean territory. There is little consensus about how serious this irradiation might be, but we might suppose it to be dangerously high (recall Chernobyl).

There would be a similar problem in a naval encounter. There is much debate as to how a very large aircraft carrier might be sunk, and it is generally thought that such a vessel would not sail very close to land, where there might be launchpads for 'swarming drones' or high-speed explosive (maybe nuclear) small ships. A naval commander might then consider the use of a tactical nuclear shell/missile to sink a large enemy carrier.

The problem then is that if such a missile misses its target (and of course the manufacturers would say that this is unlikely) it would either splash into the ocean or destroy itself. Whichever, it would mean a similarly irradiated area as on land.

The second problem is that the strategic use of nuclear weapons would be a decision made by a president or prime minister, or maybe a chief of defence staff, or an inexperienced cabinet if such were not available. They would be more in touch with the overall strategic situation than a commander on the spot. The decision to use a tactical nuclear weapon would to be in the hands of the local battle commander, who might choose a logistical chokepoint or assembly point of enemy troops. By definition, such a commander might be inexperienced in managing large bodies of troops and would certainly be inexperienced in the use of even tactical nuclear weapons. The consequences would be unknowable.

The third and consequent problem is that, whereas a NATO (say Polish) commander might be reluctant to use a tactical nuclear weapon on their own territory, it is generally considered that the Russians have no such inhibitions. (They have much more space. Recall the withdrawal of everyone from Moscow when Napoleon turned up.)

The decision to use strategic nuclear weapons is well rehearsed: rather than using them to win the war, any strategy would be based on them not being used at all. However, with a more localised battle – for example, North Korea or a Chinese decision to take over Formosa (as they would call it; now called Taiwan) – any commander, if given permission, might use a tactical nuclear device. The danger then becomes one of escalation. Land, air or naval defence depends on radar, and it would be difficult to distinguish between a conventionally armed cruise missile and one armed with a nuclear device, however small.

One might then adduce that the whole idea of tactical nuclear weapons is considered to be of very little use in what started as a conventional war.

However, one of the things that is always surprising about strategic considerations is relative lack of consideration of the orientation and capability of the enemy. As noted already (for the sake of argument) though 'the West' might be reluctant to irradiate its own territory with a tactical nuclear bomb, we might think that the Russians, the North Koreans or the Chinese might have no such reservations.

With these considerations in mind, tactical nuclear weapons were removed from the front-line armoury of NATO in 1982 and held in store. The current situation is that it is thought that the Russians hold large stocks of tactical nuclear weapons and, as considered above, they might not be reluctant to use them. Again, they have much more space. To date, no tactical nuclear weapon has ever been used in a battle situation, but there are extreme dangers of using them, escalating the conflict beyond anticipated boundaries, from the tactical to the strategic.

NUCLEAR BOMBS

In this text we consider atomic bombs, both fission and fusion, hydrogen bombs, thermonuclear bombs and just nuclear bombs. For all intents and purposes, and for strategic consideration, they are all equally terrible, but here is a closer definition of each type.

An atomic bomb derives its energy (bang!) exclusively from fission reactions, the splitting of atoms. This is a bit of a misnomer as the energy released comes from the nucleus of the atom, as it does with the fusion reaction.

A hydrogen bomb also uses a fission reaction but uses it to cause a fusion reaction, between deuterium and tritium, both isotopes of hydrogen. Actually, the fusion reactions can themselves trigger additional fission reactions.

A thermonuclear bomb is a hydrogen bomb. To date, only a few countries – the United States, Russia, United Kingdom, China, France – have developed thermonuclear weapons. India may have done so, but this is doubted. A nuclear bomb is just a short name for a thermonuclear bomb.

There are also neutron bombs, which are 'low-yield' nuclear bombs designed to maximise neutron radiation in the vicinity of the blast. They might be used in what the military call an 'area denial weapon'.

Two other relevant facts:

'Kuzma's Mother' was the largest explosion the world had ever seen. At 50 megatons of TNT (that is 50 million tons of TNT), it was simply too big to be used as it would devastate such a large area. It was dropped by parachute so that the aircraft delivering the bomb would have enough time to put sufficient distance between itself and the explosion. For reference, the Hiroshima bomb had a yield of 15 kilotons (15 thousand tons) of TNT.

Second, a rather surprising fact is that during a nuclear explosion, some mass is converted to energy, on the basis of Einstein's $E=MC^2$. But it is only a very small mass, a natural constraint of the fusion process. If a new physics were discovered, that yield might increase hundreds or even thousands of times, the results of which would be truly unimaginable.

DID DETERRENCE WORK? WILL IT WORK IN THE FUTURE?

Deterrence has worked insofar as there has not been a nuclear war between the two main nuclear-armed powers, the United States and Soviet Russia/the Russian Federation since nuclear weapons were first used in 1945. Until recently China, who acquired nuclear weapons in 1964, was not seen as a threat.

What we cannot say is how close we have come to a nuclear war, or even a war in which tactical nuclear weapons might have been used. The Cuban missile crisis in 1962 is often held up as a near miss, but modern scholarship suggests that the dangers were less than portrayed. Able Archer (see panel earlier) might have been a danger point, as was the Vasili Arkhipov incident in 1962 and the Stanislav Petrov incident in 1983 (both of these are described in Wikipedia, and it is salutary that both dangers were spotted and avoided by Russian officers).

There is no magic wand that will ensure that nuclear war will not break out: no religion, no philosophy, no ideology.

But has deterrence as a strategy been successful? The best thing that can be said is that deterrence has not failed.

But then if we take Freedman's definition, concerned with 'setting boundaries for actions and establishing risks associated with crossing these boundaries', the success is less apparent. If we then continue to ask whether deterrence has made any progress towards a reduction of nuclear arsenals or discouraging non-nuclear states from acquiring nuclear weapons, or the ultimate elimination of nuclear weapons, then this must remain an open question.

NUCLEAR DISARMAMENT

There are about two dozen organisations around the world that campaign for the elimination of nuclear weapons, nuclear power and general worldwide peace. The British version is called the Campaign for Nuclear Disarmament (CND), and represents a model for other campaigning organisations. CND advocates unilateral nuclear disarmament by the United Kingdom and other countries. It supports the Nuclear Non-Proliferation Treaty and opposes any military action that may result in the use of nuclear weapons (undefined) and, incidentally, chemical or biological weapons. It also opposes nuclear power in the UK, thereby obstructing efforts to achieve fusion power.

CND opposes NATO, which, notwithstanding many reservations, has kept us safe for many years. From its website, it says NATO has recommitted to an interventionist military agenda that sets back the cause of peace and nuclear disarmament. No rationale is offered. CND opposes NATO's 'expansion of its area of work to *counter-terrorism, cyber-security, and the proliferation of chemical, biological and nuclear weapons*'. There follows many other 'antis', such as Trident, 'American missile defence', and war in general. It forebears to mention being against sin.

Whereas one must respect such noble goals, it reminds me of sitting in a pleasant square in Naples having lunch one day. The main street was just a few dozen yards away. Suddenly there was a great clamour with trumpets, cymbals and shouting. Turning to our tour guide, we asked who was protesting and he explained that it was policemen, firemen, nurses, students and council workers. Being rather alarmed at this, we asked exactly what they were protesting about. The guide simply shrugged his shoulders and said, 'They're just protesting about everything. It happens regularly in Napoli!'

The point is that CND would do far better to engage with the defence community and refute their arguments rather than just complain. One of the most famous generals of the Second World War, Field Marshal Bernard Montgomery, used to dismiss anybody he thought was simply 'bellyaching'. But there is a point, one that CND misses. One of the doyens of strategy and arms control, Thomas Schelling (1921 to 2016), was an American economist and professor of nuclear strategy, and arms control. He argued in his monograph, *A World Without Nuclear Weapons?* that '... drastic reductions make sense ... but considering how much intellectual effort in the past half century went into the study of the "stability" of nuclear deterrence ... it ought to be worthwhile to examine contingencies in a nuclear-free world to verify that it is superior to a world with (some) nuclear weapons'. CND might attempt to refute, or at least comment, on this theory.

INTERNATIONAL EFFORTS TO CURB THE SPREAD OF NUCLE-
AR WEAPONS
Many countries in the past have considered developing their own nuclear weapons. Today, nine states are nuclear armed, about the same

as there were twenty-five years ago. If we include Iran as an aspiring nuclear power, then we get just into double figures.

It looks, then, as if efforts to curb the spread of nuclear weapons has been successful. After the demise of the Soviet Union in 1991, the 'peace dividend', which saw an eighty per cent fall in the number of warheads held by America and Russia by 2010, looks inspiring, but progress since then has been slow or even non-existent. Commentators are no longer optimistic about any further cuts. Indeed, the focus has shifted to the proliferation of nuclear weapons among what are currently non-nuclear states. The ultimate goal of the non-proliferation treaty (NPT) is the total elimination of nuclear weapons, but despite this treaty, there are many dangers on the horizon.

But neither is it clear that nuclear-aspiring states are the real problem. As long ago as May 2018, *The Economist* was suggesting that 'it would be a tragedy for the world if it took an existential scare like the Cuban missile crisis, or worse, to jolt today's complacent reckless leaders back to their senses'. It quoted Michael O'Hanlon, a strategist at the Washington-based Brookings Institute suggesting that '... arms control is an extraordinarily valuable tool and it is one that the nuclear powers risk losing through a mix of complacency, neglect, ignorance and malice ...'. In terms of the more measured tone of most commentaries on international relations, words like *complacent*, *reckless*, *neglect*, *ignorance* and particularly *malice* are remarkable, and demonstrate the strength of feeling about today's politicians.

Reducing nuclear stockpiles, and indeed all arms control, looks comparatively straightforward: agree a target, a timeframe and a verification programme and away you go. Unfortunately, nuclear arms control is unusually complicated. The 'Security Dilemma' (My weapons are for defence, yours look like they're for offence) remains the backbeat for all negotiations. So, we might now be tempted to think so far, so good:

nuclear tests have declined, non-proliferation seems to be effective and, despite concerns about North Korea and Iran, the world seems to be, not exactly safer, but with the risks more clearly identified, and may thereby be more manageable. In the past, an enormous amount of effort from politicians, diplomats, technical experts and military personnel went into intelligence, analysis, negotiation and treaties but, given superpower rivalry and some suspicion on all sides, we are probably in the best place that we can be. However, given complacency and lack of attention, we may be heading for an era when nuclear postures are unconstrained for the first time in half a century. Of course, in the past there have been many nuclear treaties, some more successful than others.

NUCLEAR TREATIES (SEE APPENDIX FOR REPRESENTATIVE LIST)

So, it can be seen that an enormous amount of effort has gone into maintaining contact with the other side (until recently the Soviet Union / Russian Federation) and that there has almost always been some sort of negotiation going on, and a potential treaty to finesse. It would be a gross extrapolation to suggest that black letter treaties were less important than the contacts and the negotiation stances, but these certainly contributed. For example, after the Iran deal (The Joint Comprehensive Plan of Action, 2015) was signed, it was obvious in the press release photographs that the teams had got on well together. Also, recall that in an anarchic international environment there is no real remedy for the breaking of a treaty provision, except retaliation. So, are the current threats of the same type and order as historic threats? There are five areas for concern:

First, is inattention. The price of security is eternal vigilance. 'Summits', 'Arms Reduction Talks' and 'Ballistic Missiles' have all but disappeared from news headlines and Parliamentary topics. The debate about Vanguard / Trident replacement focuses exclusively on cost and a vague concept of deterrence, without any accompanying (diplomatic) narrative on how we might need to deter an aggressor. For a tiny fraction of the cost of the new Dreadnoughts or F-35 fighter planes that the RAF and Navy imagine they need, we could restore our intelligence and diplomatic efforts (to include arms reduction talks) manyfold.

Second, has there been deterioration in the legal basis, the processes and even expectations for the International System? Trump's abjuration of the Iran deal will have many and unforeseen implications. Although treaties and agreements have been broken – probably more times than not – in the past, that particular agreement was entered into voluntarily, and with only limited guarantees of what the Iranians were really worried about: *security*. Coupled with the American distain for the United Nations, concerns about the viability of NATO and the failure of the European Union to agree, devise and execute a coherent foreign, security and defence policy, the future looks bleak. The first responsibility of any state is to look to its citizens' security. Without confidence in the International System, many states may feel that they have no choice but to actively seek nuclear weapons.

Third is the cyber risk. According to a recent Chatham House report, 'Cyber vulnerabilities within nuclear weapons systems and structures present a whole set of dangers and risks. At best, cyber insecurity in nuclear weapons systems is likely to undermine trust and confidence in military capabilities and in the nuclear weapons infrastructure. At worst, cyber-attacks could lead to deliberate misinformation and the inadvertent launch of nuclear weapons.' The terrifying, aspect of the report is that Chatham House also suggests that 'Future research with current or former military officials, technical officers, and political figures in nuclear weapons states … is carried out, to identify how confident they are ... with the nuclear weapons complex and digital systems while making decisions.' This does not inspire confidence. They then pose an important question: 'do key decision-makers have sufficient knowledge with regards to the integrity and trustworthiness of nuclear weapons systems?'

Chatham House is the UK's leading think tank on international relations. The thought that they feel moved to ask such questions does not inspire confidence. Even so, the main problem with a cyber-attack on the nuclear command and control systems is that such attacks may simply be considered mischievous and debilitating, but could equally be interpreted as a prelude to a nuclear first strike. Without confidence in the available intelligence, political and military leaders could be put in an invidious and dangerous position.

Fourth, we need to consider rogue acquisition. It is generally thought unlikely that a terrorist group could acquire a complete nuclear bomb. These are closely monitored and kept under strict security, but even if one was stolen or acquired by some other means, the delivery mechanism would prevent it from being projected far. The real danger is that a terrorist group would get hold of some radioactive material. As we know from polonium poisoning, radioactive material is extremely toxic, and introducing it into the atmosphere would cause widespread public panic.

Fifth, is the consideration of cruise and other missiles. We cover this in the chapter on technology.

WHERE ARE WE NOW?
Much of what goes on in the world of nuclear weapons is secret and classified. However, to placate journalists and the commentariat in general, the United States, France and the United Kingdom all publish what appear to be details of their nuclear arsenals and delivery methods.

Where such is not available, the International Institute for Strategic Studies (IISS) also publish a report entitled *The Military Balance*, which pulls together the best intelligence on all armed countries, including nuclear arsenals and delivery methods.

THE UNITED STATES

The United States publishes from time to time a *Nuclear Posture Review* (NPR) to consider their nuclear policy and strategy. The 2010 Review, requested by President Obama, asked how a world free of nuclear weapons could be achieved. It covered nuclear proliferation and nuclear terrorism, a considerable departure from the usual consideration of a nuclear confrontation between states. As such, an objective was to reduce the focus on nuclear weapons in American policy. In the event, though, the Obama administration triggered a modernisation estimated to cost some $1.2 trillion over the next thirty years.

This changed dramatically under President Trump. Trump's NPR was published in February 2018 and the focus shifted back to deterrence rather than disarmament. The NPR foresaw other great powers as competitors, as well as recognising the threats posed by the nuclear ambitions of North Korea and Iran. Nuclear terrorism was also identified.

So far in the history of nuclear weapons and deterrence, there has been an underlying assumption, sometimes explicit, that the focus of any state was on another nuclear-armed state using nuclear weapons. It is this aspect that changed dramatically. The U.S. now saw non-nuclear strategic attacks, including cyber, as worthy of a nuclear response albeit in 'extreme circumstances'. One might observe that any armed attack or attack on vital infrastructure like energy or telecommunications might be considered an 'extreme circumstance'. Only for the gallery, one imagines, but, to be fair, Trump's NPR commits the United States to the long-term goal of disarmament, although there is a heavily caveated approach to future arms control, suggesting that 'further progress is difficult to envision'.

This changed again under President Biden. During his election campaign, he pledged to reduce the American reliance on nuclear weapons. Indeed, although he has not yet published a new NPR, in March 2021 (with only a few days to go before expiry), he agreed with President Putin of the Russian Federation to extend the New Strategic Arms Reduction Treaty (New START) for five years, until 2026.

Biden is known to see the U.S. nuclear arsenal as a deterrent, one to use in the event of a nuclear attack. The world, or at least those countries involved, breathed a great sigh of relief. Biden has also indicated that he will review the American policy that reserves the right to use nuclear weapons first in a conflict – virtually a 'no first use' promise. It may just be rhetoric or it could be the first step to a dramatic reduction in the worldwide number of nuclear weapons and even, optimists might hope, a world free of nuclear weapons.

By way of possible contrast, let us look at how the two European members of the United Nations Security Council Permanent Five have developed their nuclear strategy.

FRANCE

France is one of the five recognised nuclear states under the Nuclear Non-Proliferation Treaty of 1968 (NPT). France has a policy of 'strict sufficiency', where the nuclear arsenal is maintained at the lowest possible level compatible with the strategic context. Although France does not, like the UK and the U.S., subscribe to the 'no first use' undertaking, they only contemplate using nuclear weapons in 'extreme circumstances' of self-defence. Unlike the UK, France does not participate in NATO's nuclear plans and its nuclear forces are not assigned to NATO. They seem to be good nuclear citizens; although the Comprehensive Test Ban Treaty (1996) is not yet in force, France has maintained its moratorium on testing.

THE UNITED KINGDOM

Here, there are two relevant documents that we have already explored and will encounter again in a later chapter. These are the *Integrated Review of Security, Defence, Development and Foreign Policy*, known as *The Integrated Review*, and *Defence in a Competitive Age*, which focuses simply on defence issues.

Regarding nuclear strategy, the *Integrated Review* asserts that it is essentially *threats based*. It frets about threats from major nuclear-armed states, emerging nuclear states and state-sponsored nuclear terrorism.

Then, curiously, it suggests that, although the government wanted to reduce the nuclear warhead stockpile from a maximum of 225 to fewer than 180 by the mid-2020s, this is *no longer possible* (my emphasis) and the UK will now move to a maximum arsenal of no fewer than 260 warheads. This, the government says, is the minimum destructive power needed to guarantee that the UK's nuclear deterrent remains credible and effective against the full range of state nuclear threats from any direction. No rationale for this is revealed. This reverses the policy of non-proliferation and could have unintended consequences in terms of other states, whether signatories to the NPT or not, wishing to acquire more nuclear weapons.

Of 'no first use' there is no mention, and no undertaking to examine this policy, as per President Biden. Instead, the IR asserts: 'We would consider using our nuclear weapons only in extreme circumstances of self-defence, including the defence of our NATO Allies … we will remain deliberately ambiguous about precisely when, how and at what scale we would contemplate the use of nuclear weapons.'

There is, thankfully, one caveat: 'The UK will not use, or threaten to use, nuclear weapons against any non-nuclear weapon state party to the Treaty on the Non-Proliferation of Nuclear Weapons 1968 (NPT).'

The document *Defence in a Competitive Age* goes into more detail and suggests that 'Russia continues to pose the greatest nuclear, conventional military and sub-threshold threat to European security and also that Iran and North Korea will continue to pose regional challenges and their nuclear programmes threaten global stability.' In terms of nuclear posture, *Defence in a Competitive Age* confirms that nuclear deterrence will remain at the heart of UK force posture. The UK remains fully committed to NATO, maintaining 'well-supported and equipped nuclear and conventional forces at high readiness, across all domains, capable of high-intensity warfighting'. Yet the word 'nuclear' only appears once, in conjunction with 'chemical, biological, radioactive and nuclear' threats. *Defence in a Competitive Age* is a great document, imagining Britain's role in 'keeping the peace', Ranger Regiments and worldwide deployment.

The overwhelming problem though is one of resource. We do not have the budget to meet all these needs and can hardly recruit the necessary technical personnel. Questions abound but as far as *Defence in a Competitive Age* is concerned, Professor Paul Cornish's testimony on it, from Cityforum, judges it to be 'incoherent, understrength and overstretched.' Notwithstanding this, my own judgement would be that there is far too little attention given to the nuclear aspects.

WHY THEN DOES THE UK HAVE NUCLEAR WEAPONS?
The need to achieve nuclear strategic stability is because of the decision to acquire, and hold ready for use, nuclear weapons. This is a choice that states make in order to enter the very small and select club of nuclear-armed states, in spite of there being over 190 states around the world

who do *not* hold nuclear weapons. The problem for the UK is that that particular decision point has been forsaken and the decision made. It cannot be undone.

First, it would be electorally unpopular. Surveys confirm that a good proportion of the population think we should be nuclear armed, and that some of the objections to nuclear armament are cost based rather than ideological. In the absence of intrusive verification treaties, any other nuclear-armed state would not believe that any of the club would forsake nuclear weapons.

Second, if it is our objective to reduce nuclear stockpiles and delivery capabilities around the world, then we would not wish to go 'naked into the negotiating chamber' as Aneurin Bevan put it as long ago as 1957. The UK needs to demonstrate an interest in nuclear weapons if we are to partake, or possibly lead, nuclear disarmament talks.

CONCLUSIONS

The risks of war, and war itself, have always been part of international society. Until the Napoleonic catastrophe, wars were generally thought of as being part of the normal backbeat of life and international relations. Napoleon had a dramatic effect on the instigation and progress of war. A similar disjunction happened when nuclear weapons were first used in anger. Despite many mistakes and near misses, political leaders and statesmen have managed to avoid a slide into nuclear war, largely through maintaining a dialogue with the other side, even in the darkest days of the Cold War.

However, in February 2017, in their first telephone conversation, President Vladimir Putin asked President Trump about extending New START beyond 2021. On the basis of a short mid-call conversation with his aides, Trump denounced the treaty, claiming that it favoured Russia and was 'one of several bad deals negotiated by the Obama administration'.

However, the treaty remained in force until 2021, still (just) within Trump's term of office. President Biden has now agreed with President Putin a five-year extension (envisioned in the original treaty). Following Trump's repudiation of the Joint Comprehensive Plan of Action (JSCPOA – the Iran deal), we are in uncharted territory. According to the CEO of the Nuclear Threat Initiative, Ernest Moniz, this is 'a major strategic mistake that not only damages the United States' ability to prevent Iran from acquiring the material for a nuclear weapon, but also impairs our ability to prevent the spread and use of nuclear weapons, to work with allies and partners on issues of global concern and to protect our interests in the Middle East for years, if not decades, to come'.

Quite.

Again, President Biden has suggested that he is prepared to re-negotiate a treaty with Iran, but the international consensus is that it's not going to be like the old one. It looks likely that it will include not only nuclear weapons, but delivery methods as well. At the time of writing, it looks as if this whole issue has stalled, with some commentators claiming that the whole thing is dead in the water.

Nevertheless, it's worth noting that after the JCPOA (the Iran deal) was signed, a picture was published of the negotiating teams sitting round the conference table. The participants were the American team, led by John Kerry, plus P5+1 (the five permanent members of the United Nations Security Council — China, France, Russia, United Kingdom, United States — plus Germany) together with the European Union. The Iranian team was led by Mohammad Javad Zarif. All parties were smiling at each other. It was obvious that they had got on well during the negotiations. Sure, there was a lack of trust at the beginning of the negotiations but – and every picture tells a story – very little animosity. It was a triumph of diplomacy and also one of the 21st-century's greatest tragedies that Donald Trump repudiated this deal.

And hereby hangs a tale; nobody would suggest that treaties should not be renegotiated, but an outright rejection damages the credibility of not only the party who rejects the treaty, but the whole idea of treaties in general. The United Sates' international reputation was and remains badly damaged by Trump's antics.

There is no single, simple answer to the problem of how to avoid nuclear war and how to achieve a nuclear-free world. As H L Mencken quipped, 'there is always an easy solution to every human problem – neat, plausible, and wrong'. But to see international relations solely as threat-oriented rather than countries seeking their own legitimate security, will mean seeing more and more threats.

The UK's *Integrated Review* mentions *threat, threats, threaten* and *threatened* 130 times. To see other countries as belligerent, again rather than just seeking their own legitimate security, will mean that everything they do will look belligerent. If all you have is a hammer, everything will look like a nail.

A good start in putting deterrence and the whole of a nuclear strategy into perspective would be to put more effort into understanding and realising Lawrence Freedman's concept of deterrence: less about fear, doubt, danger and trouble, and more about boundaries, risks and, by implication, communication. Even then, deterrence alone is not a strategy. It may contribute to a strategic approach but it is, of itself, not a comprehensive strategic posture. Formulating strategy is challenging; it goes to the heart of who we are, our values and beliefs and how we interact with the rest of the world. Strategy is challenging, and unpicking any strategy in general is also challenging. I have spent hours, days and weeks working with commercial/industrial managers discussing whether what they plan to do is essentially strategic, tactical, expedient, contingent or if it simply 'seems like a good idea at the time'. Realising whatever strategy or strategies you choose is even more challenging.

The danger is that the United Kingdom is losing the ability, and the even desire, to define any vision or long-term strategy with respect to nuclear weapons. Given our position as a nuclear power and our place on the United Nations Security Council Permanent Five, we *could* lead the world in encouraging the reduction in the number of nuclear weapons. But, as the Brexit negotiations have painfully demonstrated, we lack the diplomatic effort, the intelligence and the technical expertise to lead such an endeavour. We also lack the appropriate processes, but most of all we lack the aspiration. It is a sad reflection on a country that has played such a major part in international affairs over the centuries.

There are many references, but one in particular stands out. In a talk at RUSI in January 2021, the Chief of the General Staff, General Sir Nick Carter, admitted that:

'On our side, we don't have the same level of understanding that we had of each other in the Cold War, and the tried and tested systems and diplomatic instruments are not what they once were – confidence building measures, arms reduction negotiations, public monitoring and inspection of each other's military activity, etc.'

Considerably more effort, diplomatic, political and technical, should go into understanding other countries' security concerns. For example, few commentators recognise Iran's security situation, surrounded by nuclear states: Russia on the other side of the Caspian Sea, Israel within missile range, a common border with Pakistan, and with India on the other side. Add a dozen or so American bases on the other side of the Persian Gulf and who would not be worried? It's not a perfect analogy, but if the Islamic Republic of Iran were actually Iran plc, then the CEO would be in dereliction of their duty in not seeking nuclear weapons.

The United Kingdom, in conjunction with our European allies, requires far more active involvement in advocating more and better diplomacy, confidence building measures, verification protocols, high-level military contacts and summits, discussions, conferences or whatever, on nuclear arms reduction. The technical, diplomatic and negotiating efforts currently applied to the issue of nuclear arms are simply not commensurate with the threat. One must ask whether there is sufficient will to do so.

The government of the United Kingdom is in dereliction of its duty to provide for the security of its citizens and that of the world in general. Distracted by what are trivial matters compared with the risks of nuclear war, some administrations are driven by a craving to stay in power rather than any desire to act responsibly. In the modern era, the political and diplomatic efforts are not adequate to the task. Even more worrying is that the world is seen through the prism of threats rather than opportunities. It is over a hundred years old, but Teddy Roosevelt's injunction to 'speak softly and carry a big stick' seems to have been forgotten. Yes, we carry a big stick, but where is the speaking softly?

Whatever the exact topic, be it proliferation, hypersonic missiles, ICBMs, mid-range missiles, test ban treaties, the existing nuclear powers should immediately start negotiating, maybe with aspiring nuclear powers as observers. We would allow that negotiating nuclear deals is complex, detailed and requires intense and comprehensive technical knowledge. But experts exist and should be used. Negotiations can review the other side's views and insights into their decision-making process, their red lines and other features their nuclear stance.

Politicians have a sacred duty to preserve the country's security and integrity. Most of all, though, they require political will, of which there is little.

Nuclear weapons so appallingly awful, not just in the effect they have, but in the political implications, that even the slightest risk of a nuclear war – and that is certainly conceivable – from the point of view of the effort put in, should be treated as a near certainty.

11. TECHNOLOGY, MISSILES AND STRATEGIC SECURITY

Technology might look as if it enhances strategic security, but this should not be taken as a given.

INTRODUCTION

In this chapter we ask what influence technology has had on warfare, although that might be evident, and what contribution technology has thereby made to war, recalling that war should be the use of organised violence to achieve a better relationship between polities.

TECHNOLOGY

Technology has always had a profound influence on warfare. Even in the Palaeolithic times, where spears, and bows and arrows were used largely, we imagine, for killing game, they would also be used in warfare. Technology? Before schoolchildren used consoles to play computer games, they would frequently cut down a stick from the tree, bend it and put a string in it and call it a bow. Any piece of twig would serve as an arrow. The pull weight of such a bow might be half a kilogram or so. But to make a bow capable of killing an animal – or a man – the pull weight of the bow has to be something between 20 and 30 kg. This takes a lot of knowledge, skill and experience in terms of selecting the right tree – yew was used for war bows – in cutting down the appropriate part, perhaps with a stone axe, and fashioning it into a bow. We can imagine that Palaeolithic man made bowstrings from animal sinew or gut.

Nevertheless, we can see a lot of technology here. For contrast, a replica warbow along the lines of one from the Middle Ages, might cost something like $1,000 in today's value, which evidently represents a lot of technological skill and expertise.

From then on technological advancements greatly helped in the production of weapons: bronze to steel, armour, gunpowder providing the motive power for cannons and muskets and eventually aeroplanes, radio and radar.

Modern military technology dazzles and appals at the same time. Bullets that can change direction mid-flight, stealth planes that have almost no radar signature and missiles that can fly around the world and land within a 100-metre radius of their targets must be counted as a current high point of man's technological rise.

This chapter is about the application of technology to warfare. True to the central message of this book, we look more at a selection of the latest technological applications focused on missiles: ICBMs, cruise missiles and, the latest development, hypersonic cruise missiles. We ask if the availability of such technologies helps or hinders in the implementation of any chosen strategy and whether they enhance or detract from the true meaning of war: the establishment of a better political relationship between polities. We address this through the concept of strategic stability.

STRATEGIC STABILITY

The word *strategic* is often heard on the news, as in 'strategic town' lost or gained, or 'strategic crossroads'. Quite what distinguishes a 'strategic town' or a 'strategic crossroads' from any other large town is not revealed – perhaps they are just bigger. Certainly, weapons are often described as 'strategic' on the basis that they are bigger or more sophisticated than the precedent.

Ideally, any strategic weapon should contribute to a durable peace, but the link from *weapon* to *peace* seems contradictory. But let us posit that strategic weapons may contribute to at least a stable international environment, which might provide a basis for peace or at least a path to it. How so? MAD, Mutually Assured Destruction, is often thought of as the basis for deterrence, although underlying MAD was second-strike capability as explained in the chapter on nuclear deterrence.

During the latter stages of the Cold War, the United States, United Kingdom and the Soviet Union had an enormous stockpile of nuclear weapons and several ways of delivering them, such as ICBMs, bombers and submerged ship ballistic missiles (SSBNs). But, and this is the vital aspect, they were all in almost constant contact and negotiation in terms of arms control talks to limit the number and deployment of the warheads.

A modern weapons system is more complicated, involving not only the armed forces themselves, but politicians who would not, despite the old political saw about 'there being no votes in defence', countenance the public thinking they were weak on the security of the country. There is also the research, development and manufacture angle: defence contracts, may be cheaper than when they were remunerated on a cost plus basis but they are still highly profitable. See *About War* and the comments on QinetiQ. It is the updated, but now public-relations curated Military Industrial Complex again.

And don't forget the think tanks, consultancies and university departments that all make a good living out of commentating on defence matters. It is an open question as to whether the sum total of these contribute very much to this overall problematic. Often referenced as a leading think tank, the Carnegie Endowment for International Peace (CEIP) is a nonpartisan international think tank in Washington DC with offices in Europe, South and East Asia, and the Middle East. The organisation describes itself as being dedicated to advancing co-operation between nations and promoting active international engagement by the United States. They also have an office in Moscow. Carnegie Moscow Centre explains strategic stability thus:

'The concept of strategic stability was formally agreed on for the first time by then Soviet leader Mikhail Gorbachev and then U.S. president George H.W. Bush during the final negotiations on the Strategic Arms Reduction Treaty (START I) in June 1990. Strategic stability was defined in terms of removing incentives for either side to launch a nuclear first strike. More specifically, strategic stability incorporates at least three elements:

First, strategic offensive and defensive arms should be configured so that neither side's defences can undermine the other's retaliatory strike capability.

Second, strategic stability requires reducing the number of warheads carried by each strategic missile. Doing this makes it more difficult for a single incoming missile to eliminate several enemy missiles, each armed with a large number of warheads, before they are launched.

Third, strategic stability puts a premium on the survivability of nuclear weapons, which would make it more difficult for an enemy to destroy them in a disarming first strike.'

We might also add arms control measures, both offensive and defensive, in the widest sense of the term, and also efficient and secure communications to prevent escalation.

Of the many technological applications that we find in warfare today, there is one general category of weapon that is particularly pertinent to this enquiry: missiles – in the form of the ICBM, (Intercontinental Ballistic Missiles), the SSBN (Submerged Ship Ballistic Missile), cruise missiles, and hypersonic cruise missiles.

MISSILES IN ANCIENT TIMES

Warfare has always involved throwing things at the enemy. We can imagine Palaeolithic man throwing stones at an enemy and graduating to spears, and then to bows and arrows. Cave paintings have been found showing battles between archers and, although these were difficult to date, some remains of bows and arrows have been found and dated to about 18,000 years ago.

It is not thought that ancient bows, such as those used by Palaeolithic man, or even by the Roman auxiliaries, had the same pull weight as the English mediaeval warbow or longbow. At about 25 kg pull weight, these older bows were probably about half as powerful as the longbow, though still lethal.

Roman legionaries would throw their 'pilum' – a long, heavy javelin – when the enemy was within range. Roman artillery also comprised siege engines such as the onager, a stone-throwing device that relied on generating tension in ropes to fire its missile. It is not clear what weight of rock or bolt was used, but something in the region of 25 kg would sound realistic, with a range of about 100 metres. We could conclude that such missiles would be useless against stone walls, but may have been effective against timber palisades, and certainly for terrifying the opposing troops. The onager should not be confused with the ballista, a slightly smaller weapon that was used in Greek and Roman times to throw a bolt or stone. They had a good range of up to 400m, but effective combat range for many targets was much shorter and the projectile lighter than the onager missile. Whereas the onager relied on tension to throw the missile, the ballista used a very strong bow *plus* a tensioned rope, for its projectile power.

In the film *Gladiator*, onagers were used to throw pots of burning olive oil to discourage the attackers. I cannot find any historical reference to such a practice, but it is well understood that, during a siege, the attackers would throw in rotting bodies, dead dogs and the suchlike to lower the morale of the defenders. Both onager and ballista are often confused with the counterweight trebuchet, a much later weapon, described as the 'most powerful weapon of the Middle Ages' by Peter Purton in 2010. There's a story that when Edward I acquired the first pair in England to his delight, he was nonetheless piqued by the attempted early surrender of a Scottish castle. He refused the surrender to give himself the opportunity to try it out.

MEDIAEVAL MISSILES

The counterweight trebuchet could throw an 80 kg missile, which could be handled by several men, about 200 metres – safe enough from the defending city. Such cumbersome weapons fell out of use later in the Middle Ages when gunpowder and the idea of the cannon took over.

Gunpowder was invented by the Chinese in the 9th century. They invented rockets, with exploding heads, used in the early 13th century, trying to repel the Mongol invaders (they failed). Actually, the Mongols brought the first counterweight trebuchets to China: cannon couldn't compete with the counterweight trebuchet, which used superior technology at that time. Apparently, Kublai Khan hired trebuchet operators from the Middle East for his invasion and paid them handsomely. Gunpowder was used in the West from about the 14th century onwards. At the Battle of Crécy in 1346, Edward III used six great cannons against the French. They did not take much of a toll against the French army, as each gun fired only a few rounds during the entire battle, but the *fire and noise* certainly frightened the French horses and also the French troops. It seems the terror of new weapons may have been greater than their destructive power.

WEAPON SYSTEMS

It may seem odd to think about counterweight trebuchets and bows and arrows in a chapter about the technology of modern war, but it is useful to identify these as part of a 'weapons system'. A weapons system considers every aspect of the weapon's technology, development and manufacturing base, the logistics of getting it to the battlefield, the way it is managed, provided with its projectile, targeted and ultimately appraised, as well as training troops to use the weapon effectively. Almost all weapons fall into this category in one way or another.

The mediaeval counterweight trebuchet is a good example. Some of them were massive, requiring a good knowledge of ballistics and woodworking, and the operators needed to be trained. Transporting them over mediaeval roads must have been difficult and when in place, the counterweight would have had to be loaded, transported to the machine and probably chipped into the right size and weight for the range and the target, as would the projectile. Then, ultimately a decision would have to be made as to whether the effect of the weapon was worth the effort and expense of having it at all.

Skipping forwards 700 years, missiles are now in a different league. We look briefly at the recent developments in cruise missiles, ICBMs (Inter Continental Ballistic Missiles) and then at the prospects for hypersonic missiles. We then consider the strategic implications for each weapon system and for the whole.

ICBMS (INTER CONTINENTAL BALLISTIC MISSILES)

The ICBM is the big daddy of missiles. They are *Intercontinental* in that they have a range of 5,500 km or more, the longest range being about 12,000 km. They are *Ballistic* in that for most of the flight they are unpowered. The multistage rocket that launches the missile takes it into high altitude (100 km) and at the peak altitude the missile reaches speeds of up to 7 km/s. They are primarily designed for nuclear weapon delivery, with one or more thermonuclear warheads, and they can also carry conventional, chemical or biological weapons or a selection. The modern ICBMs support MIRVs (Multiple Independently Targetable Re-entry Vehicles), each of which can strike a different target.

WERNER VON BRAUN (1912 TO 1977)

Von Braun was a German aerospace engineer and the prime mover in the development of rocket technology in Nazi Germany. He designed and developed the V-2 rocket at Peenemünde during World War II. In all, some three thousand V-2s were produced, the first hitting London in September 1944, and then Antwerp and Liège. Casualties amounted to about 9,000 civilians and military personnel and – the nastiest part of the story – some 12,000 concentration camp inmates died as a result of their forced labour in the factories making the missiles. (This part of the story is outlined in the novel The Good German by Joseph Kanon, an American writer.)

Operation Paperclip was a more or less secret United States post-war programme moving more than 1,600 German scientists, engineers, and technicians from the former Nazi Germany to the U.S. for government research on rocket development. It formed the basis of the American space and rocket programme, and the development and production of the first ICBM: the SM-65 Atlas.

There is a whole range of ICBMs: intermediate, medium and short range, and tactical. This may seem arcane to the general public, but in terms of arms control, this differentiation has a vital significance. Early designs were not particularly accurate in terms of targeting, which made them useful only against the largest targets, such as cities or naval bases. The latest designs have dramatically improved accuracy so that even the smallest targets can be successfully targeted *if you know where they are.*

An up-to-date American ICBM is the LGM-30G Minuteman III, weighing some 36 tonnes, standing about 17 m high and with a diameter of 1.7 m and a range of nearly 10,000 km. The Minuteman delivers one, two or three independently targeted warheads, each with an explosive yield of 475 kilotons, giving the missile a maximum yield of over 1.4 megatons, about one hundred times the power of the atomic bomb dropped on Hiroshima.

British and American submarines use the Trident missile, a submarine-launched ballistic missile (SLBM), which is equipped with MIRVs. The Trident is massive: it stands over 13m tall (44 feet) and has a diameter of over 2m (7 feet). At launch, they weigh nearly 60 tonnes and have a range of nearly 10,000km.

Each of the British Trident missiles carries three 100 kiloton warheads, each giving the missile a maximum yield of over 300 kilotons, about twenty times power of the atomic bomb dropped on Hiroshima. The American Trident carries four, six, or eight 475 kiloton warheads.

HOW DO ICBMS CONTRIBUTE TO STRATEGIC STABILITY?

As described in the previous chapter, deterrence as a concept relies on second-strike capability, sufficient communications to facilitate escalation control, arms control measures, verification and treaties all contributing to strategic stability in that the tensions of the nuclear-armed states are apparent and well understood. Together, these measures reduce the risk of miscalculation or misperception of the other nuclear-armed state's actions. Strategic stability is essentially about the reduction or absence of incentives for the first use, or even the use at all, of nuclear weapons.

Recall the observations in the previous chapter about deterrence being based on 'fear, doubt, danger and trouble' and Freedman's rejoinder about 'setting boundaries for actions and establishing risks associated with crossing these boundaries.'

ICBMs can be launched from ground-based silos or vehicles. Where is it is possible for an enemy to identify the location of the silos, it is much more difficult to identify where vehicles are located, so retaliation is more possible in some circumstances. The element of the triad used exclusively by Britain and France is the SSBN, and we consider this in detail here.

THE SUBMERGED SHIP BALLISTIC MISSILE

The UK's Current Nuclear Deterrent is based on the SSBM, a Submerged Ship Ballistic Missile. The nuclear-powered, nuclear-armed submarine is probably the most sophisticated example of what we might call 'extreme tech', the apotheosis of technological achievement. Able to remain underwater and undetected for months, such a boat could happily sail around the world and still be fully functional. The only constraint would be the availability of on-board food for the 135 crew.

Currently the five members of the Security Council permanent five operate SSBN: the United States, China, Russia, France and the United Kingdom. India also operates, at the moment, just one boat. For a reason that only mariners will understand, and although they are officially called 'Submerged Ships ...', the Navy calls them 'boats'.

The UK has four Vanguard Class nuclear-powered ballistic missile submarines, each armed with 'up to' sixteen Trident II missiles, each with a maximum range of 12,000 km. Each of these missiles has 'up to' four independently targetable warheads, meaning a total capability (classified) in terms of nuclear blasts of between forty-eight and over sixty, quite enough to wreak devastation on any enemy country, however large.

SSBNs cruise mainly between at a depth of between 60 m and 100 m below the surface. They operate on a covert basis, in that the location, speed and direction of the boat is not known to the home Navy. This is because the boat cannot send a message to its home base without revealing its position to an enemy's electronic submarine detection facility.

They can surface and trail an aerial to pick up any messages from the home base, which presumably they do regularly. If this were an order to fire a missile, then this message would be encoded and would have to match some codes held on the submarine itself.

Thus, the largely undetectable SSBN is the ideal delivery vehicle for an ICBM and one that contributes greatly to strategic stability. Also, given the technology found within a nuclear submarine, there is a very high technological barrier to overcome for any competitive nation to attempt to acquire and operate such a boat.

Deterrence, and thus strategic stability, is primarily based on the 'mutual vulnerability' of an all-out nuclear attack. But there must also be sufficient communications to facilitate escalation control. This can be seen clearly in the event of an accidental launch, though the credibility of the source of the communication might be called into question by the other side. The fictional BBC programme *Inside the War Room* (shown in 2016) illustrated this. The Russians had detonated a nuclear weapon over a American nuclear carrier group in the Baltic and said it was the actions of a rogue commander, quickly arrested and executed. The British were unsure what to do and could not reach a consensus, and the U.S. president decided to launch one nuclear missile on a Russian city. SSBNs, largely undetectable, contribute to strategic stability by ensuring the second-strike capability. However, the leaders of nuclear-armed states around the world have not used this to manage a reduction in the overall nuclear arsenal. Also, given the technology found within a nuclear submarine, there is a very high technological barrier to overcome for any competitive nation to attempt to acquire and operate such a boat.

France has four *Triomphant*-class nuclear-powered, nuclear-armed submarines, each armed with sixteen M45 missiles or M51 missiles.

China has one Type 092 submarine, an older version and five *Jin*-class submarines (Type 094), each armed with twelve JL-2 missiles.

Russia has four active SSBNs of the Borei class and up to another eight older boats.

India has one *Arihant*-class SSBN in service and another three S5 class SSBN planned, but not yet in service.

As one might expect, the United States has ten Ohio-class SSBNs. Four of the original boats have been converted to cruise missile submarines.

CRUISE MISSILES

There are many different types of cruise missile. What distinguishes them from other classes of weapon is that they are guided, either by assigning a target or by a real-time camera in the nose relaying back to an operator. Generally subsonic, flying less than the speed of sound, they are powered by a turbo fan engine, rather like a jet liner, and they have a considerable range. Cruise missiles that fly faster than the speed of sound are known as 'hypersonic', and are covered presently.

Rather than being ballistic – flying a trajectory – the cruise missile is powered through its whole flight and can therefore fly at very low altitudes. Cruise missiles generally use Terrain Contour Matching, in which their on-board computers match the terrain the missile is flying over and adjust their course accordingly. This means they avoid flying into mountains and it also makes it difficult for the intended target to detect, as it flies 'under the radar'.

The American Tomahawk cruise missile is a good modern example, although it has been in service with the U.S. (since 1983) and the Royal Navy (since 1995). Of its 1,600 kg weight, it carries a 450 kg high explosive warhead, which is enough to sink, for example, anything but the biggest ship. Tomahawks are 5.5 m long and have a wingspan of about 2.7 m. They fly at about 900 km an hour and have a stated range of about 2,000 km. There are many different types of Tomahawk, and a whole list of the variants, plus other countries' cruise missiles, would be considerable. Since 1991, 2,200 Tomahawks have been fired, and at a (current) unit cost of over $1.5 million, add up to a whacking great $3 billion – useful revenue for the manufacturers.

Another example would be the Indian/Russian BrahMos, a larger cruise missile at 3,000 kg weight and a length of over 8 m. It carries a 200 kg warhead and has a range of nearly 300 km, though this is being upgraded to about 800 km. There are also rumours of this missile being made supersonic, which we come onto in the next section.

Cruise missile are generally used to attack high-value targets such as airfields, ships, logistical hubs, bridges and dams, with modern guidance systems facilitating highly accurate attacks. The unit cost of the missile, coupled with the logistical back up, makes them expensive to use, and thus targeting has to be accurate. Cruise missiles are a true *weapons system* in that they are the result of much technological research, need considerable logistical back up and, of course, at over $1.5 million each, they are quite expensive to use against anything but a vital and identifiable target.

HYPERSONIC CRUISE MISSILES

The speed of sound in air at 20°C is 1,235 km an hour. Most aircraft fly at a lower speed although Concorde flew at Mach2, meaning twice the speed of sound and many modern jet fighters can also fly at this speed. The RAF require permission to fly at greater than the speed of sound over the United Kingdom, as doing so creates a sonic boom which can be heard for miles around the flight path. *Supersonic* refers to speeds up to five times the speed of sound (Mach5), and anything faster than this is usually referred to as *hypersonic.*

Hypersonic cruise missiles are the latest preoccupation, or one might say obsession, for the arms industry, military commentators and the military itself. *The New York Times* warned in June 2019 that 'Hypersonic missiles are unstoppable. And they're starting a new global arms race.' The strap line is: 'The new weapons – which could travel at more than 15 times the speed of sound with terrifying accuracy – threaten to change the nature of warfare.' Later on in the article, it says there is no defence against the hypersonic missile as they are 'fast, effective, precise and unstoppable'. Ballistic missiles (ICBMs) also travel at hypersonic speeds – over Mach20 – but these are not dirigible in their final stages. What makes hypersonic cruise missiles so worrisome is that they can, while in-flight, evade anti-missile defences and only commit themselves to a target at the last stage.

There two main types of hypersonic missiles, both of which will, eventually, be able to carry nuclear weapons. There is the HCM, the Hypersonic Cruise Missile and also the HGV, the Hypersonic Boost Glide Vehicle. The HCM is powered by a scramjet, which is a supersonic development of the ramjet. The scramjet relies on the missile getting to a very high speed before it will actually work – something like Mach4. This means they have to be launched with a rocket, such as an ICBM. Otherwise, the characteristics of the cruise missiles are similar to their subsonic cousins. The HCM can be equipped with all the navigation devices, including a camera, which relay the view from the missile back to an operator, who can change the last-minute target or abort, if necessary. The HGV is unpowered in its final form, and because it is going at hypersonic speeds it can bounce along the upper atmosphere. It is equipped with small orientating thrusters for control. Because they can orientate themselves and change target, the unpredictability of where the HGV will land poses a large risk factor.

As we have mentioned in several places in this book, the idea of deterrence being based on mutually assured destruction is not the whole story. The real factor in deterrence is the fact that, given that an enemy cannot identify every source of a nuclear retaliation, the enemy retains this second-strike capability.

If one of the protagonists imagined that they could identify every nuclear silo containing ICBMs, every airfield with bombers standing ready to deliver the nuclear bomb and every SSBM cruising under the oceans, and, incidentally, had a way of neutralising them all, then it could attempt to try and eliminate an enemy with a first strike. What is stopping this happening is the concept of Ballistic Missile Defence, BMD.

This might thereby destroy the idea of a second-strike capability and diminish strategic stability. It is absolutely vital that worldwide treaties are negotiated and agreed that prohibit the development and use of such hypersonic vehicles. It would be a jolly sight cheaper too!

12. DRONES AND DRONE WARFARE

Death From Above?

Most people will be familiar with the grainy black and white footage shown on the evening news broadcasts: a building, tank, group of people or vehicle in the crosshairs of what must be an aircraft flying above. Suddenly, there's a big flash and it's obvious that a missile has struck. 'Terrorists' or 'enemy combatants' have been destroyed. When he was the Prime Minister of the UK (2007 to 2010), Gordon Brown claimed that actions against Afghan terrorists 'made the streets of Bradford or the homeland in general safer, and that people could sleep easier in their beds'. Quite tricky to prove, one imagines. Welcome to the world of drone warfare.

WHAT EXACTLY IS A DRONE?

Drones are Unmanned Aerial Vehicles: UAVs in American parlance, although the RAF prefers to call them RPAS: Remotely Piloted Air Systems. More recently, the RAF, like everyone else, calls them drones.

Drones can vary in size from small models not much bigger than an insect, to very large cargo drones, carrying up to 1.5 tonnes. Tiny drones, one of which could fit on your fingernail, could be used as a 'cloud' to attack incoming aircraft or missiles by confusing its navigational system or damage the propulsion. Small model aircraft with a wingspan of a few feet are used for battlefield intelligence to see 'over the hill', and the mighty Global Hawk, a surveillance aircraft with a wingspan of forty metres, can fly for twenty-four hours continuously and can survey as up to 100,000 square km of terrain a day.

Drones operate through a combination of advanced technologies, including video connection with the pilot, who may be proximate to the aircraft, or through satellite communication on the other side of the world. There may be video and radar surveillance of the ground below, some aspects of artificial intelligence, and avoidance technology. None of this is particularly novel; an ordinary civilian could possibly pilot a small model drone from the other side of the world by attaching an iPhone to the front of the drone and calling it up. Drones can be aerial vehicles, land or sea vehicles and occasionally underwater.

DEATH FROM ABOVE

Although some articles are headed with titles like Death from Above, the vast majority of drones by number are used for a wide diversity of peaceful purposes: such as the delivery of medical supplies to remote locations; spotting rustlers; mapping uncharted territory; catching smugglers; detecting forest fires; and, my favourite, the inspection of high, difficult to access places such as towers, bridges and even the tops of jumbo jets. They can even 'climb' to the top of church towers to inspect the brickwork. The vast majority of military drones are also used for surveillance rather than targeted assassination.

An example of a modern drone would be the American-armed General Atomics MQ-9 Reaper. The United States Air Force operate nearly 200 of these aircraft; the RAF in Great Britain have about five, with another five on order. The Reaper is 11m long with a wingspan of 20m and weighs over two tonnes. It can carry nearly two tonnes of armaments. It can be 'piloted' remotely from, for example, Creech Air Force Base in Nevada, U.S.A., or, for the British drones, RAF Waddington in Lincolnshire, United Kingdom. Fully loaded, it can fly for fourteen hours, meaning that it can fly for several hundred kilometres, 'loiter' over the target area for several hours while waiting to acquire a target and then fly back to base. It can carry a variety of missiles, including the AGM-114 Hellfire, the GBU-12 Paveway II and the 230 kg (a lot of bang!) GBU-38 Joint Direct Attack Munition (JDAM). The Air-to-Air Stinger (ATAS) has also been tested.

WHAT EXACTLY ARE DRONES USED FOR?

Drones have been around for years. Surveillance drones were tested in the First World War, but not used operationally. Surveillance drones were used on a large scale during the Vietnam War (1955 to 1975). During the Yom Kippur War in 1973, Israel flew target drones as decoys over Egyptian positions, causing Egypt to fire most of its anti-aircraft missiles. This enabled Israeli pilots to exploit the depleted Egyptian defences.

Surveillance drones contributed greatly to the first Gulf War in 1990/1991. Encouraged by this, and in conjunction with satellite technology, the United States developed the remotely controlled combat UAV, or armed drone. The first successful attack by an American UAV was in October 2001, in Kandahar province, Afghanistan, only a few weeks after the 9/11 attacks.

Now, drones fly high above a target area and observe, through human intelligence, people and their patterns of behaviour, buildings or vehicles on the ground and then launch a missile to destroy them. The idea is that drones can undertake work that would be more dangerous and expensive using ground troops or piloted aircraft – and pilots cannot fly in an aircraft for fourteen hours, even if the aircraft had the capacity to do so.

Ascertaining the exact number of drones held by various countries around the world is difficult: much data are classified. What we do know is that many countries have developed and continue to develop their own drone technology or have copied that of other countries. Certainly, the United States has its own drone programme, as has China, Israel, Iran, Russia, Pakistan and Turkey.

Counting the number of lethal strikes in war situations is more challenging. The U.S. does not release much useful data, partly because drone strikes increased under President Barack Obama and even more under President Donald Trump. But, in March 2019, Trump signed an executive order banning reporting of drone casualty details. The data differs between sources: government sources suggest that almost all drone strikes are successful in killing a known terrorist, with, regrettably, some collateral damage – civilians killed. Fortunately, the London-based Bureau of Investigative Journalism (BIJ) kept a close tally of strikes, civilian deaths and child deaths. Their dataset is large, but to take a couple of examples:

THE BUREAU OF INVESTIGATIVE JOURNALISM

The BIJ ceased reporting drone strikes in February 2020, releasing a statement to the effect that: the American covert warfare is no longer the underreported area that it was when we began, it is increasingly difficult to pursue this kind of reporting, and we believe our drone data work is now better placed with Airwars – an organisation monitoring civilian casualties – than with our investigative journalism team.

In Afghanistan alone, between the years of 2015 and 2020, there were over 14,000 American air and drone strikes. Somewhere between 4,000 and 10,000 people were killed in the strikes, including somewhere between 300 and 900 civilians, of whom between 100 and 200 were children. Between sixty and 1,700 people were injured.

In Yemen, in the same period, there were about 230 American air and drone strikes. Between 200 and 800 people were killed, of whom between 100 and 150 were civilians. Also, a dozen children were killed. Between 100 and 300 people were injured.

By way of complementing this data, according to *The Guardian* newspaper in November 2019, between 2014 and 2018 the UK flew 2,423 Reaper drone missions over Syria and Iraq, striking 398 times.

Although a different theatre of war, one statistic that stretches credibility is that, between September 2014 and January 2019, British drone and air raids in Syria and Iraq killed some 4,315 fighters, but that only one civilian was killed or injured.

The conclusion is clear: although drone strikes can kill the baddies, destroy houses used as meeting places and disrupt transport, there will inevitably be civilian deaths associated with any strike. And this will include first responders who rush to the site of a strike. Drones are militarily effective, but the collateral damage might negate them as a strategic weapon. Much depends on how the targets are chosen.

CHOOSING THE TARGETS

To identify targets, one might expect detailed and exhaustive intelligence, gathered patiently on the ground and verified, cross checked and risk assessed. Yes, of course there is some of this: human intelligence from spies or observation on the ground. But much target identification – and we don't know how much – is done by metadata, certainly in the U.S.. As NSA (the U.S. National Security Agency) General Counsel Stewart Baker has said, 'Metadata absolutely tells you everything about somebody's life. If you have enough metadata, you don't really need content.'

When challenged about this at a debate at Johns Hopkins University in 2014, General Michael Hayden, former director of the NSA and the CIA, replied that this was 'absolutely correct', and asserting, 'we kill people based on metadata'.

For the UK, and according to *The Economist* in 2015, 'RAF drones have been used for lethal strikes in Afghanistan, but only when British or allied forces were threatened by fighting.' However, in what the then UK prime minister, David Cameron, conceded was a 'new departure' for the UK, an RAF drone killed Reyaad Khan, a British citizen from Cardiff, in Syria in 2015. The strike killed two others who were travelling in the same vehicle, including one other Briton.

According to The Economist: 'Cameron's defence of the attack and its legality was based upon intelligence that identified Khan as actively engaged in the planning of 'barbaric' attacks on the West,' and the UK had an 'inherent right to self-defence'. The legal opinion of the Attorney General had been sought and he had opined that 'there would be a clear legal basis for action under international law'. As usual in these cases, the legal advice was not published. Generally, we rarely get to know what process the United Kingdom uses to authorise such killings or whether any such process takes place at all. Nor do newscasts offer any explanation or any informed legal view about whether these killings are legitimate, 'justified' or in line with International Humanitarian Law (IHL).

METADATA

Metadata is essentially data that provides information about messages, but not the content of the message, such as the text or an image.' A good example would be telephone calls. Without listening to the actual content of the call, anybody monitoring the number and duration of a telephone call could adduce information about the caller and the recipient.

So, for example, if a salesperson makes a phone call to the same number every day at about 6 pm, it might reasonably be adduced that he was phoning his manager with the results of the day's activities.

However, there can be a sinister side to this. When operating over what they considered to be terrorist-held areas, an American observation drone might observe a person crossing a border on many occasions. They might then assume that they are indeed terrorists, and launch a strike to eliminate them. Or they might observe several men in a compound doing jumping jacks. Again, ignoring the fact that they might just have been keeping fit, they would assume that they were terrorists and launch a strike.

As reported by John Norton of The Guardian in 2016, the U.S. National Security Agency's Skynet project uses metadata to help decide who is a target. In April 2014, at a symposium at Johns Hopkins University, General Michael Hayden, a former director of both the CIA and the NSA, said this: 'We kill people based on metadata.' He qualified that stark assertion by reassuring the audience that the United States government doesn't kill American citizens on the basis of their metadata. They only kill foreigners … he did not reveal how metadata could distinguish between an American citizen and a foreigner.

Supporters of drone wars claim that terrorists can be eliminated, safe houses made unsafe and convoys carrying weapons and explosives destroyed. They certainly seem to have been successful in their chosen *military* tasks: dozens of al-Qaeda and Taliban leaders have been killed, a practice known as 'decapitation' if the target is an 'HVT' (High Value Target). Many middle-ranking and working operatives have also been eliminated. It is reasonable to assert that al-Qaeda in north-west Pakistan was removed – or at least severely depleted – as a local threat in this way.

ANOTHER INTERPRETATION

But that's only one side of the story: another might be that there is something problematic with an aircraft launched from another country and controlled from yet another, launching what it claims is a legitimate lethal attack on what *might* be a potential enemy – and probably their family – in a foreign land upon which it has not declared war.

What is rarely shown, or even mentioned, on the evening news is the process by which the targets are chosen. When Barack Obama was president, he would have a morning 'kill list' meeting every week, deciding who was to be killed.

TACTICAL SOLUTION OR STRATEGIC DISASTER?

Is drone warfare just another military innovation or do drones represent a more fundamental change in the approach to war and counter-terrorism, one with profound moral, legal and strategic implications?

According to David Kilcullen, an Australian author, strategist and counterinsurgency expert, drone strikes in Pakistan have killed far more civilians than high-level al-Qaeda targets. What these air strikes *have* done is to create a lot of what Kilcullen calls 'accidental guerrillas' – local people who become jihadis not out of an ideological desire ... but because they *feel threatened by us.*

It's worth looking at comments made by Kilcullen, who from 2005 to 2006 was Chief Strategist in the Office of the Coordinator for Counter-terrorism at the U.S. State Department. He claimed some years ago that, overall, these 'accidental terrorists' (the title of his book) are the brothers, fathers, sons, nephews, cousins and friends of the people who were killed in the attack. Given the wider family associations in some of these countries, that's quite a lot of people.

The rationale is that, in the wake of the 9/11 attacks, the U.S. president was authorised to take whatever action he deemed necessary to counter the threat from al-Qaeda. But it has been suggested that a far greater number of people who played no part in those attacks have been 'vaporised by Hellfire missiles' – a stark example of what we might call 'legal creep'.

SUPPORTERS OF DRONE WARFARE

Daniel Byman, a professor in the Security Studies Program at Georgetown University, asserts that drones have 'done their job remarkably well … killing key leaders and denying terrorist sanctuaries in Pakistan, Yemen and (to a lesser extent) Somalia'. Byman claims that 'communications and logistical supply have been disrupted and recruitment inhibited'. Though he conveniently ignores Kilcullen's concerns, his whole article is really a long refutation of drone detractors' objections, rather than any demonstration of how drone strikes serve the American strategic agenda. His final assertion is chilling: 'It would be better if the militants were captured alive, but, apart from being a hazardous undertaking, what does one do with the detainees?' The answer has a chilling logic: 'it has become more politically palatable for the United States to kill rather than detain suspected terrorists.'

And if drone strikes are carried out in another country, what, then, about the 'host' governments: Afghanistan, Pakistan, Yemen, Somalia, Syria and Iraq? We may be surprised to discover that, in fact, although these governments (*government* not currently being a coherent concept in Somalia) complain publicly about drone strikes, they might actually approve of some of them. The quid pro quo seems to be that the United States is quite prepared to conduct what are called 'goodwill kills' against, for example, Pakistani militants who threaten the Pakistan government far more than they do the United States.

DETRACTORS FROM DRONE WARFARE

On the other hand, Michael J. Boyle, an Assistant Professor of Political Science at La Salle University, Philadelphia, refutes the benefits of such targeted drone strikes as espoused by Byman and others. In an article entitled 'The Costs and Consequences of Drone Warfare', he recounts the story of Faisal Shahzad who, on 21 June 2010, told a Manhattan court that he placed a bomb in New York's Times Square as payback for U.S. drone strikes in Afghanistan and Iraq, citing, in particular, the killing of Baitullah Mehsud, a Pakistan Taliban leader.

Boyle's article focuses on the strategic costs of drone campaigns in, specifically, Pakistan, Yemen and Somalia. First, he claims, drones deepen anti-American feeling and provide a good recruiting tool for Islamist networks. According to the Pew Research Center, in a survey in June 2012, seventy-four per cent of Pakistanis now consider the U.S. an enemy. It is clear, Boyle says, that drones have improved the recruitment base for terrorists and Islamists, and particularly in the Federally Administered Tribal Areas (FATA) in northwest Pakistan.

Second, it demonstrates to any indigenous population that their government, in allowing foreign offensive action within their territory, does not have full administrative control, either in terms of curbing drone strikes themselves or in using other, more legal, methods of countering terrorists.

Another view comes from Audrey Kurth Cronin, author of the

previously referenced article 'How Terrorism Ends'. In 'Why Drones Fail', an article published in *Foreign Affairs* 2013, she suggests that drones are not helping advance the strategic goals of U.S. counter-terrorism. Al-Qaeda, she says, is never going to be 'defeated' as such. Drone strikes also fail in containing local conflicts. After its drubbing in north-west Pakistan, al-Qaeda did not actually move to the Arab Peninsula (AQAP) or the Maghreb, but one could say that the concept migrated.

Only Cronin flags up the problem of the intelligence required to identify targets, which Byman and Boyle conveniently ignore. Here we find what may be the weakest link in the chain and the one with profound strategic implications. Drone targets are identified by drone observation, signals intelligence (SIGINT in military parlance) and human intelligence (HUMINT). But what confidence can drone targetters have in that intelligence? After the attack, the victims will probably be dead and any identifying equipment or documentation they have may also have been destroyed in the strike, so verification may be impossible. The strike may have been in a remote area, inaccessible to any objective observer. Also, if one is relying on local operatives, are they really serving counter-terrorism's interests, or carrying out personal, inter or intra group vendettas?

There is little middle ground in the debate about drones. For supporters, drones are a low-cost, low-risk and effective solution to eliminating those who would (or, chillingly, *might*) do America harm.

On the one hand, there have been no more large-scale, externally planned attacks such as on the World Trade Center on 11 September 2001 but to detractors, drone strikes are, in some unspecified way, morally repugnant and are of dubious legality under local, American or international law – especially the 'double tap'.

Another danger is that of strategic slippage. There is the real danger that the U.S. will come to see all countries, all races, all religions as being against them if they're not for them. Indeed, George W Bush once made this very point. And if the CIA and U.S. are so distracted by drones, they may forget the one basic tenet of all use of military action: how do you convert it into beneficial political effect? Drone warfare may become a displacement activity, crowding out consideration of any or all other solutions.

THE 'DOUBLE-TAP' DRONE STRIKE

Those familiar with SAS or SEAL films will be familiar with the concept of the 'double tap'. This is where the serviceman – it's usually men – involved always fires twice to make sure that he's got his target. This has translated itself into the 'double-tap' drone strike, with rather more sinister implications.

The 'double-tap' drone strike involves launching a missile at a target, a person, vehicle or building, waiting a period of five to twenty minutes, for the first responders – medics, fire fighters – to arrive and then launching another missile, either to deter the first responders in the first place, or to destroy them.

According to the Florida Law Review, such strikes are 'likely serious violations of Common Article 3 of the Geneva Conventions of 1949, which prohibits targeting civilians, the wounded, or those placed hors de combat'.

Thus, such attacks are likely war crimes under international law and under the War Crimes Act of 1996, a U.S. law that criminalises carrying out, or ordering to be carried out, grave breaches of Common Article 3.

The U.S. seems now to have ceased this practice but it may be that the evidence is suppressed. Witnesses are most likely dead. Evidence that the UK is involved in such practices is sparse, and there are clear suggestions from the Bureau of Investigative Journalism and Drone Wars UK that although civilians are not targeted by UK drone strikes, they are certainly collateral victims.

What then is the political end point that the U.S. is seeking? If Pakistan is an exemplar, what is the world going to look like if American drones roam freely and kill indiscriminately? What effect might this have on the targeted people? The answer really lies in choice and capability. If strategy is concerned with turning military action into political effect, there needs to be a sufficiency of political skill to render other actions useful. The omens are not good. The United States has intervened in dozens of countries since the end of the Second World War, usually, though not always, using military force. Some commentators will point out that the failures in Vietnam, Iraq and Afghanistan, not to mention Iran and Chile, are hardly encouraging. One must therefore ask whether the nexus of American political goals, the use of U.S. military force and U.S. diplomacy do, in fact, add up to any successful strategy for achieving the overall goal of enhanced security for the United States, or, as an ally, the United Kingdom.

Drones represent much more than an extension of 'indirect fire' or 'targeted killings'. Fundamental issues of strategy are raised, apart from other moral or legal considerations. But the real danger is the insidious erosion of coherent thought about 'the other', why that 'other' might wish to do the United States harm and what other resources – political, economic and social – might be brought to bear. Drone warfare is useful and effective, but it may also be a displacement activity for real strategic thinking.

How then does Drone Warfare contribute to strategic stability?

The focus in this section has been on the predatory use of U.S. drones on suspected terrorists, their houses and vehicles. The RAF has followed this lead by using jet fighters and drones to do the same thing. The *strategic* aspects are the same.

We have not considered the use of drones against tanks and armoured vehicles but there is a clear use here, although it is unlikely that these drones would be used against a peer competitor because they would have anti-drone missiles or electronic countermeasures.

One unspoken objection to drones is that they do not put the drone operator into any physical danger, and that they are thus immoral. This is hardly tenable; if a military operation can be carried out without harming one's own troops, then there is no reason why this should not be the case. Not protecting your own troops, pilots, sailors and so on, in every way possible, is irresponsible. However, there is a psychological cost to using drones in that drone operators may suffer what front-line combat troops sometimes suffer: PTSD, Post-Traumatic Stress Disorder.

We might also look at drones through the prism of the Military Industrial Complex. Consider the General Atomics MQ9 Reaper, mentioned earlier. Nearly two hundred of these have been manufactured, at a total value of nearly $8 billion. Nice work for the military contractor! But it's not just the drones themselves. Missiles are quite expensive too. For example, the AGM-114 Hellfire costs between $150,000 and $200,000 each; the GBU-12 Paveway II costs about $22,000 and the GBU-38 Joint Direct Attack Munition (JDAM) between $25,000 and $36,000. An MQ9 Reaper carrying four Hellfire missiles would cost about $700,000 to arm fully. Nice work ...

Drones are here to stay. For non-military uses, they can be used for a vast variety of purposes. They are generally cheaper, quicker and more accurate than alternative means. For military uses, the vast majority of drones will also be used for surveillance. However, most military technical innovations get countered eventually and, with drones, electronic jamming and anti-drone missiles are an obvious route. We might expect expensive anti-drone innovation any time soon. We can also be sure that militaries around the world will be lobbying their governments for the latest drone technology, citing enemies, potential and actual, as having, or developing, slightly better ones than we have. It's the old-style, well-known security dilemma, the old-style and well-documented arms race.

For the anti-drone lobby, they need to exert pressure for more disclosure of the Rules of Engagement (ROE), target selection and better reporting of civilian deaths. Some of this is happening already but not on a sufficient scale.

Alienated civilians mourning the loss of family or friends, governments losing control of the security, and the military seeing drones as a useful route to victory all combine to produce a dysfunctional picture, one that might, tragically produce simply more of the same.

But let us not forget the basis for the use of all military power: the achievement, or at least a path to it, of a better relationship between protagonists. With many American interventions, including drone warfare, one might fear that they have lost sight of this fundamental tenet.

13. ARTIFICIAL INTELLIGENCE AND THE MILITARY

Artificial intelligence will greatly help military commanders make more informed decisions, but war is an intensely human affair, and politicians should be wary of investing too much faith in AI.

"Well, this certainly buggers our plan to conquer the Universe."

© Estate of Peter Birkett, 2022

There has been much recent attention on the prospects for AI: artificial intelligence. On one hand AI will transform working life, automating dull, repetitive jobs, particularly in industries such as financial services, insurance and retailing. It will facilitate safe, driverless cars, better health diagnoses and voice-controlled computers.

On the other hand, there is much concern – fear, even – that the military use of AI will lead to 'killer robots', which will develop their own personalities, which we ordinary humans will not understand. These killer robots may eventually turn against humans and slaughter us all. This of course is vastly overblown and has more to say about mankind's fears about technology than technology itself.

Seeking an objective view of what AI is, how it works and how, in general, it might be used is challenging. This chapter explains some of the basics of AI, examines its use in the military, and posits that without serious attention to organisational structure and risks, a nightmare scenario may well develop.

Artificial intelligence is the result of human agency. It may appear to be intelligent, but most people would have difficulty in defining our own human intelligence, let alone that of a machine. It is certainly true to say that practitioners are enthralled by it and see AI as the answer to many of the world's and society's problems. Yet politics and the use of military force are intensely human activities. AI can provide background, data insights and models but it would be a great error to imagine that AI can do anything other than help and maybe facilitate strategic thinking. Everyone will be familiar with a friend or colleague who may not seem to be intelligent in the conventional sense of the word, but might have tremendous intuitive human skills, like relating to people with psychological problems or those less unfortunate than themselves. Now, we would talk about intuition, a vital quality for any international politician. And don't forget emotional intelligence.

AI is very popular. The volume of AI-related commentary is increasing exponentially, almost as fast as AI computational power. In 2018, OpenAI, a research laboratory, found that 'the amount of computational power used to train the largest AI models had doubled every 3 to 4 months since 2012.'

HOW THEN IS ARTIFICIAL INTELLIGENCE DEFINED?

There are many suggestions. These summarised definitions will give an idea of the wide interpretation of meanings, and, to a large extent, expectations. This may be tedious, but the world of AI is resplendent with subplots and subsets and it is essential to understand which are pertinent to AI and which are normal computer software-based procedures.

IBM SUGGESTS:
'The science and engineering of making intelligent machines ... combines computer science and robust datasets, to enable problem-solving ... AI algorithms which seek to create expert systems which make predictions or classifications based on input data ...'.

ACCENTURE SUGGESTS:
'A constellation of many different technologies working together to enable machines to sense, comprehend, act, and learn with human-like levels of intelligence ...'.

A USEFUL DEFINITION COMES FROM WIKIPEDIA:
'Intelligence demonstrated by machines, as opposed to natural intelligence displayed by humans ... some accounts use the term AI to describe machines that mimic cognitive functions, such as "learning" and "problem solving", but some experts prefer the term "acting rationally".'

NARROW AND STRONG AI
There is also Narrow AI, sometimes called Weak AI, which performs specific tasks like the Siri on an iPhone. It is AI for a particular purpose and cannot cope with a problem for which it is not programmed. Whereas Alexa will play dinner jazz if you instruct her to, she won't tell you the next time the news media has something on East Timor.

Strong AI is where a computer has a human-like intelligence. This exists only in theory. As an aspiration, AI engineers and practitioners dream of the day when an AI user would not be able to distinguish between what the AI system is telling them and what a human respondent is saying. It should be made clear that this *point of singularity*, where a user would not be able to distinguish between a human respondent and the computer output or where the AI system exhibits 'human-like' intelligence, is a long way off yet.

The fear would come from exactly the same source. AI may reach such levels of sophistication, especially with the self-improving subroutines within it, that it 'decides' itself to widen its franchise and – the ultimate fear – starts to question human control.

Stay with it! Just a couple more words to do with AI in general …

MACHINE AND DEEP LEARNING

Machine learning concerns algorithms that can improve themselves through experience and by the use of data. Deep learning is rather more esoteric. It is a subset of machine learning and uses algorithms that train themselves to perform tasks such as image recognition or speech-to-text engines.

ALGORITHMS

People sometimes use this word without a full appreciation of what it means. An algorithm is a process or set of rules that facilitates the achievement of a particular task. Most often, this is to do with computing, but a recipe to make some biscuits is also an algorithm: computational and physical tasks have to be carried out in the correct order and they depend on each other. A mathematical equation is not, in itself, an algorithm. An algorithm set may have several or even many sequential mathematical equations and instructions within it.

So, the key words are: datasets, intelligence, expert systems, problem solving, simulation, algorithms and acting rationally. It is all underpinned by ever-increasing computer power.

We ought also to mention the commercial angle. Management techniques are, to a large extent, fashionable and IT companies and management consultancies are always on the lookout for what they will claim as new approaches and thus new profit opportunities. Artificial intelligence sounds appealing, which might explain some of the arcane language that is used around AI ('Only we can interpret it and make it work for you.')

ARTIFICIAL INTELLIGENCE AS A CURATED PACKAGE

So, AI might be thought of as a compendium. Accenture mentions constellations – of various techniques, underpinned by massive computer power. What AI is *not* is something that you can buy off the shelf, although one can be sure that there are many organisations who will claim that you can. AI is a package of several or even many different types of application, fashioned and curated with the specific purpose in mind.

Microsoft's Excel spreadsheet has a wonderful tool called Goal Seek. This allows the user to calculate a required input which appears at many places in the spreadsheet by identifying a desired output. You might use this in identifying how much mortgage you could afford to pay, how much your pension would need to grow to provide a comfortable retirement. But if the goal you were seeking depended on a far greater number of variables than just the interest rate, you would have to know much more than Goal Seek. And here's the rub: AI requires a lot of input, some knowledge of how it all works and some experience of interpreting the output.

A GUIDE TO THE KEY FEATURES OF AN ARTIFICIAL INTEL-
LIGENCE SYSTEM

1) Data sets, which are typically too big for the human mind to
contemplate and analyse without a formidable amount of work.
(People of a certain age might recall data analysis being done by
punched cards and knitting needles. It was not only a lengthy
process, but subject to all sorts of errors. What happened if the
cards were sticky?)
   AI can do this work almost instantly and with great accuracy.
2) Algorithms that can develop new, better algorithms and generally
   improve the whole process.
3) Problems solving, in that the number of inputs and combinations
   (think of a decision tree) are too vast for the human mind to
   comprehend.
4) A decision-making facility or at least the facility to supply a
   human operator with ranked options.
5) Information networks.

WHAT APPLICATION MIGHT AI HAVE FOR THE MILITARY?
Much current AI research is going on in healthcare, internet search and
autonomous (self-driving) vehicles.

   At first sight, AI could be most useful in military terms for equipment
procurement, intelligence, long-term planning, campaign planning, battle
management (tactics) and weaponry. The military are now enthusiastic
about 'Operational Art', but it may be that art is the keyword here: might
AI be applicable to something that is essentially an art? Here, we consider
the two applications of AI: first the strategic level and then weaponry.

STRATEGIC ASPECTS

War is about much more than warfare, so how might AI contribute to aspects of strategic analysis, such as information gathering and intelligence, cultural appreciation and risk assessment? How might it contribute to the key decision of any and every war: whether to use kinetic force at all, and if so, how best to use it? How, we might ask, does AI contribute to *changing the political balance between protagonists* – our definition of war. How might we programme an AI system with the ultimate goal of lasting peace? By any token, this must be a long way off, possibly in the realms of impossibility, or it might involve relinquishing so much human control as to be unworkable.

The fear angle is illustrated in a Christopher Coker's book *The Improbable War* (2016). In the introduction, Coker quotes a novel by John Updike *Towards the End of Time* (1997). In it, Updike's hero, perhaps anti-hero (nicely described, or even condemned, by Updike as a 'white, angst-ridden, middle-class male') is contemplating the aftermath of 'the improbable war' between the United States and China. Updike writes 'that the war had mostly been inspired by highly trained young men and women in sealed chambers of safety reading 3-D computer graphics'. Coker goes on to suggest that it is precisely these highly trained young men and women, locked behind their screens, who are likely to be the principal characters in history's next great power war.

There might well be highly trained young men and women they might well be the principal characters but they will not, we pray, be in a position to *inspire* war. Updike is confusing strategic analysis and management with tactical management, and while Coker is correct to say that these highly trained young men and women might be principal characters, they will surely not be making the decision to go to war, or negotiate a peace.

The big question yet to be addressed, let alone answered, is that although AI can contribute to strategy by offering insight into the politics of the enemy and their political leadership, much of the data used to input the model might be based on historic and largely subjective judgements. Intelligence, such as that put forward to justify the invasion of Iraq in 2003, was based on a few unreliable sources.

In an article in *Survival*, an IISS journal, Kenneth Payne suggests that '... strategic AI will not be subject to the myriad individual and collective psychological processes at work in human decision-making, including groupthink, confirmation bias, bureaucratic politics, excessive optimism and poor risk judgement ...'. This seems to refer to an over-perfect world. If we are talking about strategy in the sense of the relationship between the civil, political side and the military, then there must be a good measure of subjective judgement. Most organisations suffer from groupthink and bureaucratic politics. Let us just look at one example of a misconceived military adventure.

In terms of the superpowers, let us assert that it would be impossible to imagine completely objective judgements on their relationship between each other. Would the Soviets have believed the Americans if they said their intentions were entirely irenic? What about vice versa? Modelling what they imagined another superpower's objectives were, they might have been tempted to put in 'world domination', which would have skewed the results. There is bound to be an inherent psychological bias when considering an enemy's intentions. A keen eye might also spot here a lexical issue. Whereas during the Cold War the Russians were seen as a potential *enemy*, China is now seen as a global *competitor*. Good. The more we see enemies, the more we might be tempted to take action against them. The more we see competitors, the more we might be able to define the rules of the competition.

ARTIFICIAL INTELLIGENCE AND WEAPONRY

The U.S. Long Range Anti-Ship Missile has what is called 'autonomous targeting capabilities' in that, once 'instructed' as to its target, it can navigate by the best course to the moving target, evading as it does, hostile active defence systems. The Israeli Harop is a drone that can spot radio transmissions itself and then attack the target by self-destructing into them. The drone can do this autonomously, using its anti-radar system or it can be controlled by an operator, called 'human-in-the-loop' mode. The Sea Hunter is a U.S. venture imagining an unmanned ship cruising the oceans, searching for enemy submarines. At least one has already been made and can be seen on YouTube.

But is this really artificial intelligence? Does it live up to the implied promise outlined above in the various definitions of AI? Without being overly sceptical, the long-range anti-ship missile uses what one might call AI, but is it any different from a heat-seeking missile? Similarly with the Israeli Harop: it identifies radio and radar signal as the Sea Hunter simply identifies enemy submarines. The key differences are that these weapons systems are programmed to destroy themselves or launch a missile upon finding a target. Yes, this could be termed AI, but is better seen as a straightforward or even non-AI development of existing technologies.

But there is a long way to go between heat-seeking missiles and the Israeli Harrop, and truly autonomous war. It might also be noted that the examples above are essentially *tactical*, including the performance of military force on the battlefield.

ARTIFICIAL INTELLIGENCE: FIVE MAIN RISK AREAS

There is no doubt that the integration of several different computer-based applications, such as the management of data sets, the identification of trends, the self-improving algorithm, the management of decision trees and neural networks that together make up an artificial intelligence facility is a major step forwards. There is no doubt that AI will be useful in many aspects of business, civic and social life and also the military. However, we must be wary of the hype, much of which is commercially inspired, and we must focus on the real benefit of AI to strategic and military applications. And, although the mist may be clearing, AI professionals are still really at the stage of trying to identify a way forward.

With business, civic and social life, an AI system that does not work as expected, might cause huge difficulties. With the military, an AI system not working as expected, or even malfunctioning, might mean more death and destruction than intended, both to the enemy – who may retaliate more robustly, thus escalating the conflict – and also to our own side. It is therefore important to take a risk-based approach to artificial intelligence applications. There are five main risk areas: *Intrinsic, Cultural, Organisational, Autonomous* and *Strategic* stability.

INTRINSIC OR CODE-BASED RISK

Code-based risk is the chance of unexpected results from the AI system and their potential for a bad outcome. This software risk is considered a combination of security, sturdiness, performance efficiency and transactional risk as it occurs throughout the system. While we can be sure that people who write code have systems and checks for ensuring that their code is correct, the control software to run a U.S. military drone uses 3.5 million lines of code. A 0.001% error could mean thirty-five lines of bad code!

CULTURAL BIAS

It is very difficult to collect data that is value free. For example, market research is carried out into new or existing products or people's voting intentions. What is not mentioned very often is that what the polling really covers is those people who have got time to stop and chat to a researcher or fill in an online survey. We have covered above the problem of strategic input, but it also applies to weaponry. Ask any arms manufacturer or weapons commentator about Russian or Chinese weapons and there may be some hyperbole in terms of what they can claim as their capabilities. At the very least they might say that Russia and China are developing or 'working on' this or that. And Russia's and China's militaries might also game the system by doing exactly the same thing.

ORGANISATIONAL STRUCTURE

This covers the shape of the organisation, the way that information and decisions are made (process), control, span of responsibility and executive skills and knowledge. A military officer's training is inevitably long and hard, ranging from team leadership, project management and strategic management through to IT skills, cultural appreciation, civil management and language skills. The world of AI might require a different set of skills, despite an officer being fully IT literate.

Here (see panel on MBA teaching) it is vital that any officer, particularly in a conflict situation, is fully conversant with the limitations of the input dataset, the way that the system works and particularly the way that the output is presented.

MBA TEACHING

For the military use of AI, it is useful to take a leaf out of the way that business schools teach MBA students. This has three legs.

First is an exhaustive reading of the available texts and relevant, and deliberately not so relevant, case studies.

Second, tutor-led case studies explore aspects of organisational, commercial and corporate practice, with a strategic focus on profitability, sustainability and social responsibility.

The third aspect is an outcome of the first two: MBA students must understand every aspect of management without necessarily becoming a practitioner. So, for example an MBA student might choose to do a module on Operational Research without intending to become a researcher. The same might be true of Strategic Human Resource Management, Linear Programming or Management Accounting.

The student does not need to know how to become a practitioner of these different practices, but simply to understand the concept, its place in the organisation and its application and limitations.

AUTONOMY

You cannot study much by way of operational art or military tactics without coming across the OODA system, or loop, which stands for Observe, Orientate, Decide, Act. A simple diagram of this is reproduced below.

People with no military experience might smile at this and imagine that it's a pretty simple thing for operational commanders in the field to do. What they miss, and this is a problem with applying a lot of learning and procedural notions to the military, is that the military commander might have to make these decisions after thirty-six hours on his or her feet, in a wet and cold environment and with insufficient information. OODA looks pretty simple in the classroom, but in the above conditions, it is useful to remember it.

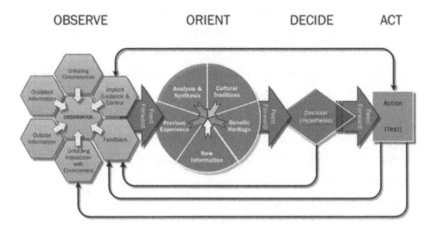

Image courtesy of the Operational Excellence Society

Implicit in the OODA diagram above is that the whole of that system is managed by a human. Take any one of the hexagons on the left, and you can see a commander rejecting 'outdated information'. Yet it might also appear that almost every aspect of that OODA system could be automated, with an artificial intelligence system. There is much current discussion about whether a human should be in the loop at all, and whether the final act, and attack, should be authorised and initiated by the AI system. At the moment, a human operator is always in the system. Another suggestion is that human being should be 'on the loop', monitoring the orientation and decision-making. The risk factor is that this is actually very difficult to control, even though there may be proper procedures in place for doing so. It's 'man-in-the-loop' versus 'man-on-the-loop'.

STRATEGIC STABILITY RISK

There is an inherent paradox in nuclear deterrence theory presented by the advent of hypersonic cruise missiles, and this maybe also applies to AI. The thinking at the moment is that no nuclear state can be absolutely assured of neutralising an enemy state's nuclear weapons in a pre-emptive strike. Some tactical applications can have strategic implications. We noted above that the SSBM provided and maintained a second nuclear strike capability in the event of an enemy considering a first nuclear strike.

Suppose though, that underwater drones, widely deployed along the GIUK (Greenland-Iceland-UK) gap could detect an SSBM manoeuvring ready for a launch. If that submarine could be destroyed, either by the drone itself or by a remotely positioned missile, it might remove that second-strike capability. The strategic conundrum would come from it seeming eminently sensible to seek out and destroy enemy submarines. *If* an aggressor imagined, with an AI system, that they knew the location of the defender's launch sites and SSBMs, *or* that they had all been neutralised *and* that their AI system could locate a retaliatory (second) strike *and* that their hypersonic missiles could be undetected by the defender, they might be tempted to attempt this first strike.

At the moment, this is not the case, and this provides *strategic stability*. No state could be a first mover. There are a lot of *ifs* and *ands* in the above statement, but then all nuclear strategy is based on it never having to be used! Strategic stability is largely subjective, and even treaties and negotiations aimed at limiting the number and types of weapons and defensive measures are precarious. These factors combine to present a substantial risk to strategic analysis, strategy formulation and control, campaign and battle management.

THE FUTURE FOR ARTIFICIAL INTELLIGENCE

The word computer was first used in the 17th century to describe people who … well, did computations. They must have had a very hard time: doing long division of hundreds into millions, which a few older people might now remember, was a comprehensive pain. There were devices called computers in First World War battleships for calculating the position and trajectory of shells, and getting them to land on an enemy battleship. It was in 1936 that Alan Turing invented the concept of the modern computer. The key to this and subsequent computer developments was digitisation, which really began in the 1950s and has not looked back since then. Digitisation of almost everything means not just raw numerical data but photographs, videos and so on.

It is not then an exaggeration to suggest that computers have revolutionised life. Even in the wilds of the African savannah, tribesman will consult their mobile phones to check current market prices. Many commentators write about an RMA, a Revolution in Military Affairs, where new military doctrines and tactics, mostly based on new technologies, fundamentally and irrevocably change the conduct of warfare.

The extent to which *warfare* has changed the conduct of *war* has been one of the themes of this book and we will not expound on it here. Nevertheless, there have been some RMAs in the past that have changed both war and warfare: the development of a professional army; the whole idea of projectiles; gunpowder (though the change was not as great as some people imagine); indirect fire, where the enemy could not be seen; and air power. RMA is also associated with the reorganisation of each or all of the arms of the armed forces.

A common assumption among military people, commentators, think tanks and journalists is that artificial intelligence will provide another RMA, a 'force multiplier' and a strategic edge in terms of campaign or battle management. Military command at any level, strategic, operational or tactical, requires the gathering and interpretation of a vast amount of disparate data. It then requires clear decision-making and communication of those decisions down the line. There is no doubt that artificial intelligence will make this quicker and more accurate.

But war is a political act, undertaken with a view to improving the political relationship between states, with the ultimate goal of a lasting peace. War is an intensely human activity, where judgement, intuition and leadership are paramount. AI will provide an invaluable contribution to decisions about war in terms of the enormous amount of information that can inform those judgements and stimulate intuition. It will not provide any guidance on leadership.

Even then, there are clear risks as outlined above. These need to be thoroughly comprehended if the output of any AI system is to be relied upon, which leaves the whole issue of autonomous systems. Through pre-programmed algorithms, the weapons system could make decisions on whom, where and how to attack. If this is not already a reality, it may very well become so and will provide many moral and tactical judgements to be made in a battle situation.

Imagining that artificial intelligence could make judgements about going to war or the progress of a war leads into very dangerous territory and ultimate folly. Given the current state of artificial intelligence, it is inconceivable that any AI system could make those judgements or help in converting military action into political gain, particularly in terms of ending a war. A better political relationship and a lasting peace may prove to be even more elusive.

Politicians, civil servants and the military must realise the strategic implications and the risk factors of using AI, and particularly the AI process. AI will really revolutionise life in general, and particularly the military, but it is essential that it is thoroughly and comprehensively understood, and that the inputs, process and outputs are treated with a caution.

14. CYBERSPACE

Will cyber capabilities take over the way war is prosecuted, or will they be just another tool?

The digitisation of ... well, almost everything was one of the great achievements of the 20th century. Now, almost all information in the form of images, art photos, videos, text, maps, engineering designs, chemical formulae, industrial processes, press releases, TV reports, can be stored and transmitted in digital form. The list could go on. The computer was the first step in this process, but now computers are almost all connected to the internet via broadband and satellite links.

Computers and the communication between them have created *cyberspace*, a term coined by one of the most well-known authors of the late 20th century, William Gibson, who created the science fiction genre known as 'cyberpunk'. His novels were noir, near-future tales that looked at the combination of technology, cyber capabilities and computer networks (we would now say the internet), described rather nicely as 'a combination of lowlife and high-tech'. Gibson coined the term *cyberspace*, which he described 'as widespread interconnected digital technology', a term that has hardly been improved on. We see cyberspace everywhere: the UK government's publication *National Cyber Strategy 2022: Pioneering a Cyber Future with the Whole of the UK*, recognises this and identifies:

Online experience: email accounts; gaming profiles; social media accounts; bank account login; contactless travelcard ID; fitness tracker profiles, etc.

Software, systems and data: enterprise IT systems; databases such as HMRC's tax records; industrial control systems; Windows/OS apps, such as WhatsApp, Facebook and TikTok; programming languages, such as Python, C+.

Physical devices and communication: routers; hubs; servers; wi-fi, ethernet; radio antennas; smart fridges; contactless travelcard readers; phones; PCs and other personal devices.

One could think of more. Together with digitalisation, and very high-speed optical fibre links, cyberspace provides enormous benefits to mankind, ranging from grandparents talking to their grandchildren in another continent via their computers to a widespread dissemination of data on every subject under the sun. It also means an improvement in the workings of democracy, in that everybody can now download the latest statement in Parliament and also get instant comment from journalists and think tanks.

Inevitably, as one might expect, there is a darker side, represented by such relatively simple things as malware and phishing software but also, at the top end of the scale, massive malign cyber-attacks by hostile states on infrastructure or power supplies, the ultimate nightmare being that a hostile state might hack into the nuclear codes and prevent or invoke the launch of retaliatory missiles. Such a move might end the whole basis of deterrence, with terrible consequences.

Cyberspace in general is a vast specialist subject, dominated by systems analysts, computer scientists, code writers, engineers, and mathematicians. To a large and not necessarily advantageous extent, cyber has created its very own world with its own language, norms, culture and, ultimately, a virtual reality.

This chapter concerns how cyberspace provides another dimension for relationships between autonomous states. This is often conceptualised as cyber *war*, and thus something to do with the military. Now, although the military must anticipate their own use of cyberspace, both in terms of defence and offence, cyberspace may well involve many more dimensions of governments' relationships with other states than the use of force. The question is whether cyber takes us into a new dimension, one where we will need a new cyber *strategy*, one that will fundamentally change the nature of warfare?

Cyber operations fall into what has become known as the 'grey zone'. This is a new conceptualisation of operations that do not quite breach the physical violence level. Over the past years, this grey zone between war and peace has grown considerably, with the use of not only propaganda ('twas ever thus), but also misinformation, attempts to corrupt elections, assassinations and 'little green men', or 'vacationers' disowned by the (usually Russian) government, but in fact special operations troops with specific tasks. Despite expectations or even threats the expectation was that Russia had enormous cyber-attack capabilities, but very little of this seems to have been apparent in their attack on Ukraine.

The cyberworld has also facilitated the growth of conspiracy theories like certain anti-vaxxers, QAnon and the Flat Earth Society. There is, though, a darker side, exacerbating societal divisions and even inciting citizens to violence on the basis that their human rights are being destroyed by 'the other side'. It's extraordinarily difficult to think what the government might do about this, without compromising the right to free speech.

GREY ZONE ACTIVITIES

In this chapter, we look at the implications of the cyber world in the context of war and near war, now known as 'grey zone'. There is no single agreed-upon definition. The Cambridge dictionary describes it as 'activities by a state that are harmful to another state and are sometimes considered to be acts of war, but are not legally acts of war'.

The U.S. Special Operations Command defines grey zone as

'competitive interactions among and within state and non-state actors that fall between traditional war and peace duality'. Philip Kapusta, writing in Special Warfare, continues that definition and defines grey zone challenges as 'characterised by ambiguity about the nature of the conflict, opacity of the parties involved, or uncertainty about the relevant policy and legal frameworks'.

Whatever operations are undertaken, they remain just below the threshold of a military attack. A domestic legal parallel would be tort, defined as a civil wrong but not a breach of contract (which would have no remedy under international law) that causes one side to suffer loss or harm. It can include intentional infliction of disruption of civil systems, financial losses to private individuals, plus many other things. However we precisely define it, the grey zone between war and peace has grown considerably.

So, cyber power is new and it is novel, but does it produce a winning formula, either on its own or in combination with a conventional approach? To answer this, we need to make a little diversion into one of the military world's favourite topics, the Revolution in Military Affairs or RMA.

CYBER SPACE: STRATEGIC RESPONSES

Strategically, cyber will give a new dimension to relations with other states but the parameters are either reasonably clear or becoming so. Many of the issues remain the same as they've always been: what are our strategic objectives; how do we ensure a consistent, congruent approach across all the arms of government and the military, and how do we monitor and control progress? Is it accountable to democratic control? Cyber operations can be used in five ways:

1) Peacefully, to improve the relationship between states.

2) As another dimension of a conventional military attack.

3) As a force multiplier: small (let's say 'Ranger'?) groups achieving much more than they would do without the cyber dimension.

4) As a means of attacking another state's systems and infrastructure without using military force (known as OCO: Offensive Cyberspace Operations, or cyber-attack).

5) As a defensive measure against another state attacking our own systems and infrastructure: cyber security.

The use of cyber capability is sometimes taken to include such enduring dimensions as intelligence, counter-intelligence, disinformation, psychological pressure and propaganda. All these things existed before cyberspace existed. There is no harm in lumping all these together but, again, this chapter looks at simply the cyber aspects of these. The use of cyberspace is simply that: using digital technology and communications to achieve a specific aim. Let us consider each one of these in turn.

PEACEFUL USES OF CYBER POWER

Cyberspace is conceptualised with an associated need for cyber security or OCO (Offensive Cyber Operations). there is very little concern about how cyberspace could actually *improve* relationships between states. A large and cyber-competent state could offer another smaller, less developed state all sorts of help and assistance with good computer programming and high-speed communications. Examples might include help with constitutional matters, elections, education or the administration of law, but one rather obvious example is that of health, and particularly public health.

AS A DIMENSION OF A CONVENTIONAL MILITARY ATTACK

This is where cyber operations – offensive and defensive – assist a military attack that has already been decided. Using cyber as an attacking force on its own is covered below. It is a well-understood military tactic to strike against the enemy's command and control systems. Weapons systems can be sabotaged by, for example, changing the coordinate instructions so that the force attacking you might go in the wrong direction or that missiles might fly into to the sea.

But because of the need to communicate between each arm of your services, and possibly back with politicians in the capital, your own cyber networks are also vulnerable. Whereas normal munitions (airstrikes, missiles, artillery,) can be used against any target, cyber-attacks can usually only be used against *specific* targets. A cyber-attack using a particular piece of software might, for example, knock out communications between a capital and the commanders in the field. It would not be suitable for changing the coordinates of a missile. The ultimate problem for cyber-attacks is that of escalation, and we deal with this specific issue below.

AS A FORCE MULTIPLIER

Small Ranger units may achieve much more than they would without the cyber dimension. Perhaps where a small armed group might fight their way into, say, a computer installation, a command hub or a launch site, instead of a kinetic attack, they would simply wreck the operating system.

OCO: OFFENSIVE CYBERSPACE OPERATIONS OR CYBER-ATTACK

This is where the attack is relying simply on cyber to disrupt communications or systems within an enemy's country. It may or may not cause physical damage. Some well-known examples of this is would include the American / Israeli Stuxnet attack on Iran's nuclear facilities in 2010. The malware was actually imported into the Iranians' system on a USB thumb drive! Eventually, it infected systems at Iran's Natanz nuclear power plant, causing about one thousand centrifuges (essential for enriching uranium) to spin out of control and fail.

In 2015 and 2016, Russian intelligence agencies hacked into the Democratic National Committee Compute network, leading to massive data breaches. Ruining nuclear facilities and trying to influence elections is one thing but, for sheer gall, it's difficult to top what happened in 2016 when the North Koreans hacked into the Bank of Bangladesh's / SWIFT interbank network to steal foreign currency. The amount was computed to be in the order of one billion American dollars, some of which was recovered.

CYBER SECURITY

Whatever the peaceful uses of cyber power might be, or the possibilities for OCO, most focus is on cyber security: the protection of your own country's computer networks and systems. Some commentators declare this to be the 'Wild West' of cyberspace.

There are many definitions of cyber security, mostly reflecting the interests of the organisation proposing the definition. At its core, it is about protecting computer and communication systems and networks from enemy, criminal or unauthorised access, which could result in the theft, disruption, denial or misdirection of the services they provide. It concerns attacks from inside (disgruntled employees or spies) or outside (the enemy). Cyber security is not simply about software and applications or files. It is a portfolio of practices, processes and protocols designed to protect computers, networks and data from unauthorised or incompetent access and corruption.

THE UK'S APPROACH

The UK's approach to the cyber world was outlined in the *Integrated Review of Security, Defence, Development and Foreign Policy*. In the subsequent *National Cyber Strategy 2022*, published on 15 December 2021, the government claimed that 'we have established the UK as a cyber power, building cutting-edge cyber security and operations capabilities and a leading cyber security sector'.

In recognition of the complex and involved nature of the cyber world, the government plans to (note the tense) 'reinforce the application of international law in cyberspace in addition to promoting the agreement of voluntary, non-binding norms of responsible state behaviour and the development and implementation of confidence building measures'.

THE NATIONAL CYBER FORCE

In November 2020, Boris Johnson, Britain's then prime minister, announced a major programme of defence spending, one of the key themes being technology. Johnson also confirmed the existence of the National Cyber Force, which had been operating for some time. The NCF brought together the GCHQ in Cheltenham, the Ministry of Defence and MI6, Britain's foreign intelligence agency, and also the Defence Science and Technology Laboratory (DSTL) in Porton Down. The aim was to increase the number of staff there to about 3,000 over the next ten years. There is no mention of MI5, the UK's domestic counter-intelligence and security agency.

Regarding Offensive Cyber Operation (OCO), the UK government has set up a National Offensive Cyber Programme (NOCP), designed for 'deliberate intrusions into opponents' systems or networks, with the intention of causing damage, disruption or destruction'. This is intended for 'both deterrence and operational purposes, in accordance with national and international law'. The UK also plans to develop the ability of our armed forces to deploy offensive cyber capabilities as an integrated part of operations, thereby enhancing the overall impact we can achieve through military action.

One particular insight here is that having a world-beating cyber strike capability sounds great to members of the general public, and to policymakers, who love offensive cyber in the same way that they love special forces. Politicians imagine they can achieve policy objectives with 'surgical strikes' which could be largely denied. Unlike any major military operations, such strikes would not have to be disclosed to Parliament.

BUT IS IT THE NATIONAL CYBER FORCE THAT BRITAIN NEEDS?
Government publications on the National Cyber Force may have more to do with aspiration than actuality. In April 2021, the Policy Institute at King's College London, together with Cyber Security Research Group (University of Wales) and the Offensive Cyber Working Group (OCWG, an academia-led initiative to: 'examine the conceptual, policy and practical implications of offensive cyber activity in the UK') published a report entitled *The National Cyber Force that Britain Needs?* The question mark is intriguing.

The report suggests that cyber operations in general have had far too little public attention; but this is a feature of most intelligence- and defence-related matters anyway. Also highlighted are the issues of governance, the organisation of offensive cyber operations and the relative rules of the intelligence arms and the military, not yet fully resolved. A major recommendation is that 'the security of domestic cyberspace should retain primacy', and the report sets out what they call 'a clear, hard account of how the many challenges facing those tasked with building the National Cyber Force might be addressed'. It has an echo from the comment of the previous head of the National Cyber Security Centre (GCHQ's defensive arm) when he warned that 'in all my operational experience, I saw absolutely nothing to suggest that the existence of Western cyber capabilities, or our willingness to use them, tutors attacker', as reported in *The Economist* in December 2020, which also claimed that a former British spy chief agreed with this: 'the reality is that non-military uses of offensive cyber are massively overplayed'. The key guidance seems to be that the best form of defence is defence.

Other findings from the KCL / CSRG / OCWG report, echoing the above comments, were that the starting point for national cyber power should be cyber security and that the NCF cannot pursue all its putative missions equally well, and that the balance of counter cyber operations and support to military operations, along the lines of operations against Islamic State, would be the best. In addition, they recommended the appointment of a National Security Advisor for Cyber, which they say will enable central strategic thinking. Such a recommendation sounds sensible, but it risks a danger that strategy will become more diffuse and that such a security adviser for cyber would either see everything through the cyber optic, or simply become no more than a secretary.

The report also mentions that the strategic co-operation between Five Eyes (FVEY) and NATO should be continued, but it should be remembered that NATO also has some very small members, and ones with limited cyber capabilities. There is also the problem of Turkey, which may be the most wayward of all NATO members, particularly with its antipathy towards Greece, another NATO member. Given the problem of coordinating action across all the arms of government, coordinating with the Five Eyes and NATO represents a major challenge, yet to be fully addressed.

The UK's approach to cyber has been laid out here in a fair amount of detail, in order to compare it with the American approach, which is also a more policy/strategic approach.

THE FIVE EYES INTELLIGENCE ALLIANCE

Five Eyes is regarded as the world's most important intelligence alliance.

Its origins date back to the Second World War where sharing information between Britain and the United States was vital in ensuring a close war effort.

Initially, it concerned only the UK and the United States, and it expanded to also include Canada in 1948 and Australia and New Zealand in 1956

Thus, for more than 70 years, the post-war alliance of the five English-speaking nations has provided surveillance with a global reach. FVEY remains one of the most involved and far-reaching intelligence and espionage alliances in the history of intelligence.

It comprises NSA Headquarters, Fort Meade, Maryland, United States, GCHQ in Cheltenham, United Kingdom, CSE in Ottawa, Canada, ASIO in Canberra, Australia, and the GCSB in Wellington, New Zealand.

THE UNITED STATES RESPONSE TO CYBER OPPORTUNITIES

Project Solarium was an American exercise in strategy and foreign policy convened by President Eisenhower in the summer of 1953. The White House solarium was where they met. The objective was to produce consensus among politicians, senior officials and academics in the national security community on the most effective strategy for responding to Soviet expansionism in the early Cold War. Until recently, this was largely forgotten as the results of the exercise largely confirmed the previously adumbrated Truman Doctrine.

Refreshingly, the idea was resurrected in 2019 and, in March 2020, the Cyberspace Solarium Commission presented its findings. This stretches over several pages, but the key points are:

- Deterrence is possible in cyberspace.
- It relies on a resilient economy.
- It requires government reform.
- It will require private sector entities to strengthen their security posture.
- It is vital for election security, which must become a priority.

There's nothing one might argue with in either the UK or U.S. approach; it's all very worthy stuff. Though it becomes apparent that, given the catastrophic effects on a country's civil and military capability, cyber-attacks and the cyber world have some parallels with a nuclear attack. Indeed, there has been much thinking about what lessons might be learned from nuclear deterrence thinking over the years. We have to proceed carefully here as with all lessons gleaned from history; it is as important to put them into the contemporaneous environment as it is to identify the lesson itself.

Ariel Levite, a senior fellow at the Nuclear Policy Program and Cyber Policy Initiative by the Carnegie endowment, made the following points, edited for brevity:

- The challenges of developing rules of the game in the cyber field are bigger than those in the nuclear field because many more players are involved and some of the most important among them are not states, but big corporations. The lessons of the Non-Proliferation Treaty do not apply in any great sense.
- The odds are that the world will not experience catastrophic attacks, which is good news. The bad news, however, is that we are likely going to witness an ever-growing number of smaller attacks, a trend we are already witnessing.

- Cyber networks do more for militaries than any other single previous technology, greatly boosting the defensive and offensive capacity of states and their militaries.
- He identified two priorities. The first is to get governments to commit to refraining from undertaking premeditated cyber-attacks, which could undermine the dynamic stability of the international system. Second, is to minimise the unintended miscalculation and escalation in and through cyber actions.

RUSSIA'S RESPONSE TO CYBER OPPORTUNITIES

In 2014, Russian military forces took over the Crimea. This was originally part of Russia, but in 1954 the Soviet Union transferred Crimea to Ukraine. The Crimea is an almost perfect archipelago, although there is in fact a land bridge between metropolitan Russia and the Crimea.

Later that year, Russian forces entered the south part of the Luhansk region in Ukraine and also the Donbas region, ostensibly to aid a separatist pro-Russian movement. At the time of writing, the situation there is at stalemate, and although there have been up to 15,000 deaths from military action and twice that number wounded, it does not look as if that situation will change immediately.

The attack was a prime demonstration of the way in which 'grey zone' activities, such as propaganda (ethnic Russians were being abused); false reports (little green men were Russian troops on holiday) – and cyber-attacks on Ukraine's communication systems, all worked to facilitate the military occupation. Russia even pre-positioned malware in some of the Ukraine' government's systems, ready to be woken up during the attack. The details are not vital to this narrative.

In a paper entitled *Cyber War and Strategic Culture: The Russian Integration of Cyber Power into Grand Strategy*, James Wirtz, Dean of the U.S. Naval Postgraduate School in California, asserted that the cyber domain, including cyber-attacks, cyber war and cyber power often seem detached from the broader strategic and geopolitical context. He goes on to ask how states will integrate their cyber capabilities into the overall strategy to achieve what we describe in this *Making Sense of War* trilogy as a better political relationship between contesting states. From the western point of view, this is not clear, but for Russia, Wirtz suggests, the best illustration comes from David J Smith, writing in the Defense Dossier of the American Foreign Policy Council that:

'Russia holds a broad concept of information warfare, which includes intelligence, counterintelligence, deceit, disinformation, electronic warfare, debilitation of communications, degradation of navigation support, psychological pressure, degradation of information systems and propaganda. Computers are among the many tools of Russian information warfare which it carries out 24 / 7 in war and peace. Seen this way, Distributed Denial of Service Attacks (DDoS), advanced exploitation techniques and Russian Today television are all related tools of information warfare.'

We contrast this later with NATO's position on this. (We should note here that Ukraine is not part of NATO.)

STRATEGY AS STRATEGY

At a cursory level, it looks as if the UK, despite its considerable cyber power, feels that new organisations are the answer to the cyber problems/ opportunity. The United States seems still stuck in the 19th century interpretation of Clausewitz, seeing strategy as a theory of victory: strategy provides guidance as to how military violence facilitates the state achieving its political goals and how to use violence to compel enemies to back down. On the other hand, Russia seems to see cyber capability as an important, but not the only dimension in its efforts to provide for its security. Recall our assertion that, at core, much warfare is about security.

So, it is pertinent to ask what is the best policy regarding cyber, and this must be related to the strategic aim. Strategy is defined in detail in *About War*, and it is essentially about reconciling internal and external ends, ways and means. The definition goes on to say that any strategic approach must incorporate *political imagination* and an anticipation of competitive moves. It is therefore dynamic and contingent. The strategic aim must therefore be more than just attack / deter / defend / counter-attack. Fortunately, there are historic and current precedents to guide our thinking here.

Historically, war, or at least battle, was never quite the free-for-all that is often portrayed on the TV and in movies. Although quite often honoured in the violation, ancient war was tempered by the possibility of surrendering before things got too sticky. Mediaeval war must have been very messy, but in some mediaeval battles heralds would act as referees; one from each side would sit on a hill above the battle and decide who had won and who could go home. In the Georgian era, ships could always 'strike their colours', that is, surrender, and the crew taken into captivity or, more likely, recruited to the other side. The ship itself would be claimed as a prize. Almost all naval ships would fight under their own colours. In the more recent modern era, there is a considerable amount of law, conventions and protocols concerning war, not always followed, but there at least to deviate from.

A similar protocol might apply to cyber capabilities: in the same way that the world must do everything it can to avoid a nuclear exchange, unrestricted cyber warfare would be catastrophic for both state parties, although we must still look to cyber defence to guard against rogue regimes, terrorists and 'Boys in Bedrooms'. A sensible strategy for cyber would therefore be to aim for a stable cyber situation, where there would no doubt still be minor attacks, but nothing catastrophic. Cyber defence would still be absolutely necessary. The problem then becomes one of escalation, a subject which will be covered in my third book, *Making Sense of War*. This is where experience from the nuclear world would prove useful.

LAWFARE

Lawfare is an American blog which discusses national security issues, published by the Lawfare Institute and the Brookings Institution, a U.S. research group. In an article published in February 2019 entitled *What is Agreed Competition in Cyberspace*, and with reference to the classic work on *Escalation* by Herman Kahn, they outlined the concept of 'tacit agreed competition'.

The authors, Michael P. Fischerkeller, a research staffer at the Institute for Defense Analyses, and Richard J. Harknett, Professor at the University of Cincinnati, focus on grey zone strategic spaces, conflict and the positive space short of armed conflict, which includes cyberspace.

The thesis put forward is that, through persistent engagement, a concept recognised in the UK's *The Integrated Review of Security, Defence, Development and Foreign Policy*, a tacit bargaining approach will emerge. This will produce an expectation of acceptable and unacceptable behaviour. They recognise that the associated danger with persistent engagement is escalation, contradicting, or at least questioning, Clausewitz's implicit warning that, in war, an irresistible momentum tends to escalate engagements and, one might add, things get out of control.

An illustration of 'tacit agreed competition' might be that an aggressor state launches a cyber-attack on a defending state which, for the sake of argument, wipes out the traffic lights in an enemy's major city. Everyone in that city is inconvenienced, particularly the police who have to mount human traffic control. Because of persistent engagement, the defending state, having recognised the attack and identified the attackers, has two choices:

The first would be to respond with a similar modest attack, wiping out the traffic lights in a similar city in the aggressor's country. Or, the defending state could escalate, and wipe out the traffic lights in the whole region. The problem here is that the aggressor state might then decide to escalate, and make a more damaging attack on another aspect of infrastructure, such as national power supplies or, horror of horrors, air traffic control. Indeed, the original purpose of 'an eye for an eye' was not to advocate revenge but to setting a maximum, with no escalation. If both states can keep to similar, low-level cyber-attacks, then a *tacit bargaining approach* might yield *tacit agreed competition*. This may seem rather too aspirational, but a parallel logic has kept the world safe from a nuclear exchange for seventy years.

RMA: REVOLUTIONS IN MILITARY AFFAIRS?

We need to distinguish between eternal verities about the place of war in international relations, and real innovation in war – though bear in mind that most of what we think of as innovation in war is actually innovation in warfare, a constant theme in About War and in this book.

Innovation in terms of the relationship between polities has amounted to, for example, the emergence of the nation state itself, the Westphalian settlements, which conferred theoretical sovereignty and autonomy on each nation state, the emergence of the concept of international law, right through to the United Nations.

Several years ago, there was a flirtation with the concept of RMA, the so-called Revolution in Military Affairs. This was adumbrated on the basis that at various points in history, new military ideas or tactics, but mainly new technologies, would dictate a permanent change in the conduct of warfare, requiring new organisations, new doctrines and even, rather hyperbolically, new strategies. We have no need to go through all the candidates for this, but these included, for example, the idea of projectiles, steel weapons, armour, artillery, the longbow, indirect fire, gunpowder, and airpower.

More recently there has been the whole idea of technology-enabled C4ISR, Command, Control, Communications, Computers (C4) Intelligence, Surveillance and Reconnaissance (ISR), which gives a commander total control of the three-dimensional battle space. Much of this was overblown, and one conclusion of the most recent RMA was that it was little more than an elaborate marketing exercise on behalf of arms manufacturers and military leaders.

So, we must approach cyber with some caution: does it indeed provide the opportunity for a real Revolution in Military Affairs, or is it more along the lines of the graduation from telephone lines to radio communications?

RMA / grey zone operations / cyber-attacks / do not in themselves represent an answer to the strategic problems facing any state. Any account of RMA must be treated not with cynicism, but with a degree of scepticism, taking note of the interests of the commentators.

COMMENTARY

According to Victor Davis Hanson, author of many books about ancient Greek war, the 'Western Way of War' originated in ancient Greece and represents a 'traditional ideology that wars should be fought in short pre-arranged and decisive military clashes between armies without the use of deceptive war tactics. Guerrilla warfare and retreat are deemed cowardly, while honour and glory can be achieved only through direct confrontation with the enemy. Also, the Western definition of a successful or unsuccessful war rests entirely on its decisiveness, meaning a war can only be decided by having a distinct winner and a clear loser at its conclusion.'

The relationship between competing states has developed considerably over the years. For example, diplomacy is now a much more mature practice. However, there are some faint resonances of the Western Way of War that we can see in modern times:

First, war and peace are seen as a duality: we are either at war or at peace. Both conditions are quite clear, with well-understood protocols. Looking at war through a different lens (as Russia and China might do), might mean that they see themselves permanently in a state of non-war / non-peace …

Second, some aspects of offensive operations against an enemy are not honourable, such as attacks on civilians (notwithstanding that civilians seem to be among the main casualties of modern war) or assassinations of heads of state.

… through a different lens (as with Russia and China), competitors may not have the same moral framework as the west. In the west, political leaders would frown on this, and tend to dismiss it, but competitors might cite the number of casualties in Iraq and Afghanistan and ask to what effect?

Third, there is a yearning for a panacea, a simple, elegant solution to the problems of interstate relations. There is no such thing. Cyber power does not provide it.

through any lens, there is always the solution which is 'simple, elegant and wrong'. (HL Mencken)

Cyber power is an enormously useful dimension of the relationship between nation states, mainly in terms of conflict, though we might aspire to helping in normal relationships in peacetime. Cyber power needs to be developed in all its aspects, and there is a clear consensus that, in of all those aspects, cyber defence is the most important. Witness:

The Oxford Handbook of Cyber Security (Ed. Professor Dr Paul Cornish) is a mighty tome of nearly 900 pages costing £125! It suggests that offensive cyber operations might have some utility, but that these must not detract from this key task. In any case, OCO carry numerous risks, some of them currently unknown.

But somewhere lost in all the commentary about cyber power is what ought to be the ultimate goal of all interstate – and also intrastate – relations, which is a lasting, peaceful relationship, one which will allow civilisation to achieve its undoubted potential.

Cyber is not a distraction, but there is a danger that politicians, military leaders, civil servants, commentators and those with a responsibility for implementing cyber will become distracted by its undoubted potential.

Also lost in much of the commentary about cyber power is the locus of responsibility for implementing it on a day-to-day basis. Cyber-security clearly has to be 24/7, not just to emulate the Russian practice but because this is clearly a constant danger. Certainly, for the UK, it is not clear who would have overall responsibility for monitoring and countering cyber-attacks and it must be recognised that to achieve a *tacit bargaining approach* that might yield *tacit agreed competition*, will need very tight control, monitoring and governance. Organisation structure and decision process flows tend not to be the subject of discussion in the political/military world, but they would be vital to manage a cyber approach to good effect.

Compare, for example, David J Smith's comments on Russia's practice in 2012:

'Russia holds a broad concept of information warfare, which includes intelligence, counterintelligence, deceit, disinformation, etc.'

With a document drafted by NATO's Stratcom Centre of Excellence (COE) and the NATO Cooperative Cyber Defence COE, NATO's response was to recommend a number of actions, all very worthy but difficult to audit and realize fully, namely:

Integrate StratCom functions with an emphasis on cyber operations;

Identify which populations and infrastructure are the most vulnerable to cyber and information attacks;

Enhance interoperability by increasing cyber-attack crisis management exercises that include other functions of strategic communications;

Support EU and national governments in enhancing digital security, such as through advocating better data privacy;

Booster deterrence; working with partners such as the EU and the private sector;

Foster a whole of government approach;

Finally, one that will go down in the annals of diplomatic history:

'Impress on Russia the futility of creating a closed information space.'

Wow, that's the stuff! Sure to save our bacon in the face of an 'increasingly aggressive Russia', until you realise that David Smith's comments were made in 2012 and the NATO comments in 2021. It is commonplace to state that the *nature* of war stays pretty much the same over the years, centuries or even millennia. Yet the *character* of war changes and develops all the time. Of course, technology influences war considerably and new organisations, new doctrines and new processes will always be necessary because of technological change. Yes, it is a mistake to imagine any one factor influencing the conduct of war any more than any other. Clarity of purpose, and assessment of relative strengths and a cogent strategy, well communicated, were always, and will always be, necessary for the conduct of work.

There is still a long way to go before we can claim that the UK and the U.S. has answered that call in the context of cyber operations. The West needs to catch up, and catch up quickly: a ten-year delay, implied above, is too much and suggests an abnegation of responsibility. In an article in the *Small Wars Journal* for February 2021 on Russian cyber strategy, they have a heading: *Russian Grand Strategy – Mother Russia actually has one*! The next heading is:

NATO needs to wake up.

15. MILITARY EXPENDITURE, ARMS AND DEFENCE

How much military expenditure is enough?

The UN Charter, drafted in 1945 and accepted by all member states, enshrines, in Chapter VII, Article 51, *the inherent right of individual or collective self-defence if an armed attack occurs*, although this fundamental provision had governed, though not prevented, war in the past.

In short, states have a right to defend themselves. We call this a 'right' but only under international law, for which there is no absolute remedy if that law is contravened. The United Nations can issue resolutions and other states can impose boycotts but, ultimately, in an anarchic system, there is no remedy for the contravention under international law.

There are, of course, other views about the use of armed force, which might include pre-emptive war: if enemy troops are massing on your border, does a state have a right to attack them? Does a state have a right to go to the aid of a friendly state if they are under attack? If so, does that cover proxy wars? And also, incidentally, a point we covered in *About War*, does this right extend itself to an individual *polity* within a state, if that polity is being abused. The obvious example here is Palestine. Insofar as Israel has the right to defend itself against armed attack, does Palestine, who would see themselves as an oppressed minority, have a right to defend themselves against Israeli aggression, as they would see it? Such questions would keep lawyers happily occupied for years.

In short, states have a right to defend themselves against armed attack, and they therefore have the right to resource, to maintain and to develop their own military forces.

Military expenditure varies from country to country, with bigger countries spending a greater proportion of GDP than smaller ones. This might seem unexceptional, but as the figure is a proportion of GDP, it means that countries with larger economies spend many, many times more in dollar terms than smaller countries. And, although there are many arms manufacturers in the world, it's only the largest states that make technologically based weapons. Small arms, mines, grenades and so on, are manufactured by many thousands of producers around the world.

HOW MUCH IS ENOUGH?

There is no general model of war and there is no universal model or rationale for identifying a viable, sustainable level of military expenditure. In terms of all-out war – such as the Second World War – the United States spent in the last year of the war some 40% of its GDP on the military. In the United Kingdom, at the height of the war, the figure was nearly 53%. The United Kingdom ended the war with enormous debts, and to a large extent only survived economically with help from the United States.

In 2020, world military expenditure was nearly $1,981 billion, or 2.6% of world GDP. Nearly two-thirds of that was spent by the five major spenders: the United States, China, India, Russia and the UK. The United States was by far the biggest military spender at about $780 billion, or 40% of total world spending. These figures are from SIPRI (The Stockholm International Peace Research Institute). There are wide variations across countries and regions, and some distortions because of smaller GDPs. For example, high-income countries spend on average 2.6% of their GDP on the military, whereas low-income countries spend roughly half that (1.4%). The UK spends between 2.2% and 2.5% on defence, about the same as on alcohol as a percentage of GDP.

Of course cost, being based ultimately on labour costs, varies considerably across the world, as does the capital investment. Thus, the

UK spends roughly the same dollar amount as Russia on defence. Two things come from that: the first of course is that the amount represents a higher slice of Russia's lower GDP than the UK's. But the second is that Russia's spend goes much further. When Russia spends, say, £5 million on providing a tank, the same tank (putting to one side, of course that the tanks would not be the same) would cost the UK £10 million. So, Russia and other low-cost economies (China, India, Pakistan) gets almost twice as much bang per buck than higher cost economies in Western Europe or North America. Also, it is said that much of the defence spending in Russia disappears through corruption and even straightforward theft.

MILITARY EXPENDITURE IS NOT JUST ON ARMS

For statistics, 'military expenditure' includes all expenditures on military and civil personnel (salaries and benefits of troops and civilian staff), peacekeeping forces, operations (general supplies, services and transport), military research and development, and military aid. The procurement of military equipment – 'arms' – is also included. Civil defence and pensions are generally *not* included in SIPRI figures.

In general, spending on arms as such, including research and development amounts to very roughly one third of military spending in arms-producing countries and much more in non-arms-producing countries. Nevertheless, at nearly $700 billion spent *every year*, this builds up to an enormous stockpile of military equipment.

SO, WHAT DRIVES MILITARY EXPENDITURE?

The immediate answer to this is simply *security* in its broadest sense, but there are many other drivers, all interrelated.

SECURITY-RELATED DRIVERS OF MILITARY EXPENDITURE

In addition to having a right, under international law, to maintain their own military, states have a duty to their citizens to provide national security. Although the notion of security expanded considerably over the course of the 20th century, now covering such aspects as economic security, environmental security, and health security, etc., *physical* security, the protection against external aggression, remains fundamental. Also, to many states, the security of the government and its institutions rather than of its people is also core; they may not have a popular mandate or there may be rebellious factions within the country. With the increasing cost of military hardware and infrastructure, many states rely on alliances with other states for their security, of which NATO, of course, is an example.

TECHNOLOGICAL DRIVERS OF MILITARY EXPENDITURE

Hitherto, military leaders would anticipate what hardware they would need to fight their battles, specify the relevant equipment and then work with defence manufacturers to resource, develop and make the equipment operational. That model no longer applies. To quote from Price Waterhouse Cooper's *23ʳᵈ Annual Global CEO Survey Defence Trends 2020: Investing in a Digital Future*, 'waves of innovation and technology coming from commercial firms have upended what had been a relatively stable sector. Leading technologies are no longer proprietary to defence, and in some cases they're no longer classified.'

This assertion is focused on digital capabilities but could also be applied to prime movers (engines), materials science, missile technology and space vehicles in the form of launchers and satellites. It is also significant that this comment comes from a consultancy, reflecting the need that politicians, civil servants and military leaders have for guidance in an increasingly perplexing technological world. PWC goes on to say that 'governments are now far more willing to look at commercial technology, to work with non-traditional contractors, and to acquire products and services in new ways. Space is a good example, with multiple players competing to offer services to government procurers.'

It is a moot point as to whether this is a result of the increasing privatisation of defence, which might provide more opportunities for directed R&D and thus innovation, or whether there is too much of a marketing focus here. There is limited evidence to suggest this, but it could be a matter of what millennials call FOMO, fear of missing out! Certainly, some of the cyber technology that is currently being talked about with reference to defence suggests rather too many demands being put onto military officers who, it must be recalled, may have troops to command and battles to fight.

INDUSTRIAL DRIVERS OF MILITARY EXPENDITURE
Only Trump was honest enough to say this in public …

On 2 October 2018, Jamal Khashoggi, a prominent Saudi journalist was murdered in the Saudi Arabian Consulate in Istanbul. Global outrage followed. Although it was never proven, the finger was pointed at the de facto Saudi ruler, Prince Mohammed Bin Salman, although Saudi authorities have denied any such accusation.

Whatever the truth of the matter, there were the usual calls for sanctions against Saudi Arabia, but only Trump, then U.S. president, was honest enough to admit that this was not possible because Saudi Arabia bought a large volume of arms from the United States. He was correct in that: arms sales and employment trumped (sorry …) censuring state-sponsored murder, if that was the case. SIPRI reports that from 2015 to 2019, Saudi Arabia was the world's largest arms importer. Between 2015 and 2020, the U.S. agreed to sell over $64.1 billion worth of weapons to Riyadh, averaging $10.7 billion per year. Over seventy per cent of Saudi Arabia's arms came from the U.S. and thirteen per cent from the UK.

We do not need to analyse this in excessive detail, but the UK defence industry employs between 130,000 and 170,000 people, less than half a per cent of total UK employment, but for the politicians this is too many to put at risk. The U.S. aerospace and defence industry employs some 2.2 million people, or 1.4% of the total U.S. workforce. Senators and congressmen lobby hard to get defence expenditure in their state, which also mitigates against secession and the breakup of the union.

POLITICAL DRIVERS OF MILITARY EXPENDITURE

To a large extent, all decisions on the composition and spend on military forces are political. In the case of a small country, with no chance of resisting an attack from a much larger neighbour, it might be thought unnecessary to have any military force at all. In fact, this is an option rarely taken. Very small countries such as Haiti (population 11 million) have only 150 active military personnel, and fifty paramilitary, yielding a total of 200 military personnel. Going up the scale, there are then many countries with fewer than one active military person per thousand capita. The UK has about 150,000 active service personnel and 78,000 reservists (Territorial Army), bringing it to a total of over 220,000 military personnel or 2.3 people per 1,000 capita. France has more, with over 200,000 active service personnel and over 40,000 reservists and 130,000 paramilitaries ('Gendarmes'), bringing it to a total of over 375,000 military personnel, or three people per 1,000 capita. The United States is much larger with nearly 1,400,000 military personnel and nearly 850,000 reservists, bringing the total to over 2.2 million, or 4.2 per 1,000 capita. It is no surprise that North Korea has nearly 1,300,000 active military personnel and, with 600,000 reservists and 5.8 million paramilitaries, the total military personnel amount to nearly a staggering 7.8 million, or over 50% of the population. Another political decision might be where troops are stationed overseas. So, for example, the UK has military forces in Gibraltar, the Falklands and Cyprus, and several other places. France has military forces in Polynesia, the West Indies and French Guyana and the United States has military bases in over 80 countries worldwide and, it is said over 700 bases in all.

It is clearly a political decision for any country, if so invited, to become a member of NATO. This carries the obligation – met by only a few of the thirty NATO members – of spending at least 2% of GDP on military forces. The famous '… attack on one …' obliges each member country to come to the aid of any of the members who are subject to enemy – external – armed attack. It is often imagined that this means that any or all of the members providing troops and military force but, in reality, Article 5 obliges any and all members to *take actions it deems necessary* to assist the Ally attacked. It is the basic principle of collective defence. Article 5 has only been invoked once, and that was after the 11 September 2001 attacks on the World Trade Center and Pentagon in the United States. It might be recalled that Tony Blair, then the UK prime minister, promised to stand shoulder to shoulder with the Americans. Other political decisions might mean participating in UN-mandated peace support operations, which could include peacekeeping, peace enforcement, humanitarian aid and a certain element of counterinsurgency, but this now seems to be going out of fashion.

MOMENTUM … OR INERTIA?
Another driver for military expenditure is momentum. The lead time on military equipment is long. A colleague involved in some technical military development (he would not say what) was told that he had a 'job for life', and he was 40! It is also claimed sometimes that cancelling a project is more expensive than carrying on but this may be a reflection of poor contract drafting or a gross exaggeration.

To this can be added to this interservice rivalry, where the three or four services, Army, Air Force, Navy and Marines, compete on the basis that there is an egregious threat that only their service can deal with, that the putative enemy has way more resources in that particular field, and that they cannot possibly do without such and such equipment.

A FINAL WORD FROM CAAT

The Campaign Against the Arms Trade (CAAT) makes a value judgement about the UK government's 'high military spending', although that is pretty much a global average figure. Also, they are somewhat sceptical about the UK's support for arms exports. The UK government, they claim, asserts that it is necessary to maintain employment and to protect what the government calls 'high skilled manufacturing jobs' (notice not 'highly' skilled). It is somewhat of a contradiction to their main argument, but CAAT then say that the economic importance of the arms industry is overstated by the government and that the 300,000 jobs that the government and the industry's trade association claims 'is overstated and incorrect', and that the real figure is considerably less than this. Again, it's one of the problems about considering arms sales, human rights, and foreign policy.

THE 'MIX' OF EFFORT

There is one other angle that perhaps trumps all others. Nowhere, it seems, does the government look at the whole spectrum of international relations: intelligence, diplomacy, aid, peace support operations, and then military force and consider whether not only the total spend was appropriate, but whether the money was being spent to best effect to meet the United Kingdom's overall strategic objectives.

The integration of the Department for International Development (DfID) with the Foreign & Commonwealth Office was generally well received and this may provide more opportunities for integration of their respective efforts, but there does not seem to be the integration that there needs to be with their responsibilities and that of the Ministry of Defence. Any senior civil service servant or politicians would scoff, and call this nonsense. But consider this: over the past few years, the FCO (now the FCDO) has had its budget slashed considerably. Now compare the cuts to the FCO / FCDO with the cost of one F35 plane, which we know to cost somewhere between £100 and £150 million, depending on how you add up the figures. This goes to the core of what military force is all about: how does it provide the opportunity for a lasting peace and a better (peaceful!) relationship between nations. Think of Korea, Vietnam, Suez, Afghanistan, Iraq and Libya. The list could go on.

WHAT'S THE ANSWER?

Before we try and make sense of all the various influences on military spending, let us recall two old American soldiers from the Second World War. Eisenhower's 'Military Industrial Complex', outlined in *About War* cautioned against the malign influence of commercially oriented companies, warning politicians against falling behind in terms of military technology. Today, we might also add other organisations such as consultancies, think tanks and university departments. A certain amount of this is reasonable and to be expected, but where there are inadequate safeguards against commercial companies' profitability, there is always the danger that there will be some exaggeration in terms of the competitive threat and what their technology can achieve. Eisenhower was president of the United States from 1953 to 1961. A very close colleague of his was Douglas MacArthur, a famous and well-known general, unfamiliar with modesty, who master-minded the defeat of Japan and went on to direct the Korean War (1950 to 1953). He was dismissed by President Truman in 1951 for not complying exactly with Truman's policies. Nevertheless, in 1957, at the age of 77, he made this statement:

'Our government has kept us in a perpetual state of fear – kept us in a continuous stampede of patriotic fervour – with the cry of grave national emergency. Always there has been some terrible evil at home or some monstrous foreign power that was going to gobble us up if we did not blindly rally behind it by furnishing the exorbitant funds demanded. Yet, in retrospect, these disasters seem never to have happened, seem never to have been quite real.'

It is an intriguing opinion, coming from a fighting general who had been involved in defeating the fascism of Japan during the Second World War and defeating the communists in Southeast Asia. One inevitably wonders what Eisenhower and MacArthur might now think of a post-Soviet Russia, and (can we say) a post-Communist China?

Given so many factors, it is impossible to assess whether the end result – in terms of spend, mix and deployment – ends up with an optimal, consensual solution or the lowest common denominator. Perhaps the answer is that the UK government will do what it has always done: approach any problem with an innate suspicion of over intellectualisation – *and for God's sake don't look as if you're trying* – a reliance on intuition, muddling through. We'll get there in the end, and, when the going gets tough, we can always invoke the Dunkirk spirit, conveniently forgetting that Dunkirk was a complete disaster. The problem with this is that the rest of the world, allies and putative enemies all have moved on. They have learned modern management techniques. They can cope with complex international relations issues. They have great cyber capabilities, etc. etc.

No commentary on arms would be complete without something on 'arms dealers'.

Generally speaking, the public's perception or any arms sales is of deadly weapons being sold to unsavoury regimes or rebel armies, the proceeds being hidden in overseas tax havens. There is no doubt that this goes on, but the UK, like some other arms-producing countries, have strict rules about what and to whom they can sell arms. And whereas arms can include deadly weapons such as missiles and bombs, it might also cover equipment that could be classed as purely defensive, like body armour.

Unpicking what the UK exports in terms of arms and to whom might seem like a straightforward business; there *appears* to be much government data on the subject. But almost every aspect of it is, while not exactly disputed, possibly open to different interpretations.

A discourse on this might take up another book, but it may be worth looking more closely at CAAT, the Campaign Against the Arms Trade, who lobby for 'a just world where conflict is resolved without the use of force'.

One of their current campaigns got the UK government to admit that Saudi Arabia has used UK-made munitions in its attacks on Yemen. CAAT point out that this may violate international humanitarian and human rights law. CAAT also campaigns against UK arms sales to Israel. One of CAAT's claims is that, 'whereas the Single Individual Export Licence permits a company to export a fixed value of arms to one country for two years, they also offer an Open Individual Export Licence which allows the export of unlimited amounts of specified equipment'. For the sake of completeness, there is also the Open General Export Licence, which is for companies to export an unlimited number of specific categories of equipment to a long list of countries. We are hardly in a position to query the government's or the CAAT's positions on this, but it is evidently difficult to pin down the exact facts of arms exports and even more demanding to put together a legal challenge, even if you had the resources to do so.

ARMS CONTROL

Armies, navies and air forces are expensive. Even at the NATO level of 2% of GDP, that still represents what some would see as an unnecessary drain on the Exchequer, money that might be better spent on health or education. Some might also see a small proportion of that being better spent on intelligence, diplomacy and aid.

Nevertheless, overall defence spending is (dare we say) *only* about twice as much as the UK spends on overseas aid. This was before that aid budget was cut from about £15 billion to about £10 billion to pay for the costs of the COVID pandemic. The essential point is that defence spending is still at a level that invokes the security dilemma, without being large enough to fund sufficient resources to resist a committed invasion from an enemy – admittedly, a remote possibility.

In 1964, the War Office was incorporated into the new Ministry of Defence but there is no doubt that, with the level and composition of Britain's armed forces, they are meant to operate 'out of area' and, with the nonsensical notion of 'Global Britain', anywhere in the world. In the latest *Integrated Review*, this is confirmed, though without any detail of where or what role the United Kingdom's armed forces might have. We assume 'Ranger Units' are to be used for much more than simple defence.

Given the cost of military hardware and the problem of the security dilemma, states around the world negotiate various arms control agreements. Most focus on nuclear arms agreements but arms control in general covers all classes of weapons from small arms up to ICBMs.

ARMS TREATIES AND PROLIFERATION

One of the many paradoxes of war is that peacetime militaries, excluding the United States, are generally large enough to invoke a security dilemma but not large enough to fight a major war. Wars large enough to involve a threat to national territory or sovereignty generally require a lengthy build-up of arms, the recruitment of soldiers, sailors, airmen and marines and officers to command them.

Given an annual worldwide spend on militaries of nearly $2 trillion (that is two thousand billion dollars) and an estimate of between one quarter ($500 billion) and one third ($660 billion) of that being spent on military equipment *every year*, it means that there is an enormous accumulation of armaments around the globe. For example, and though estimates are difficult to establish, it is reckoned by the UN that there are about one *billion* small arms in the world. 'Small arms' are defined as handguns (pistols, revolvers), rifles (including sniper weapons and automatic and semi-automatic rifles), submachine guns, and light machine guns. More startling is that 86% of these are in civilian hands. Nearly half of these are in the United States, which is (UN quote) *more than those held by civilians in the other top 25 countries combined*. Forbes reckon that there are nearly 73,000 tanks in the world, though not all are operational.

We do know that there are nearly 13,000 nuclear warheads in the world, ninety per cent of which belong to Russia and the United States. Not all of these are operational, with some awaiting dismantlement.

There are many themes to proliferation, non-proliferation and counter-proliferation. Most major western countries appear to take this issue seriously. The UK has a Counter Proliferation and Arms Control Centre and a Counter Proliferation Strategy. The United States has the FBI Counterproliferation Center and other players, and many other countries support this effort through the United Nations' Office for Disarmament Affairs, though that seems to focus mainly on nuclear issues.

There is general concern, alarm even, about terrorist groups or rogue states acquiring CBRN weapons – Chemical, Biological, Radiological and Nuclear. This is not to say that small arms have been forgotten – many civil wars in Africa are fuelled by small arms – but the risks of a CBRN attack anywhere, from the point of view of the damage they would cause and also public panic, is considerable.

Conventional, or non-nuclear arms control has a long and

undistinguished history, despite the efforts put in, with few absolute successes. Arms control agreements about nuclear weapons are more respected and have generally fared better, but have not achieved the ultimate aim of a considerable reduction of nuclear stockpiles, though these are much lower than at the height of the Cold War.

The first arms control agreement is thought to have been in ancient Greece, with the Amphictyonic League defining who could be attacked and how, but this did not necessarily have much to do with arms per se.

Charlemagne (Frankish king in the eighth century) banned the export of Frankish swords and chain mail armour, but it is difficult to cite this as a real arms control. The second Lateran Council of 1139 prohibited the use of crossbows against other Christians, although it did not mention non-Christians. And it didn't work.

The first mention of chemical weapons was in 1675 with the Strasbourg Agreement, which covered poison bullets. It did not prevent the horrors of gas attacks during the First World War, though these were dealt with in the Geneva Conference of 1925.

In the 19th and 20th century, arms control largely concerned the conduct of war rather than just arms. The 1817 Rush-Bagot treaty demilitarised the Great Lakes region of North America. The 1899 Hague conventions led to rules about the conduct of warfare, which were modified in 1907. After the First World War, the League of Nations was set up in 1920 which attempted to promote peace and eliminate war. The United States did not join the League and although it is usually thought of as a failure, many of the ideas were incorporated into the United Nations. The 1928 Kellogg-Briand pact, covered in *About War*, was ineffective but, again, some of the ideas were incorporated into the United Nations at its inception in 1945.

Arms control in general is now seen as an agreed way to restrict and even eventually eliminate the development, manufacture, distribution and deployment of all classes of weapons. Arms control can be bilateral or multilateral and can be brokered by the United Nations or by the United Nations Security Council permanent five members (the United States, Russia, the United Kingdom, France, and China). A minor but important point is that some treaties are agreed and signed by national delegations at the relevant conference – some lasting years – but not ratified by their governments when they get back home.

A full list of arms control treaties would be lengthy, with very variable results in terms of implementation. We therefore focus here on the list of banned weapons, and then on some of the major nuclear treaties that have been mooted, successfully, since Russia, and later China, acquired nuclear weapons.

COMMENTARY

How much to spend on what is a perennial problem for governments. Reconciling that with the willingness of people to pay tax is always challenging. It's even more difficult if taxpayers don't see the immediate benefit. It might be obvious that we need new or better schools or better infrastructure but all these expenditures compete with each other and with the military. Professional leadership in whatever area of national life, such as Social Security, policing, health or local government will all have their own agendas and feel that they should take precedence, so compromise is essential.

Justifying military expenditure is more difficult in that it is contingent on security threats as yet unknown, and that might even apply to those threats known and controllable, such as in peacekeeping. Ministers in the Ministry of Defence are not only having to cope with the competing claims of other spending departments but also interservice rivalry, where each arm will claim priority – they've been doing it for years – on the basis that they are best able to cope with whatever are seen as current security threats.

So, it might be somewhat futile to claim that military expenditure is a special case. We might claim that officers capable of leading the Army, Navy or Air Force in times of war might need years of training and practice, but of course the same thing might be said of headteachers or hospital consultants. We might point out that developing new weapons would take years; so would new schools or hospitals. Yet, nuclear submarines might take over four years or more to build, and that's not including the design and development. An interesting side-line here is that the average time for a Liberty Ship to be built in the Second World War was forty-two days.

Finally, the figures must add up, and then it falls to the Treasury to contribute to the final decision-making.

Benchmarking, the practice at looking what other organisations in similar circumstances do, is not a management panacea but it is a useful pointer for judgement. The UK's military expenditure amounts to a little more than 2.1%, with the inevitable caveat that it depends how you add up the figures. This is about on par with our nearest neighbour, France, and about on par with global expenditure as a percentage of global GDP. To some extent, these figures are distorted by the enormous level of American expenditure. For reference, a benchmark of health spending at 10% of GDP, and education at about 4% of GDP would be reasonable.

No political party would get elected on a platform of slashing the military even more than it has been slashed over the past few years. And, although there may be many detractors from this comment, by and large, the United Kingdom gets quite good value out of its military. The RAF has participated in bombing ISIS from its Akrotiri base in Cyprus; the Royal Navy, even though they're currently a bit short of ships, can deploy warships in the Gulf and Indian Ocean and, of course, the British Army is deployed on many peacekeeping missions, largely to do with training, around the world. With reference to the section on problems in our own backyard, all arms can operate in the Arctic.

United Kingdom citizens are proud of their armed forces, as they should be. We could slash them further, but this would mean they did not have a 'critical mass' of capability and we could find ourselves incapable of meeting our strategic objectives. Yet, as in any organisation, we could spend much more on the military, but would this be to good effect?

But in general, despite known and unknown security threats and in conjunction with our allies in NATO, the UK military does a pretty good job.

16. PACIFISM

War is and has always been invoked by state leaders, sometimes through the abrogation of the constitution, sometimes through assuming monarchical powers and sometimes out of sheer machismo

Most people would claim to believe in peaceful solutions to the world's problems and would generally claim to be against violence. A proportion of those would also claim to be pacifists but a little probing would reveal many caveats: are we under threat? Is military force the only remaining option? Indeed, is the problem itself resolvable? See Luttwak's comments above on 'Give war a chance'. 'Pacifism' can range from being virtue signalling to deeply held belief. It also depends on whether the conversation is about our own security, or that of another people in a 'far-off country of whom we know little'. Would peaceful solutions apply when it comes to some dreadful and murderous war in such a country where there is a clear breach of international law, or people are being murdered for their religious or political views? Other states – with whom we might have reasonable relationships – might be helping on one side or the other. Should we, here in Europe, rich, stable and with a sizeable military force, intervene?

It is noticeable that there has been very little comment from people who might call themselves pacifists on the occasion of Russia invading Ukraine.

In this chapter, we try to identify whether the concept of pacifism, the beliefs of those who claim to be pacifists and an version to violence. and the use of military force

Those of a certain age might remember late March 1982. Research conducted in the UK along the lines of 'are you a pacifist?' might have yielded a general reluctance to use military force, and a preference for the 'peaceful solution'. But then a further survey in early *April* 1982 would have shown an entirely different result. The difference? On 2nd April 1982, Argentine forces invaded the Falkland Islands, a British Overseas Territory in the southern Atlantic. Suddenly, the whole population was filled with patriotic fervour, with banners on the dust carts (as refuse removal vehicles were then called), saying, 'On your bike, Argies!' There was little doubt in the country that we should retake the Falklands Islands by military force. There was some talk of negotiation, but Margaret Thatcher, the then prime minister of the United Kingdom, absolutely refused – one of her 'no, no' speeches – to engage with President Galtieri of Argentina. Just one caveat: when we mention military force, it might be noted that there were still alive many people who fought in the decolonisation wars of the 1950s and 1960s, and indeed some people living who fought in the Second World War – my father included. Many of these thought that the Falklands were not worth a single British life, echoing Bismarck's view that the Balkans were not worth the bones of one Pomeranian grenadier. He was probably right, too, at least about the Balkans.

It does not take long to adduce that pacifism as a concept is both contextual and contingent. This is not to say that people who espouse pacifism are not sincere.

WHAT IS PACIFISM?
The question is just the tip of an iceberg. The term was first used and coined by Emile Arnaud, a peace campaigner, at the Universal Peace Congress in Glasgow in 1901, though the concept of pacifism goes back many millennia. In the context of that peace conference, pacifism was about opposition to war, militarism and violence.

Active Pacifist say on their website "that pacifism is a commitment to peace and an opposition to violence, and in particular war'. They also add that: 'some pacifists extend its purpose to promote justice and human rights', which is sensible – 'no peace without justice' – but may have the effect of confusing the whole issue.

The BBC does not shy away from the discussion: on their ethics page, they allow that 'there are several different sorts of pacifism, but they all include the idea that war and violence are unjustifiable, and that conflicts should be settled in a peaceful way'. At its core, pacifism is about the principled opposition to war and violence as a means of settling disputes.

Does pacifism have any utility? Has it, over the years, actually worked in the task of reducing violence? Is it just moral virtue signalling? Is it a position that people take because they are not prepared to look to their own security with the associated risk of physical violence? Even then, more questions crowd in: is pacifism essentially a religious movement? Do religions ban the use of violence, or do they accommodate it? What about the humanist view?

Furthermore, we find that there are, in fact, several types of pacifism, some of which seem to refute the concept itself.

We can see that the term *pacifism* covers not so much a spectrum of views as a panorama of views, concepts and moral principles. This philosophical space might range over many dimensions, from the organisation of society to international relations, from justice and human rights to morality and from abolition of the institutions of the military and war to security considerations. There are also some who eschew any organisation of society through governmental force: this might be thought of as an anarchist position, sometimes referred to as 'libertarian pacifism'. Noticeably in the pacifism discourse, security is not something that seems to preoccupy or even concern pacifists.

DIFFERENT TYPES OF PACIFISM

There seem to be several different types of pacifism. *Militant pacifism,* is where pacifists resort to every peaceful method to oppose violence and war. This includes civil disobedience and unauthorised marches and demonstrations. Under proposed UK legislation, violence may be used by the state to stop and punish such demonstrations. In the United States, the law is slightly different but the reaction is the same.

Conditional pacifists are generally against war and violence, but they recognise that some wars, for example against a repressive regime, may result in fewer deaths and injuries overall.

Selective pacifism is largely about opposition to nuclear weapons, with chemical and biological weapons thrown in for good measure. There are indeed very good arguments against nuclear weapons, some of which ignore the reality of current international relations.

To most people, human life is sacred, and the taking of it always morally wrong, even in self-defence. *Active pacifism* is more to do with advocacy and politics but the eponymous website also covers justice and human rights. There is only one sort of *absolute pacifism*, where the belief is that it is never right to take part in war.

We must also recognise that when we are considering pacifism, we are talking about the pacifism of individuals and like-minded peoples. Pacifism as a concept will have much less relevance to the behaviour of the nation state, where, however much idealism is proclaimed, real considerations of interstate relations will usually be more realistic.

A HISTORICAL PERSPECTIVE

Very few, if any, ancient texts mention anything to do with pacifism. In contrast to a modern Christian view of war, the times depicted in the Hebrew Bible or the Old Testament were violent in the extreme. In fact, there is something of a subculture of people studying these times and trying to tease out how many people were killed either by God himself, or under his instruction or support. The website WIRED even suggests that the Old Testament God, credited with killing more than 2 million people, is a more vengeful god that the New Testament God who preached tolerance, love and peace. This is not an aspect particularly fruitful to pursue, but the Dwindling In Unbelief website comes up with the suspiciously accurate figure for how many people were killed by God of 2,476,633. Let's thank goodness – or perhaps God – that the modern representation of God is not quite so bloodthirsty.

There wasn't much pacifism in the ancient world. Ancient Greece had a general moral injunction against violence between individuals, but there was little to do with violence between states. Ancient Rome was almost always at war and probably had no concept of pacifism. However, the constant wars were not particularly unusual in those days, and one can always interpret the Romans' warlike attitude to a search for, not so much peace, but security.

The 17th century saw a number of new Christian sects, including the Religious Society of Friends, also known as the Quakers. This is an interesting perspective on pacifism in that, although they denounce war, they nevertheless participate to the extent of being bearers and medics. The Quakers aim for a better world, through human rights, social justice and simple living. Quakers are environmentally sensitive.

There was some interesting peace, as opposed to pacifism as such, during the 19th century. The early 20th century saw much interest in pacifism and there was a thriving European peace movement before 1914. Like many societies of this nature, the movement had many internal divisions and collapsed at the outset of the First World War.

In the modern world, pacifism as a concept operates more as a conscience than a campaign. It was the wish for a pacific future that gave rise to the League of Nations in 1920. The league never really got off the ground; the Americans never ratified the treaty and it was replaced in 1945 by the United Nations.

An argument which trumps pacifism is of course the Second World War, seen as the archetypal just war, certainly by the Russians. When it ended and the full horror of Nazi crimes were made manifest, WWII became a powerful, go-to rebuttal for those arguing against pacifism.

RELIGIOUS ATTITUDES

Most religions are more or less pacifist, but most religions also recognise that violence may in some instances be necessary for self-defence, or to right an egregious wrong as a last resort, after strenuous efforts have been made to avoid violence. Looking at the vast majority of religions and placing their beliefs in our philosophical space, as above, would cover every dimension and every part of that space. Only Jainism, an ancient Indian religion – one of the oldest – espouses absolute non-violence. Killing any person is considered completely wrong. Even killing animals for food is not sanctioned, so most Jains are vegetarians. In particular there is the Christian Just War tradition, which permits war in accordance with certain criteria. (This is described in detail in *About War*.) Judging by the high incidence of war among nominally Christian countries, this has been regularly ignored. Yet the Christian Just War tradition has contributed greatly to the international laws of war and to The Hague and Geneva conventions. It is not, as some might think, an empty concept.

Islam has the concept of 'jihad', wrongly translated as war but in fact often means the struggle against oppression. Jihad is often confused with the idea of 'holy war' but Jihad means 'to struggle in the way of Allah', and refers to the inner or personal spiritual struggle as much as it does to the idea of war. There are two levels of jihad, this inner struggle being much more important.

There's a somewhat ironic comparison here that puts misunderstandings between Muslims and non-Muslims of Christian inheritance in perspective. It is quite common for western people to talk about a moral crusade, a crusade against hunger or homelessness or alcohol or ignorance or slavery or cruelty, etc. Crusade is used as a metaphor, and in innocence, long separated from its origins relating to the medieval wars of Christendom against Islam. But the word, to Muslims, remains as specific and inflammatory as jihad is to most westerners. Witness George W Bush's description of the 'war against terror' as a 'crusade' after 9/11. The wording was innocent and ill-advised, seized upon, of course, by Islamic countries worldwide.

CONSCIENTIOUS OBJECTORS

A conscientious objector is any person who refuses to serve in the military. Many pacifists could also be conscientious objectors, but in a specific case, the objection could be about a particular war. Although conscientious objectors base their position on their conscience, they may have various religious, philosophical, or political reasons. They may also object simply on the grounds of freedom of thought. Many conscientious objectors have been imprisoned for long periods or executed because of their beliefs. In more enlightened societies, they are usually put to war work (see the earlier reference to Quakers). Another example is Maximilianus, later canonised, who refused to be conscripted into the Roman Army in the year 295 because of his religious convictions and was immediately beheaded.

The modern practice is for conscientious objectors to prove themselves not to be malingering. This would usually be in front of a military court, where the judge or chairman might ask what actions they would take if an enemy soldier raped and killed their mother / sister / wife. There is no record of the various responses that were received except one amusing response from Lytton Strachey, an English biographer and wit. When asked, 'Tell me, Mr Strachey, what would you do if you saw a German soldier trying to violate your sister?' Strachey, it is said, replied with an air of noble virtue, 'I would attempt to interpose myself between them.' Best of luck with that!

There is little international law on the subject of conscientious objection, other than that pertaining to human rights and freedom of speech. Different countries have different laws and, should it be required, different punishments.

WELL-KNOWN PACIFISTS

The experience of some famous historical pacifists is, in some instances, illuminating, in others, tragic.

Martin Luther King Jr was an American Baptist minister and a leader of the American Civil Rights Movement in the 1960s. He is famous for his 1963 speech, 'I have a dream ...'. Essentially a pacifist, he promoted civil rights through non-violence and civil disobedience, based on his Christian beliefs and the non-violent activism of Mahatma Gandhi. Tragically, he was assassinated in 1968 by James Earl Ray.

Mohandas Gandhi, given the honorific 'Mahatma' (great-souled), was an Indian lawyer, an anti-Raj nationalist and political essayist. Gandhi believed in non-violent protest and gained political potency from the way the British Raj reacted briefly to the various rights and demonstrations for Indian independence. Gandhi was a leader in the 'quit India' movement, which gained momentum after the Indian Mutiny of 1857, known in India more as a war of independence, and the Jallianwala Bagh massacre at Amritsar in 1919, where something between 400 and 1,000 Indians died. The Bengal famine of 1943, in which two million Bengalis died, greatly expanded the push for independence.

Through a campaign of non-violent resistance to British rule,

Gandhi was instrumental in ending the Raj, and in 1947 India gained independence. He inspired Martin Luther King and other civil rights movements across the world. However, his pacifist, non-violent approach may not have worked under another administration. When Gandhi exhorted Indians lay down on the railway tracks to protest, he knew that the British would not run them over and kill them. Tragically, in 1948, Gandhi too was assassinated, by Nathuram Godse, a Hindu nationalist.

It's counterfactual, but it's interesting to think about what the Germans might have done with Gandhi. Recall what they did in 1904, when they attempted to exterminate the Herero and Namaqua people in their South West Africa colony, now known as Namibia. Some 100,000 were massacred.

Other well-known pacifists include Albert Einstein, John Lennon (who was also 'assassinated'), Aldous Huxley and Leo Tolstoy.

HUMANISM AND PACIFISM

Humanism is based on reason rather than religious authority. Humanists trust in science to understand how the universe works and they thus reject the idea of the supernatural. Humanists tend to be atheist or agnostic. As a philosophical stance, decisions should be based on reason, empathy, and a concern for human beings – all human beings. Humanism is based in the natural world, which gives a basis for morality. Humanism treats all people the same without prejudice or favour. It is often held that putting humanism and pacifism together would solve all human problems. Both concepts would fit together well, but would provide overwhelming problems for both concepts.

COMMENTARY

Judging by the incidence and persistence of war as a major factor in interstate and intrastate relations over the years, pacifism as a concept has not been a great success. Neither have conscientious objectors had much effect on the rest of their societies or the march to war. Massive demonstrations, which the UK, and other countries, saw prior to the invasion of Iraq in 2003 were acknowledged by the government but largely ignored.

Oddly though, the 'Stop the War' coalition didn't march when Russia carpet bombed Aleppo or when Assad used chemical weapons, nor have we heard much of them since the Russians invaded Ukraine. This may be why 'peace' protesters cut so little ice with either politicians or voters; unfairly or otherwise, their outrage often seems to be selective, and maybe more to do with complaining about the current government than anything else.

However, it must be recognised that pacifists tend to focus on the awfulness of war; the blood and treasure cost; the misery of the individual soldier; and the effects of war on society. There seems to be considerably less focus on the constitutional constraints on war, the lack of democratic debate in the decision to deploy military force, and the information coming back from the front line. Whatever war the United Kingdom is involved in, we always *seem* to be 'winning', until as such time as we leave ignominiously. As an example, consider the demonstrations about Iraq where it is said millions of people marched through central London. Gordon Brown, when he became prime minister, promised new constitutional arrangements for the decision to go to war. From a personal point of view, I would advocate full disclosure of any intelligence, and a grilling of the intelligence people, and the military, by Select Committees. Maybe MPs should be briefed by some academics and think tankers. This should be followed by an unwhipped vote.

Pacifism provides an intellectual, philosophical and emotional anchor, reminding people that there may be, and there usually are, alternatives to war. While not rejecting Orwell's tenet that pacifists can only operate if somebody else is looking after their security, we must recognise that pacifism is a worthy cause.

Pacifism, its advocates, its principles and its inherent goodness should be taken much more seriously.

17. CONCLUDING COMMENTARY

There is no glory in war.

There might be honour, duty, courage and leadership, but no glory. War is bloody awful. Neither is there anything romantic about it, despite what Shakespeare says.

With apologies to the Bard, the Saint Crispin's Day speech by Henry V is wrong. An old soldier, airman or sailor does not actually 'strip his sleeve and show his scars and say 'These wounds I had on Crispin's day.' Most service men and women, unless afflicted by some dreadful wound, simply want to forget. We are thankful that servicemen and women suffering from PTSD (post-traumatic stress disorder) are now recognised and cared for properly. It was only just over a hundred years ago that 'Other Ranks' might be shot at dawn for this. Officers were mostly sent home to recuperate.

Henry V's speech continues '... old men forget ...'; they may affect to, but they don't forget. In the still watches of the night they recall the awfulness of it all: their best mate vaporised by an enemy shell; their beloved CO shot by a sniper. Even seventy years after the event, TV interviews with veterans still show the tears.

There would be far less war if the politician and generals had served in the mud and blood of front-line combat or had to eject from a stricken plane, or saw his ship – his home – sinking under him. William Tecumseh Sherman, the Union general in the American Civil War, famously said: 'I am tired and sick of war. Its glory is all moonshine. It is only those who have neither fired a shot nor heard the shrieks and groans of the wounded who cry aloud for blood, for vengeance, for desolation. War is hell.'

War is hell, indeed.

Another American general who went on to become the 34th president of the United States, Dwight David Eisenhower said: 'I hate war as only a soldier who has lived it can, only as one who has seen its brutality, its futility, its stupidity.' His attitude was reflected in his presidency, where, despite some distractions, he managed to keep America out of any major war – an armistice having ended the Korean War a few months after he assumed office.

It is easy to sit in a warm comfortable study and think about strategy, doctrine and tactics and the performance of various weapons systems but we must never forget that fit young men and women will have to go into the field and suffer injury or death. Neither Sherman nor Eisenhower forgot.

Wars are easy to start but difficult to control once started. They are even more difficult to end. Neat endings to war are comparatively rare, and are usually the result of titanic struggles lasting years. The Thirty Years War and the Napoleonic wars are examples but the Armistice of the First World War simply contributed to the Second. The Korean War has not technically ended; it has simply been a sixty-nine-year armistice. And although the Falkland War in 1982 looked like a comprehensive victory for the British forces, Argentina still lays claim to what they call the Malvinas Islands.

Wars are easy to start but difficult to end. But could they have achieved a new and better political relationship between protagonists peacefully? One burden is the legacy of the Second World War. This was a truly titanic war of unparalleled ferocity, 'a new Dark Age made more sinister, and perhaps more protracted, by the lights of perverted science' as Churchill sagely predicted in 1940. That legacy gives us the notion of 'victory' or, in Bush Jr.'s unfortunate phrase, 'mission accomplished'. But victory is not achieved if peace does not result.

As I write, the world is focused on the Russian invasion of Ukraine and how that war might end. Rightly, world statesmen and diplomats focus on this, but when it is over, the West will still have to deal with a recidivist, non-democratic and bitter Russia. A long-term durable peace may be elusive.

It is impossible to aim for peace or to achieve it without a thorough understanding of war, its provenance, its prosecution and its resolution. War is the most extraordinary, complex activity that mankind practises. It starkly reveals every aspect of human and social behaviour, from noble to base, from gratuitous violence to unselfish generosity and from moments of shame to acts of self-sacrifice that inspire generations.

War in Context has taken the principles outlined in *About War* and applied them to the real world, with particular reference to the UK's experience. The book has focused on the prosecution of war – the use of controlled violence to achieve political ends – rather than the wars' provenance.

War is an extreme measure and needs a thorough understating of its legal boundaries. To ignore international law or to claim legal justification dishonestly risks not just reputational damage (like Blair's after Iraq) but a lasting and rumbling insurgency inspired by justified grievance. An appreciation of the legal entity known as 'the state' is essential.

History is important, but care has to be exercised in applying historical lessons to the modern day. Take the battle of Platea in 479 BC: what possible relevance can this have for the modern day? It was fought between the Greeks and the Persian empire when it was the mightiest empire in the world, but the word 'Greek' is open to interpretation. Indeed, some Greeks fought on the Persian side. It is more accurate to talk about the Hellenistic world. But the battle is relevant today because it was one of the relatively few occasions when the Hellenistic world came together to defeat a common enemy. The Greeks, the Hellenes, won, and the Persians soon abandoned the struggle to defeat them. Might this have echoes in terms of Europe's security today, where consensus is all? Europe still looks to the United States for leadership in world affairs, despite having a greater land area, a larger population, a bigger GDP and more troops.

We all want peace. But war will never be eliminated or even mitigated unless we fully understand every aspect of war represented by my chapter headings.

Integration, a 'general management' approach, is critical; a brilliant military campaign is no good without a clear political objective. Weapons systems are useless without technicians to manage them (people might be surprised by this, but there are many instances over the years of gaps in that particular field). It is no good fighting one sort of war when the other side is fighting another sort of war. And politicians need to know what war can achieve and what it cannot. War can give statesmen and diplomats room to negotiate but it cannot, in itself, achieve peace, unless, of course, it's a Carthaginian peace.

Yet, despite all the theory, there is no general model of war, no scientific approach, no algorithm or AI-inspired method for predicting, managing or ending war. The perversity of man starts it and the genius of man must end it. War does not 'break out'; someone breaks it out. War does not exist in the passive tense. War is the consequence of human agency and it is only through human agency that we can achieve a lasting peace for all concerned: that is, *everybody*.

We look back to the lessons of the Second World War. If the threat is big enough, the leadership strong enough and the people committed enough, we, the people, can achieve anything.

Even lasting peace.

SUPPLEMENT: THE RUSSIAN ATTACK ON UKRAINE

On Thursday 24 February 2022, Russian armed forces crossed the border with neighbouring Ukraine and attacked the country from the north, the northeast and the east. Despite the enormous military build-up, and warning from the American Pentagon, the world was shocked. President Putin's plan to reclaim what he considered to be a Russian territory had been signalled on many occasions previously, but using brutal physical force to achieve this came as a surprise. If Putin's plan was to incorporate over forty million people into the Russian Federation, then bombing and killing civilians was exactly the wrong way to go about it. Subsequent pronouncements from President Putin give no idea that he has any sympathy with this view.

He also warned the United States, NATO and the rest of Europe not to interfere, and he has repeated this on many occasions, with hints that he would consider using a nuclear strike in retaliation. This further reinforces the impression that he is either deranged, paranoid or ignorant – or probably all three. Nevertheless, there was immediate condemnation of Russia and its leader, who appears to be the sole instigator of this appalling war.

The Russian – and much of the world's – expectation was that they would take Kyiv in three days and also Kharkiv, and use the eastern oblasts (regions) to launch a takeover of the whole country. The Russian troops were told they would be welcomed as 'liberators' from Ukraine's 'Nazi' leadership and were even told to bring dress uniforms for their victory parade through Kyiv, no doubt cheered on by 'liberated' and cheering Ukrainians.

The Russian plan was that the Ukrainian army would be quickly destroyed, Kyiv taken, its president, Volodymyr Zelensky, would be captured or would flee, and an interim government set up that would be friendly (Russian parlance for subservient) to the Kremlin.

The consensus then and now is that the attack was and remains wrong from every point of view: political, legal, moral and, from Russia's point of view, completely unrealistic. And that responsibility for the venture rested entirely with one man: President Vladimir Vladimirovich Putin.

As we now know, things did not quite go to plan. The oldest lesson in the history of military endeavours, *don't underestimate the enemy or overestimate your own capabilities,* was demonstrated with a vengeance as the Ukrainian armed forces, universally praised as brave and resourceful, repelled the Russian attacks in the north and held them in the east while suffering the terrible and gratuitous shelling of civilian areas and targets, causing thousands of civilian deaths.

The Russians were thrown out of north Ukraine. They claimed they withdrew as part of their plan and focused on the Donbas area where they had been, since 2016, supporting two breakaway regions, recognised by Vladimir Putin as the republics of Donetsk and Luhansk just before the Russian attack.

Since then, there has been an enormous, unprecedented effort by the United Kingdom, the European Union, other states within Europe and, most particularly, by the United States in sending arms and ammunition to the Ukrainian army. The United States also provides lavish intelligence in the form of satellite reports and counter cyber-attack facilities.

Sanctions on Russia were introduced after they had illegally occupied Crimea in 2014. Many of these sanctions were reinforced and stepped up after the February 2022 invasion, focusing on banking, trade and individual oligarchs. There was some disappointment, indeed anger, that Germany refused to stop buying Russian gas, with the maybe hyperbolic accusation that, as they were sending nearly €1 billion every day to

Russia in payments for the gas, that it was being used to kill Ukrainians.

Considering the death and devastation that the Germans caused in the last century, they should have been be prepared to suffer a small hit on their GDP for the sake of fellow Europeans. Their excuse is that they will wean themselves off Russian gas eventually, but one might recall that the Germans, despite having some Greens in the new coalition government, are still burning lignite. Though, surprisingly, the Greens appear to be the leading hawks in Germany at the moment – not only, as we might expect, not being wedded to burning fossil fuels from Russia or anywhere else, but even in terms of urging the swifter provision of more abundant arms to Ukraine.

The international community has been impressed by the Ukrainian armed forces, and also the courage and leadership of President Volodymyr Zelensky. A laconic early comment from him, when asked by the Americans whether he wanted to be exfiltrated, was, 'I don't need a ride, I need ammunition.' He also addresses the Ukrainian people every night on the television, giving an honest and factual account of the war and is seen walking round the centre of Kyiv in his now traditional khaki army issue T-shirt.

His defiance, and the performance of the Ukrainian armed forces have encouraged donor countries to step up their contributions to the war both in terms of quantity and quality. As I write, the United States is supplying 155 mm howitzers, plus ammunition, and there are currently comments that these weapons may shape the whole character of the war.

There is little point in recounting the current news, with the appalling violence and the gratuitous missile strikes, some out of vindictiveness for the sinking of the Moskva, flagship of Russia's historically vaunted Black Sea Fleet. (Sorry, *Pravda*, you told us it was an on-board fire.) The ICRC are having a hard time establishing humanitarian corridors, and with every piece of territory re-conquered by the Ukrainians, they are finding dead and mutilated civilians.

No words can describe the atrocious behaviour of the Russian troops torturing and murdering Ukrainian civilians. With some armies, such behaviour is usually attributed to ill-disciplined troops, who also loot goods and artefacts from the defeated civilians. The consensus about the Russians in Ukraine is that this is a deliberate policy of using terror tactics on the Ukrainian population and that those orders come right from the top. It is refreshing that, as I write, war crimes tribunals are trying Russian soldiers in Kyiv.

A full description of the Russo-Ukrainian war to date would fill many volumes. In the fullness of time there will be comprehensive coverage. In keeping with the spirit of this book, this supplementary chapter puts the war into context with initial comments on the Russian domestic environment, the provenance of Vladimir Putin, Russia's foreign policy, and Russia's relationship with the United States, NATO, and more generally 'the West'. We look briefly at the strength of the Russian armed forces and their supposed competitive edge. We consider how 'strategic' the Russian actions are and attempt to project this into their future stance and thus the implications for their relationship with the rest of Europe and the international community.

THE RUSSIAN DOMESTIC ENVIRONMENT

Often missed is that Russia is, in fact, a poor country. Despite being considered a 'high-income' country by the World Bank in 2013, Russian GDP per head (nominal) is about $11,000, ranking 86th in the world – about the same as Argentina (IMF figures). But this hides wide regional variations. For example, whereas Sakhalin Oblast has a GDP per head equivalent to the European Union as a whole, many oblasts (regions) have a GDP per head of less than $5,000.

The population demographics are even worse. The population growth rate as of December 2021 was *minus* 7.2%. Some of this was caused by the COVID pandemic. If this decline is not checked, the population will halve in nine years. From the 1990s to 2001, Russia's death rate exceeded its birth rate: a demographic crisis. Consequently, Russia now has one of the oldest populations with a median age of about forty. There are also reports that young, tech-savvy people are leaving the Russian Federation and seeking jobs in the West. Some reports say this may be as many as 2.5 million people in the past few years. To add to this – or rather detract – oil and gas account for about forty per cent of Russia's budget revenues. And although having low external debts, the inequality of household resources is one of the highest among developed countries.

To add to the sanctions imposed on Russia after its appropriation of Crimea, the invasion of Ukraine saw more international sanctions and corporate boycotts. France declared *'all-out economic and financial war'* with the aim of isolating the Russian economy from the global financial system, led, unfairly in Russia's view, by the United States.

All this may seem rather laboured, but these aspects are often ignored in current commentary. But the demographics might loom somewhat larger in the Kremlin's thinking. Even at this stage of what might be a long war, and despite a much larger population (Russia's 146 million compares with Ukraine's forty-one million) their army is having to widen their recruitment net and use troops with insufficient training. This harks back to Russia's 'Great Patriotic War' between 1941 and 1945 when they repelled the Nazis with what has been described as an 'inexhaustible supply of young people'. Putin has also curbed civil rights and suppressed a free press in Russia; witness the massive arrests of demonstrators against the war. In many ways, Putin's regime is worse than the old Soviet system. At least in those days they had discussions within the supreme Soviet, and Politburo and there were institutional checks and balances on government actions.

BASIC PSYCHOLOGY SUGGESTS ...

... that slights, real or imagined, can become augmented, confirmed and can grow against another party. A friendly hand can be seen as patronising, an offer of financial aid can be seen as an attempt to acquire equity on the cheap, and cultural initiatives seen as attempts to pervert established norms. This is particularly the case when the person – or state – being 'slighted' is demonstrably much weaker and less sure of their place in the family, society or, in Russia's case, the international system.

VLADIMIR PUTIN AND RUSSIA'S FOREIGN POLICY.

It is worth looking briefly at the development of the Kremlin's foreign policy and the extent to which this can be identified with Vladimir Putin or to what extent it is, and always has been, Russia's approach. Vladimir Putin considered the collapse of the Soviet Union as one of the 'greatest disasters of all time'. From being a recognised and feared (as Putin saw it) part of the bipolar world with the United States, to being a country that could almost be considered a failed state was a considerable shock. The shame that Russia felt was exacerbated by their having failed in their Afghanistan venture from 1979 to 1989 just before the Soviet collapse.

The Soviet Union was dissolved at the end of 1991 and the Russian Federation proclaimed. Boris Yeltsin became president, but Russia's economy collapsed from the shock of an attempted transition from centralised control to a market-based economy. Abby Innes, a professor of political economy at LSE, suggests that Russia has now suffered the 'catastrophe of two materialistic utopias: Soviet socialism and the Washington consensus', a neat and apposite phrase.

Poverty became widespread. Yeltsin's political opponents blamed 'the West' – largely the United States – for the failure of liberal economic reforms. The accusations were that Yeltsin had made too many concessions and had failed to oppose the initial expansion of NATO. In

1996, Yeltsin appointed Yevgeny Primakov as Russian Foreign Minister, who claimed that Russia had become led rather than a leader in foreign affairs. The Kremlin repeats these resentments to this day. Primakov's aim was a multipolar international system not so dominated by the United States, a concept that appealed to Putin. Future historians might eventually term this the 'Primakov Doctrine'.

Yeltsin and the U.S. fell out over NATO's intervention in Yugoslavia in 1999, causing a major diplomatic rift between Russia and the U.S.. Clinton authorised bombing to curtail human rights abuses by Serbian President Slobodan Milošević – an ally of Russia – against ethnic Albanians in Kosovo.

In December 1999, Yeltsin resigned and left Prime Minister Vladimir Putin as Acting President. At first, Putin focused on domestic affairs, viewing the weakness of the Russian Federation and its internal economics as existential threats. He was concerned that Russia would 'slide into the second and possibly third echelon of world states', an insight into his own psyche. He also strengthened his grip on power. His particular animus was against the United States.

Between 2003 and 2004, world events unsettled Putin and added to his paranoia, the U.S. invasion of Iraq in 2003 particularly so. The 'colour revolutions' in several former Soviet states, such as Georgia's 2003 Rose Revolution and Ukraine's 2004 Orange Revolution also upset Putin. To what extent these were sponsored by the U.S. is difficult to tell – they might have happened anyway – but, again, Putin accused the Americans of imposing 'external governance' over these states.

Between 2004 and 2012, the relationship between Russia / Putin and the rest of the world, and in particular the United States, became more confrontational. There was the cyber-attack on Estonia (by then a NATO member) in 2007, with the Kremlin seeing the engagement of the U.S. and NATO with Ukraine and Georgia as national security threats to Russia.

Putin had won re-election in the 2004 Presidential elections, but later (due to term limits) became Russian prime minister in 2008. He still dictated the policies of the Kremlin and the then president, Dmitry Medvedev. Now Putin thought it was necessary to become more confrontational. Things went rapidly downhill from there.

Somehow, either through poor diplomacy, lack of engagement or intelligence failures, Russia's occupation of Crimea in 2014 – the Russians called it the 'recovery' of Crimea – and the intervention in Syria in 2015 came as something of a surprise to the West.

RUSSIA'S GOT PREVIOUS ...

Crimea was previously part of the Ottoman Empire, controlled by a Crimean Khanate. It was annexed by the Russian Empire in 1783 after they had interfered in Crimean affairs for years.

The annexation continued for 134 years and ended with the Russian Revolution of 1917. After changing hands several times during the Russian Civil War, Crimea became part of Soviet Russia from 1921. Khrushchev transferred it to Ukraine in 1954.

The Russian Federation annexed Crimea again in 2014 though this is not recognised internationally.

Also, we should not forget the Molotov/Ribbentrop pact of 1939, with Poland as the victim.

Looking back at Putin's pronouncements over nearly two decades we can see that these were simply extensions of his worldview. The U.S. was working on the mistaken assumption that the period of non-assertive foreign policy from the mid-1980s to mid-1990s had become the new norm for Russia, the beginning of Russia becoming a democratic, liberal, free-market capitalist economy, the only possible available model. (Recall the 'end of history'.) How wrong they were: this period was an anomaly, not the model for the future.

Putin is deeply suspicious about NATO. Between 1999 and 2020, fourteen countries have joined NATO, bringing member countries very close to the border with Russia. NATO sees itself as a defensive alliance. Russia sees NATO as a threat to its integrity and security. Neither of these extremes is wholly convincing, though we must at least recognise Putin's concerns.

SO, IS PUTIN MAD, BAD OR JUST PARANOID?

The best intelligence on this comes from the CIA. The United States has the largest and most extensive intelligence apparatus in the world. Usually secretive, the current and well-respected CIA chief, William Burns, has taken a higher political profile than his predecessors. As a Russian speaking former U.S. ambassador to Moscow, Burns knows Putin well. As reported in the *Financial Times* for Saturday 14 May 2022, during a Senate intelligence hearing in March, Burns said: 'I had dealt with him and watched President Putin for many years and what I've seen, especially over the past decade, is him … stewing in a very combustible combination of grievance, ambition and insecurity …' Burns went on: '… his risk appetite has grown over the years as has his grip on power, which has tightened, and his circle of advisers narrowed …'. We might conclude, then, that Putin is mad, bad *and* paranoid. Isolated as he is, he did not take the instrument of his strategy, the Russian army, seriously enough.

WAS / IS THE RUSSIAN ARMY UP TO THE JOB IN UKRAINE?

The Russian armed forces have not performed well during this campaign. They have been pushed out of northern Ukraine despite having a safe base in Belarus and their incursion into the east of Ukraine is not making anything like the progress they had hoped.

The air force has not done very much better, and neither has the Russian navy, especially with the Ukrainian sinking of the Russian flagship, *Moskva*. Despite a defence budget of something like $250 billion (purchasing power) being three times that of Britain or France – much of it is wasted or even stolen – the performance of their armed forces is nothing like what one might expect. They have advertised their exotic weapons, their cyber capabilities and the sheer scale of their armed forces (see YouTube), but it's difficult to be sure whether these things actually exist. They also have an exotic-looking command centre in Moscow, which coordinates every aspect of their military endeavour, including propaganda, cyber capabilities, assassinations, and economic warfare. It does not appear to have achieved great success in attacking Ukraine.

What of the Russian armed forces in historical context? They did not have a good 20th century. With the heroic and costly performance in the Second World War against the Nazis being the exception, Russia has been beaten or forced to a stalemate in many of its actions. Under Czarist rule, they were humiliated in the Japanese War at the Battle of Tsushima in 1904. The First World War against the German Empire ended for Russia with the brutal and harsh treaty of Brest-Litovsk. When the German army attacked the Soviet Union in June 1941 (Operation Barbarossa), many sections of the Russian army fell away in disarray. Entire air forces were destroyed. Whole Russian armies were encircled and taken into captivity, never to return to their homeland. The loss of equipment was phenomenal.

Nevertheless, the Russians, having mobilised the entire population and economy, prevailed in the end, though at a staggering cost in blood and treasure. Four years of heavy fighting developed Russia's staff work into an efficient regime, but even at the end the Russians tended to trade troops for technology and although some of their equipment was reasonable (for example, the T–34 tank), they were unconcerned about human loss.

They were careful not to become involved on the ground during the Korean War, which they supported, but suppressing the Hungarian rebellion in 1956, and Czechoslovakia in the Prague spring of 1968 was pretty straightforward. The counterinsurgency operation in Afghanistan from 1979 to 1989, is frequently cited as one of the reasons for the collapse of the Soviet Union. During that engagement, they lost 26,000 military personnel killed, including 3,000 officers, against Mujahideen losses of 56,000 killed and 17,000 wounded. Nothing much changed in Afghanistan.

Russia was embarrassed by secessionist Chechnya in the First Chechen War (1994 to 1996) and then only won the second (1999 to 2000) by adopting bombing and artillery bombardments (they flattened Grozny) to defeat an enemy that they could not take on in a conventional way.

Georgia in 2008 was hard work for both parties, but 'successes' against Ukraine in Crimea in 2014 and then in Donbas in 2014-5 were modest affairs without much ground fighting. In Syria there was much bombing and what ground fighting there was by small units of special forces. By and large then, Russian military endeavour over the years has been at best patchy.

By all accounts, the United States 'lost' the war in Vietnam. Whatever retrospective analysis might show – one thesis is that the war was not there to be won anyway – the American armed forces then went into some deep introspection about their equipment, doctrine and command structures. It is simply astonishing that, given Russia's record, they have not done the same. Armies often look impressive because of their special forces, but an army's performance is measured by the quality of the average soldier, not the best or the worst. Perhaps Putin and his military leaders have never read one of the best books on war, which is Bill Slim's *Defeat into Victory*. I have given his final chapter to many of the senior managers whom I have counselled about management and strategy. It is difficult for people outside the military to imagine what subtle changes can be made within the military, but we cite two illustrations of this from among the many on offer.

First, the armed forces of any country are a reflection of the society from which they come. Conscripted, poorly educated boys from the far east of Russia are deployed on a 'training exercise' in friendly Ukraine, only to find a hostile reception, with many of their colleagues being killed. Leon Trotsky's thought that 'the army is a copy of society and suffers from all its diseases, usually at a higher temperature' is apposite here.

It was not much better for the officers and senior commanders. Putin and his entourage kept their plans to invade Ukraine secret from senior officers, indicating a crippling lack of trust. Disgruntled troops, fed on out-of-date rations and with insufficient fuel to move, deserted their poorly maintained vehicles.

Contrast this with the average American service man or woman: well trained, well supported and living in a society where news and comment is freely available. American schools salute the flag, 'Old Glory', every morning in their classrooms whatever their ethnic or political background. The American armed forces were once described to me as 'one great learning machine'.

A second example of how armies can differ might be offered by the devolution of decision-making. There is a world of difference between a hierarchical command structure where troops at the front line simply wait for orders, and a structure which, while still being hierarchical, can devolve decision-making and enable independent units to act. This was seen clearly in the Second World War with the German army's ability, even against considerable odds, to scrape together fighting forces to either attack or defend. This had its manifestation in what is known as blitzkrieg, which was not really a specific tactic, but more the manifestation of this devolution of decision-making.

LOGISTICS AND MOVEMENT CONTROL

Certainly, any military observer would be staggered at the logistical problems that the Russians experienced. One of the most striking images was a line of Russian tanks – nearly 50km long – nose to tail on the road to Kyiv. From the military point of view, this means three things: first, almost any enemy rocket or shell can destroy them in detail. This indeed is what seems to have happened. Second, taking out the first tank means that that has to be cleared out of the way before the other tanks can get around it. Third, it is an amazing mismanagement of armour: how on earth did the officers in charge of the movement control allow this to happen? The British Army would have sacked whoever was responsible on the spot.

Sure, there is an indication that off-road mud and swamps dictated these intractable convoys. But the Russians had every opportunity to carry out reconnaissance, even if it was from the air. There are also some reports of units going into action without their full complement of troops. This is quite frequently the case in many armies, but in some cases, this was down to fifty per cent. Some Russian intelligence officers and some military leaders have been arrested, harking back to the old Soviet system.

It is difficult to imagine that Putin had never heard the old aphorism that '… armchair generals talk strategy, but real generals talk logistics …', though he had probably never heard of the American Civil War general who said something along the lines of '… strategy? Just get there soonest with the mostest …'.

There are many more factors that could be cited in diagnosing the Russian armed forces' poor performance. The problem with this is that there is always a tendency to gloat. This must be avoided, and a thorough analysis made of their weaknesses, their ability to address them and the effect that this might have on whoever they see as their enemy. One manifestation of this that we can see from the Ukraine crisis is the Russian army falling back on artillery and missile strikes. This is not to say that this is not a legitimate tactic or doctrine, but it does have the distinct disadvantage that when you occupy a city, there's very little left.

The Russian army, air force and navy were not up to the job and Putin should have been fully aware of this. It is extraordinary that Putin did not (in Churchill's words) 'nag, pester and bite' his staff to make sure that they were up to the adventure he was embarking on. Russian doctrine still seems to focus on artillery as a decisive weapon for destroying enemy formations, while manoeuvre units mop up the survivors. Their reliance on the 'god of war' – artillery – dates back to imperial times. Hey, that was several hundred years ago! Putin's real hero, Peter I (the Great) was in many ways the father of Russia's artillery as well as its navy. After tasting bitter defeat by Sweden at the Battle of Narva, he decided that the Russian Imperial army needed more, bigger and better guns. The Russian army seems to have maintained an affection for artillery ever since.

My personal view is that the U.S. attack on Iraq in 2003 was unnecessarily destructive. Yes, 'shock and awe' won the war, but it could have been done while leaving much more infrastructure in place.

PULLING IT ALL TOGETHER: WHERE ARE WE NOW?
As I write, the Russo-Ukrainian war may be at the end of the beginning but cannot be anywhere near finished. There is much good news: the Russians have withdrawn from north of Kyiv and there are some reports that Ukrainian forces have reached the Russian border north of Kharkiv. But, against that, the Russians have taken Mariupol and are still capable

of launching missile strikes on Kyiv and other cities in the west. Here then, I present several observations, each an implied question including perhaps *the* question, which admittedly might be challenging to answer.

PUTIN'S STRATEGY

The word 'strategy' is often used in many reports about Putin and what he is doing, but it is impossible to identify what Putin's strategy is. Sure, he wants to take over Ukraine and bring it within the Russian sphere of influence. But what does that really mean? In any case, destroying the country and alienating its population makes it impossible for the Russians to control Ukraine, even if they had the resources to do so. As Zelensky mentioned in an interview with *The Economist*, Putin's thinking seems to date back twenty or thirty years, whereas Ukraine and the rest of the world has moved on.

It is almost impossible to imagine that Putin, not a stupid man, cannot understand what strategy is: *visionary, contingent, competitive* and *dynamic*, with a realistic assessment of your own capabilities – which poses the question about whether Putin was aware of the shortcomings of his armed forces. In April 2022, Professor Sir Lawrence Freedman published an article in *Comment is Freed* entitled 'Absolute Ends with Limited Means: Putin's Self-deception'. Lying to the world is one thing, lying to oneself another. Coming from a Business School / commercial enterprise / organisational background, I'm not sure I buy all this. Surely, I would suggest, the job of the Chief Executive, whether president, prime minister or even dictator, is to ensure that they get good advice. Is this possible? I hear you say.

The first book of this trilogy, *About War*, referred to a book by Eliot A Cohen, an American political scientist, entitled *Supreme Command*. Cohen analyses the leadership styles of some of the greatest war leaders in modern times.

The most intriguing leader being David Ben-Gurion, who was the main founder of the State of Israel and one of its early Prime Ministers. Very early on he recognised that Israel, surrounded by hostile Arab states, would have to look to its own defence. Ben-Gurion was assured by his military commanders that they were up to the task, but he wasn't sure. There is no suggestion that he didn't trust them, but the situation was existential. Putin conducted the plans for the attack on Ukraine within a small coterie of his closest advisers; some reports mention as few as nine. He clearly does not trust the rest of his military hierarchy. Ben-Gurion, on the other hand, undertook to interview systematically the *entire high command* of the Haganah to review its state of preparedness. At that time, the Haganah was the main paramilitary organisation of the Jewish population in the British mandate in Palestine between 1920 and its dis-establishment in 1948, when it became the core of the Israel Defense Forces (IDF). It was one of the main pillars of Zionism.

He had concluded that the Haganah was profoundly unfit for the challenge looming ahead and, even worse, the military leadership was reluctant to confront this. Ultimately, with some organisational changes, he was satisfied that Israel could stand on its own two feet. Putin is not a stupid man, and it is very difficult to imagine that he did not inform himself of the state of his armed forces, as did David Ben-Gurion.

We must assume, then, that while Putin might have thought his armed forces seriously flawed, he considered them good enough for the task, based on his delusions – and research – about the unity and morale of the Ukrainian armed forces and its population. It's ironic to report that, after Putin's adventure in Ukraine, and even with territorial losses, such as much of the eastern Black Sea coast and the Donbas regions, and despite the destruction, Ukraine will become more unified and an energetic and high-profile player on the European stage. Its courage, and that of its president, Volodymyr Zelensky, have made its mark on the world stage: everyone knows its flag, its anthem, its cities and rivers, its shape and location. There is a comparison with the American War of Independence: British ministers thought they were dealing with errant cousins, primitive backwoods men. Instead, they were giving birth to what would become one of the great nations of human civilisation. How wrong could the British have been?

There are also reports that reforms in the Ukrainian army over the past few years have had great utility. One of the jokes about the British Army is that the NCOs actually fight wars, while the officers interfere. You might guess where that come from … but elevating the role of NCOs is very important. The Russians seem to be stuck with a top heavy hierarchal Soviet structure instead. The Ukrainians have had extensive experience in the Donbas over the years since the little green men (that is, Russian troops on holiday) helped the independence movements in those areas. It didn't go well for the Ukrainian army at first, but eventually they found their feet.

Contrast Putin's strategy with Ukraine's strategic intent. In the first instance, they simply want to throw the Russians out. But it seems they have a good idea of how they will manage their security after the war is over.

THE WEST'S RESPONSE

This has been much more coherent, and much more generous than the Russians, and to an extent the West themselves, had expected. Arms are now pouring into Ukraine, some of them being very effective against Russian armour.

However, Volodymyr Zelensky claims that it is not enough, and we should respect that view. Indeed, he even suggested that had all his requests been met earlier, he could have chased the Russians out already. Despite his rhetoric, his announcements seem generally to have been truthful and objective, and we should value this. Unfortunately, full support for Ukraine is not universal. The prevarication of the German Chancellor Olaf Scholz stands in the way of a total European embargo on Russian old oil and gas, as does Victor Orbán of Hungary. Despite having been warned over the years of the strategic folly of depending so much on Russian energy, Scholz, who seems wedded to a pacifist and maybe somewhat anti-American and Russian-friendly outlook, refuses to share with the German populace that it is not simply increased energy prices for them that matters, but the security of all Europe.

Even accounting for the generosity of the United States in terms of supplying arms, the coherence that we have seen from the EU and other European leaders, and the arms supplied by the United Kingdom, I can discern no coherent strategy from Europe. Bear in mind that war is about a better relationship between polities; there must be some long-term solution to this problem. The current objective seems to be a ceasefire, stopping the war, and 'dealing' with Russia. But what we really need is to get to a better relationship with not only Russia, but the Russians in general. Somehow, somewhere, this needs to be communicated to the Russian population, despite the heavy hand of their current government.

WAS IT ALL THE FAULT OF THE 'WEST'?

Was the West, particularly the United States, negligent in terms of diplomacy or intelligence? There is certainly something in this. Insofar as the leaders of the late-stage Soviet state believed in their ideology, which they did not, the collapse of the Soviet system was a calamity for that system of government, and for the Russian people. But it is not the collapse of the Soviet system that irritates Putin; it's the fact that Russia – Great Russia – lost territory and influence in the world, particularly in comparison with the United States. One of the astonishing things, at least to the Western eye, is that this has nothing to do with, and never did have anything to do with, the Russian people themselves. Carnegie's

Christopher Bort calls this 'the disregard, if not contempt, that Russia's rulers display towards their own people'. It is a historical perspective; perhaps a legacy of serfdom.

Russia's sense of being humiliated after the collapse of the Soviet Union might have been managed more carefully by the American-led West, whose provocative triumphalism was anathema to Putin. Whatever truth there is in this, it offers no rationale or excuse for Putin's current actions, which take things to a new and more dangerous level. Do we believe everything that Putin says? Does Putin believe everything that he says, or is told? If not, it's time for him to grow up and understand the realist view of international relations in an anarchic environment.

In a February 2022 article by one Ted Galen Carpenter of the Cato Institute, and after the usual disclaimer that it is Putin's war, he claims, that NATO's 'arrogant, tone-deaf policy' towards Russia deserves a large share of the blame. He points out that the Russians had disbanded the Warsaw Pact, with the implication that the NATO countries should have done the same. And as regards Putin's complaint that NATO forces are right on his border, my reaction would be: Hard luck mate, that's because we don't trust you. Your assurances, and we could cite many, are worthless. Neither do the ex-Warsaw Pact countries trust you. They simply could not wait to throw off the shackles of the oppressive Soviet system.

Carpenter finishes his article by saying that the 'history will show [which elevates history to some sort of freestanding judgement facility] that Washington's attitude to Russia in the decades following the demise of the Soviet Union was a policy blunder of epic proportions.'

We might admit that the West's relationship with Russia could have been better managed, but so could Russia's relationship with the West. And also, let us not forget that the Russian Federation is a criminal, gangster state, hardly the fault of the West. It has enriched only a small proportion – some say about 200 – Russian oligarchs, while ignoring the welfare of the general population. The International community can tolerate regimes that oppress their citizens in some way, but not to the extent that the Russian Federation does. The West's attitude to the Russian Federation does not excuse bombing the hell out of Grozny, intervening in Georgia, bombing hospitals in Syria or, ultimately, invading Ukraine.

There is another vitally important point which Putin has missed completely. Any country's place in the international community depends to some extent on its military power: think of North Korea. However, it is much more to do with economic strength. It is here that the Russian Federation has failed. Having thrown off the Soviet system, the Russian Federation has had *thirty years* to transform its economy into a modern, technologically based success. Put simply, they haven't. Instead, they have siphoned off billions of roubles for Putin and his close coterie of advisers.

Recall what the Chinese economy has done over the past thirty years. Recall the '*Trente Glorieuses*' of the French economy between 1945 and 1975. Look at the German economic miracle. Oh yes, I hear you say, but these were because of the Marshall Plan. But Soviet Russia was offered a Marshall Plan, and turned it down. That's hardly the West's fault!

NATO

NATO, the North Atlantic Treaty Organization, is an intergovernmental political military alliance between thirty member states – twenty-eight European states, the United States and Canada. Founded in 1949, its purpose is to guarantee the freedom and security of its members through political and military means.

NATO promotes democratic values and enables members to consult and cooperate on defence and security-related issues to solve problems, build trust and, in the long run, prevent conflict. NATO is committed to the peaceful resolution of disputes. If diplomatic efforts fail, it has the military power to undertake crisis management operations. These are carried out under the collective defence clause of NATO's founding treaty – Article 5 of the Washington Treaty – or under a United Nations mandate, alone or in co-operation with other countries and international organisations.

Contrary to common belief, NATO member countries are not obliged to come to any other country's *military* aid if that country is attacked. The treaty says that they must give 'all aid possible' and it is then left to the individual countries what they do. With the end of the Soviet system, there was uncertainty about NATO's purpose. Caution about the future of the Warsaw Pact prevailed and NATO survived though with occasional nagging from the United States, who spend about twice as much as the rest of the NATO countries put together.

Eventually an agreement was reached that military expenditure was to be at least 2% of GDP, though very few countries achieve this. The United States spends something like 3.5% of their GDP on defence; the United Kingdom and France nearly 2%, as does Greece. Some realist American commentators suggest that Europe has only grown fat and rich, with the tacit suggestion of complacency, under American protection. Although most European leaders would rebut this, there is much truth here.

Despite President Emmanuel Macron of France suggesting in 2019 that NATO was 'brain dead', the Russian invasion of Ukraine, the most blatant example of state-on-state aggression since the Korean War in 1950, has proved NATO's worth. NATO could only intervene militarily in Ukraine if Ukraine were a member of NATO. Despite this, however, there is now a shared strategy among NATO members: to provide generous support to the Ukrainians; to strengthen reassurances to NATO's most exposed states, such as the Baltics, and to work with other regional blocks on a massive programme of sanctions.

Ukraine certainly needed this amount of assistance, and it is likely to need it in the longer term as this conflict looks like becoming one of attrition. One major problem of all war is the danger of escalation, particularly concerning nuclear-armed states. The worst possible way of managing this would be to have all European countries, or even just thirty NATO countries trying to manage escalation in the event of a nuclear attack. A popular aphorism is you 'never miss your water till your well runs dry', and this could well apply to NATO. It's almost impossible to imagine what the European reaction to the Ukrainian crisis could have been had NATO been disbanded in 1991 at the end of the Soviet Union, as the Kremlin claim they expected.

Putin has warned of dire consequences if Ukraine even *thinks* about joining NATO or if NATO becomes directly involved, but President Volodymyr Zelensky has already said that this is off the table – though it's a useful negotiating ploy when Russia and Ukraine finally negotiate a settlement. In reality, NATO is already involved. Ukraine is being supplied with NATO stocks of weapons and munitions. It is intriguing that, although Putin has stated that his position is to remove or at least degrade NATO's capability, he has achieved exactly the opposite. Again, it is extraordinary that anybody in such a position could make such an egregious error – or am I missing something?

Already, both Finland and Sweden have asked to join NATO. In some ways this is a great relief to the Finns and the Swedes, and gratifying for the other members of NATO. However, planning for, supplying and imagining tactics for defending Finland's 1,340km border with Russia is enough to give NATO planners a headache!

NUCLEAR WEAPONS

Putin has repeatedly declared that if the U.S., the UK, NATO or indeed anyone else interferes with his operation in Ukraine, he will retaliate in a way that implies the use of a nuclear weapon. This has been largely interpreted as sabre rattling: there are many different nations and organisations already involved in Ukraine, but fortunately this has not invoked such a reaction from Putin.

It is assumed that such a retaliation would involve a small tactical or battlefield weapon in a battlefield situation, but how? He can't really use it *within* Ukraine as that would stop the Russians occupying that part of the country. And whatever else the Ukrainians might do, it's very unlikely that they would make any incursions into Russian territory, and we can discount the possibility of a Russian tactical nuclear strike on Russian territory to drive them out. However, he might not be talking about tactical nuclear weapons …

NATO and nuclear-armed countries will have comprehensive contingency plans for a full-scale nuclear war, but these might be contrasted with the Kremlin's attitude to nuclear weapons:

First, Russia's conventional forces have always been weaker than those of NATO. Thus, they rely on nuclear weapons as a deterrent.

Second, the Russian armed forces see nuclear weapons as just bigger bangs rather than crossing a threshold. But, as we mention elsewhere, even using a tactical nuclear weapon in another country would mean a lot of irradiated territory.

Third, we must not discount the psychological effect of a nuclear weapon being used anywhere in any war. By definition, politicians would not know how to handle it and it could mean massive population movements and panic.

Fourth, Russia might believe in the idea of 'escalate to de-escalate', that is to say wiping out a major Ukrainian city would oblige the Ukrainian government to sue for peace. I do not consider this to be viable.

Defence in Depth is a blog published by King's College London War Studies Department about war-related matters. In a blog posted on 6 May, they examine some of the comments made by the state-backed media and others in Russia about the use of nuclear weapons. Very little of this has hit the mainstream UK media. In short, if NATO 'interference' in Ukraine is considered a strategic threat to Russia, then there will be a retaliatory 'lightning strike', which *Russian* observers assume to be a nuclear strike *on a NATO country*, rather than the use of a small tactical nuclear weapon on the Ukrainian battlefield. This implies a full-scale ICBM (Inter Continental Ballistic Missile) or SLBMs (Submarine Launched Ballistic Missiles), the United Kingdom being the favoured target. There are comments such as 'the nuclear annihilation of Great Britain' or 'one nuclear-armed Poseidon drone' (a kind of large torpedo) that would explode underwater near the UK's shores and create a tidal wave that would 'plunge Britain into the depths of the sea'.

To think of all the munitions and help we sent Russia during the Second World War – remember the Arctic Convoys, recently commemorated with a medal! But then gratitude has no place in international relations: the Americans sent $608 billion's worth of aid (in 2020 money) to Russia during World War II. Thanks?

Another chilling threat comes from Margarita Simonyan, the head of the media giant 'Russia Today' who is one of Putin's chief propagandists. According to her, Vladimir Putin is more likely to push the nuclear button than lose the war in Ukraine. It was 'more probable', she suggested that Putin would 'turn to his nuclear arsenal than admit defeat'.

These comments may be sardonic, in which case they are intriguing, or made on the instruction of the Kremlin. It is difficult to tell. But if it gives a hint of current Kremlin / Russian thinking, we need to take these threats very seriously. Even if there is only a minuscule possibility of that happening, we need to have a comprehensive, agreed contingency plan for how then to proceed. It will be heavily influenced, even dictated, by the American view, but the UK/EU/Ukraine must have their view as well. At the moment, there seems to be no such plan, and actually, no clear strategic objective either.

However, in the event of a full-scale nuclear strike on a NATO European member, Europeans should appreciate that the Americans would *not* retaliate on their own account. There might be demands from many hawkish quarters in the U.S. for a retaliatory strike, but this would only have any utility if it were within Russia. So, the complications multiply: the Americans would not want to start a nuclear war. The U.S. would never 'sacrifice New York for Paris', and we should not expect them to.

In the event of a nuclear strike on the United Kingdom, how might we respond? This raises the immediate question of how independent Britain's nuclear deterrent is, and my guess is that the British prime minister would be very reluctant to launch a retaliatory strike without the agreement of the American president. And to add to woes, the French would not *dare* to launch their nominally independent nuclear deterrent for fear of escalation.

We cannot cover the contingencies here for a full-scale nuclear attack on the United Kingdom or any other NATO country. *About War* referred to a book by General Sir John Hackett, *The Untold Story: The Third World War* (1982). In short, he intimates that, in the event of an outbreak of nuclear war, it would be limited to a single nuclear exchange. He suggested Minsk (now in Belarus) would be sacrificed for Birmingham (UK, not Alabama!). It is a conclusion echoed in a BBC drama *World War Three: Inside the War Room* (2016), where a single nuclear exchange (two weapons) happens. Both parties pull back and sue you for peace. In theory, this might provide a scintilla of comfort, but given the depth of Putin's resentment, and also concerns about his health (it is said that he may not have long to live), he might just risk a full-scale nuclear war. We can only hope that if Putin decided on this course of action, that wiser heads in the Kremlin would prevail. There is a possibility that the officials concerned would refuse to carry out the order or that Putin would be deposed; we really can't tell. Intelligence from the Kremlin is pretty thin as it always was.

Sleep well tonight, my children.

In the event of a battlefield nuclear weapon being used, either within Ukraine or on another NATO country, my suggestion would be *not* to escalate via a retaliatory nuclear device, as portrayed by Hackett or the BBC's *Inside the War Room*. The best solution would be for NATO to become involved because the use of a nuclear weapon anywhere in Europe would represent a grave threat to European and NATO security.

I would advocate a massive *conventional* strike on all Russian forces on either side of the Russian / Ukrainian border, at least as many GBU-43/B MOABs, with a bomb blast radius of one mile, as the U.S. can spare. An aside might be to leaflet all the Russian forces to the effect that their cause was unjust, that they cannot win, that the whole world is against them, AND the leaflet would advertise the conventional strike (in which case it would have to be carried out), and this might cause panic in the ranks, mutiny or, given their predilection for gratuitous violence, senior officers being 'fragged' (an expression from the Vietnam war, where disconsolate soldiers would kill what they considered to be a foolhardy officer by throwing a fragmentation grenade at them. It was estimated that up to **1,017** fragging incidents may have taken place in Vietnam, causing 86 deaths and 714 injuries of United States military personnel, the majority officers and NCOs.)

We also need to realise that this is simply a strategy to end the war and revert to border peace: *subjective strategy*. We still need to consider how to live with the Russian Bear in the future – not necessarily the current government, but the Russian people: *objective strategy*.

PROGNOSIS

It's difficult to imagine how this war might proceed. It seems that every day we get more frightening pronouncements from Russia about their hideous plans, and they obviously want to take Odesa to open a land bridge to Transnistria, where Russian troops have been deployed ever since the collapse of the Soviet Union. Moscow's propaganda machine gives out completely false ideas about how the war is going. The consensus is certainly that they do not have the military capability of achieving their aims. On the other hand, every day seems to bring news of fresh arms for Ukraine, not only in terms of numbers but in terms of capabilities, from the United States, NATO and European countries.

All in all, though, the most likely scenario is a stalemate; a long slogging war of attrition. It is this scenario that provides the biggest headache for the Ukrainians and also for the Russians. The Ukrainian / Western hope is that with the sanctions on Russia's economy, they would not have the capability to keep up a long war. Also, it may be that their popular support would diminish. Germany, please note …

More chillingly, William Burns, CIA Director, speaking two days before the parade in Moscow (9 May), said that he was 'in no doubt that Putin would eventually go back on the offensive.' The war, he said, 'was probably entering a period of attrition in which Russia would seek to consolidate and expand its land grab in the east before regrouping for another assault on Kyiv.'

Nonetheless, mid-May brings news that the consensus among military observers – the Pentagon, NATO and the MoD in UK – that Ukraine may actually win this war, *winning* being the ejection of Russian troops from the whole of Ukraine, though Crimea is sometimes not included in that aspiration. Commentators have even gone as far as identifying the date, with August/September thought to be likely.

There is no shortage of international views about the negotiating parameters for Ukraine, though these views are typically expressed with the swift caveat that it is up to Ukraine to decide its own future. Cop-out or Noblesse? Obviously, Ukraine wants to recover the territory currently lost to the Russians: Donetz and Luhansk, Kherson and Mariupol. They would certainly not wish to cede a land corridor between Russia and Transnistria.

That leaves the question of Crimea, and the unspoken assumption is that this is Russian, and will remain Russian. Yes, it gives a problem about territorial waters in the northern Black Sea, but that can probably be resolved.

BUT THERE ARE DANGERS: BE CAREFUL WHAT YOU WISH FOR …

In the *London Review of Books* for 11 March 2022, Neil Ascherson, the author of a book entitled *Black Sea: Coasts and Conquests from Pericles to Putin* makes some alarming comments about the various 'statelets' around the Black Sea. He suggests that, should Putin win the Ukrainian war and for that country to become a vassal state, Putin would simply add it as a 'pendant on his necklace', together with these 'statelets'.

But there are risks too if he loses. Some of the statelets; Ascherson suggests Artsakh (aka Nagorno-Karabakh), South Ossetia, Abkhazia, the two Donbas republics of Donetsk and Luhansk and Transnistra, will 'explode in blood', causing an exodus of even more refugees. One can only hope that somewhere in foreign policy establishments, there is a good intelligence on this and some policy to cope with it.

Indeed, dateline 23 April 2022, there is a news report that Ukrainian President Volodymyr Zelensky warns that 'Russia is eyeing other countries after Ukraine'. Of course, this might just be a sabre-rattling threat but, as above, we hope that this is a hot topic with western governments.

But whatever happens in Ukraine and whatever happens to Russia, we must recognise the dangers and threats that a criminal, gangster state on our doorstep presents. Let us hope that the current regime in Russia is displaced and a more open, democratic and human-rights-oriented regime takes its place. Whatever its past misjudgements, the West must have a role in this, and the ultimate goal of any diplomacy, sanctions or military action, should be that of living in peace and prosperity with this neighbour.

Is it going too far to suggest that, notwithstanding Putin's stated desire of re-establishing the Soviet empire or greater Russia, notwithstanding the supposed 'threat' from NATO and even given Putin's warped mind, that the real problem with Russia is its lack of development, and a chronic lag in terms of keeping up with the industrial revolution? In the time since the end of the Second World War, Western Europe has enjoyed great advances in technology, industrial production and material wealth. It cannot have gone unnoticed in Russia that it has also benefitted from seventy-seven years of peaceful coexistence.

Yes, this breeds an element of complacency but, paradoxically, Putin's adventures in the Ukraine might shake that somewhat, which, although tragic for the Ukrainians, might be just what Europe needs. Germany, please note …

A CHANGING WORLD ORDER: THE WORLD AFTER UKRAINE
Commentators thinking of the longer term have been considering the impact of this war on world security, which will be considerable. This is often presented in terms of a changing world order, with a contrast between democracy and authoritarianism. However, a better description of the new dividing line is one between the existing powers who operate under the current international order and revisionist, revanchist powers who seek to overturn it. Many of those powers are autocracies, and we

might hope, against hope, that their populations would put pressure on their governments for more democracy and human rights. History does not provide much comfort in this area.

But in all the commentary on the new world order, there is little about what that order might look like. Certainly, the West hopes to influence this, but it is not clear in what direction. This is a huge area to study, and not one that we can consider here, but there are some comments about the Black Sea above. Indeed, whatever we think of the existing international order and however much we recognise that it is indeed developing, it has served most of the world reasonably well over the years since the Second World War. The reasons why it has not served most of the poorer countries (think of Africa) is only partially to do with the system itself.

About War and this volume, *War in Context*, have made much of the need for clear strategy – focused on the ultimate goal, long-term, contingent, competitive and embracing every aspect of the state's governance – strategy as protocol, strategy as the core function of government.

When the Ukraine crisis broke, my first reaction was that the West could easily resolve the issue with enough will, but it would be the lack of consensus among the various parties: NATO, the European Union, United Kingdom and the United States that would provide the biggest barrier to an agreed and coherent strategy. And so it has turned out: already there are signs of divergent views between the United States and the United Kingdom and France, Germany and Italy. But none of these parties seems to have addressed the main issue. Putin will eventually disappear, and the international community will have to live with a disconsolate and brutalised Russian population.

The current U.S. Secretary of Defense, Lloyd Austin, may be right in saying that he wants to degrade Russian capability to the extent that they could not try this on again, but it is not clear that he has thought through the implications of this. Surely the answer is for Russia to become a modern industrial state, not so dependent on natural resources and putting considerably more effort into the welfare of their citizens. And, internationally, with a desire to live in peace and harmony with the rest of the world, as part of an agreed international system. Most commentators would say this is difficult; Russia resents what they see as interference in their own affairs, but that should not deter us from trying.

This supplementary chapter has reproached Germany for not cutting off their supplies of gas from Russia, but we must recall that Germany, after the excesses of two world wars, has rehabilitated itself – actually rather too much – as a peaceful, responsible European country.

Let us hope that Russia, in co-operation with the rest of Western Europe, can achieve the same.

APPENDICES

Appendix 1: Definitions, from 'About War'

WAR DEFINED

War is a hostile act of coercion or the threat or use of organised violence designed to change the political balance between polities.

A polity is a social organisation which is coherent and largely supported by its members.

Such a polity must be capable of providing security and other social goods, such as governance and justice. The obvious example is the nation state.

WARFARE DEFINED

Warfare is the practice of planning for, managing and using organised violence, be that military force or any overt hostile action (such as a cyber-attack).

It has many dimensions: doctrine, 'operational art', tactics, but it is essentially subordinate to the (political) essence of war ...

Strategy Defined

Strategy is about planning for the future, about how any polity uses its incumbent resources (people, process and hardware and those they can develop) to achieve their long-term goals.

It is about reconciling (internally and with outside actors) ends, ways and means.

Any strategic approach must incorporate political imagination and an anticipation of competitive moves. It is therefore dynamic and contingent.

Strategy is manifest in plans and processes, but the crucial dimension is that those involved think strategically.

Appendix 2.

Illustrative List of Britain's Military Interventions Since 1945: not exhaustive

Deployment	Rationale	*Political* Result
British forces involvement in the **Greek Civil War** (1944-1947) was partially successful in liberating Greece from German occupation but financial pressures meant a withdrawal of forces in 1947.	Obligatory, to resist communism	**A British necessity but an American success**
Jewish forces in **Palestine** battled British troops occupying Palestine during the mandate (1920-1948). The Mandate was relinquished, handed over to the Americans.	Obligatory under League of Nations / UN mandate but UK was exhausted after 2WW.	**Partial failure: no peaceful settlement left behind.**
Deployment	Rationale	*Political* Result
British troops re-occupied Japanese-held **Indonesia** until the Dutch colonial administration could resume rule, coincident with the Indonesian Revolution (1945-1946). The Dutch eventually withdrew.	Discretionary / obligatory, and an overhang of the Dutch empire which, like Britain's, collapsed.	**Neutral: holding operation; There was, ultimately, a political settlement.**
The counterinsurgency campaign in **Malaya** involved British forces battling CTs (communist Terrorists) guerrillas in Malaya.	Obligatory: again, to resist communism.	**Benchmark political success: Malaysia emerged as a democratic, wealthy Southeast Asia country.**

Deployment	Rationale	*Political* Result
British forces made a major contribution to the **Korean** War (1950-1953), defending South Korea from North Korea and eventually from China. Stalemate was achieved in the form of an armistice (still current), but since the line of demarcation remained where it was, the whole operation can only be called a no-score draw. 6) At the very least, it gave succour to other South East Asian states that they would not be abandoned to communism.	The war was sanctioned by the United Nations (Soviet Russia was boycotting the UN at the time, so did not exercise their veto in the Security Council). The war was essentially about countering communism.	**Partial success: British troops performed well but North / South Korea still not settled. And political tensions remain.**

Deployment	Rationale	*Political* Result
The Anglo-**Egyptian** War (1951-1952), where government guerrillas attacked British forces stationed in the Suez Canal zone was followed by the debacle of **Suez** (1956) where British, French and Israeli forces invaded **Egypt**. The Eisenhower administration in Washington obliged Britain to withdraw: a major turning point in Britain's self-image and foreign policy.	Hubris	**Humiliating** *political* **failure**

Deployment	Rationale	*Political* Result
Mau Mau insurgency against British rule during The **Kenyan** guerrilla war (1952-1956), was a nasty, brutal campaign on both sides. Although technically a British 'win', the uprising had put Kenya and other African colonial states on an inexorable path to independence from colonial rule.	Obligatory; this could be seen through many prisms; there were British white settlers in Kenya who 'owned' the land, but an increasing nationalist fervour among Kenyans to run their own affairs.	**Military success. Moral and political failure.**

Deployment	Rationale	*Political* Result
EOKA, the Greek Cypriot militant group fought to force the withdrawal of British from **Cyprus**. The goal of the rebels was to unite Cyprus with Greece. This was **ENOSIS**: never happened, and Turkey invaded Cyprus in 1974, the island is still partitioned.	Obligatory, post empire	**Partial military success. Political failure. There are still tensions on the island of Cyprus.**

Deployment	Rationale	*Political* Result
British troops aided the government of **Oman** against rebels. The Jebel Akhdar War.	Obligatory, supporting democracy	**Great success: Oman remained peaceful.**

Deployment	Rationale	*Political* Result
Pro-Indonesian rebels launched a rebellion in **Brunei** in in 1962; British forces defeated them.	Discretionary / Obligatory: Demonstrating to the new Indonesian state that they could not acquire territory by military force.	**Great *political* success**

Deployment	Rationale	*Political* Result
During the **Malaysia-Indonesia** Confrontation ('**Confrontasi**', 1963 to 1966), Indonesia launched a guerrilla war against Malaysian Sarawak in Borneo. British forces supported the Malaysians.	Discretionary / Obligatory: Demonstrating to the new Indonesian state that they could not acquire territory by military force.	**Great *political* success**
British forces who put down the revolt of the **Ugandan** Army, who mutinied in 1964.	Discretionary, but could be seen as obligatory as Uganda was an ex-British colony	***Political* success**

Deployment	Rationale	*Political* Result
During the **Dhofar** Rebellion British air and ground forces aided the **Omani** government in defeating the Marxist rebels (1962-1976).	Discretionary: Resisting communism	*Political* success
Rebels in the British-ruled **Aden** waged a guerrilla war against the British and associated **Yemeni** forces (1964-1967). The British withdrew, following which the new nation of **South Yemen** was formed.	Obligatory	*Political* failure; not predicated on military performance

Deployment	Rationale	*Political* Result
The British Army fought a long, nasty war in **Northern Ireland** (1969-1998). Known as 'The Troubles', the 'Provos' (The Provisional IRA) were, according to the Army, eventually defeated or at least obliged to negotiate the Good Friday Agreement., though religious and Brexit tensions remain.	Obligatory. Northern Ireland has been a thorn in the side of a British government ever since the partition of Ireland in 1920. Troops were deployed to protect the population, both Catholic and Protestant	**Partial military success. Partial political success, but there are still tensions within Northern Ireland, and between the province and the Irish state.**

Deployment	Rationale	*Political* Result
After Argentina's invasion of the **Falkland Islands** in 1982, British land, air and naval forces, aided by American intelligence, re-took the islands in a short, well-fought campaign.	Discretionary: Many ex-service people said that recovering the Falklands was not worth British lives (in fact, British casualties amounted to over 250), but Margaret Thatcher (in the words of the chronicler of the war) 'never looked back'.	**Great military success, but there might have been other solutions.**

Deployment	Rationale	*Political* Result
Britain and other allied nations (a 'coalition of the willing') joined together to evict the Iraqis from their illegal occupation of **Kuwait**. Also known as the First Gulf War.	Discretionary, although it was essential to eject Iraq on the basis of safeguarding the international order.	**Great *political* success; International order was upheld.**
After the First Gulf War, British warplanes assisted American air power to enforce a 'No-Fly Zone' in Saddam Hussein's **Iraq** to protect Kurdish and Shiite forces, (1991 to 2003).	Discretionary	**Partial success, though Saddam Hussein remained in power.**

Deployment	Rationale	*Political* Result
During the protracted **Yugoslav** civil wars (1992 to 1996) British forces engaged in NATO peacekeeping operations, including some combat during the Bosnian War.	More or less obligatory, on the basis that problems in the Balkans (as ever) might have impacted on Europe's security overall.	**Partial success, eventually.**

Deployment	Rationale	*Political* Result
Similarly, during the **Kosovo** War in 1999.	Discretionary	**Partial success, eventually.**
British military intervention in **the Sierra Leone Civil War** (2000 to 2002) helped legitimate the government forces to conclude the war. British troops remained in Sierra Leone to confirm the peace and train government forces.	Discretionary, although as an ex-British colony, Sierra Leone was worth saving.	**Great, textbook *political* success.**

Deployment	Rationale	*Political* Result
British troops participated in **Afghanistan** (2001 to 2014) as part of ISAF and many other NATO countries. Despite enormous efforts, little was achieved, and the war against the Taleban continues.	Discretionary, although there was some obligation for the United Kingdom as a member of NATO. On the other hand, why was NATO, a European security alliance, fighting on the other side of the world?	**Disaster: Afghanistan has reverted to what it was before the invasion. Much to many people's surprise, for much of the 20th century, Afghanistan was a progressing state – from the 1920s to the 1980s. What we see now is far from how it has always been.**

Deployment	Rationale	*Political* Result
Following the Second Gulf War, the invasion of **Iraq** to oust Saddam Hussein in 2003, British troops remained to assist American forces, leading to the embarrassing withdrawal from Basra.	Discretionary	**Humiliating failure: what political Achievements there might have been a dwarfed by the horrendous casualties, and the resurgence of enmity is between Shia and Sunni Muslims.**

Deployment	Rationale	*Political* Result
British air and naval forces bombed **Libya** during the Libyan War in 2011. Billed as 'humanitarian assistance', it was more accurately about regime change. Muammar Gaddafi was deposed and killed (unpleasantly). British Special Forces were also involved. Nominally a success, the country descended into warlordism with many casualties.	Hubris	**Although a vicious and murderous thug, at least Gaddafi kept a lid on sectarian violence: a *political* disaster.**

Deployment	Rationale	*Political* Result
The Royal Airforce undertook a bombing and drone attack campaign against **ISIS** (Islamic State of Iraq and the Levant, also known as Daesh) (2014-Present) to degrade their capabilities in Iraq. British Special Forces were also involved.	Discretionary	**Partial success: ISIS simply moved, and is still active 'somewhere' in the Middle East.**

Deployment	Rationale	*Political* Result
The British army and the RAF are also deployed in **Mali**, assisting French troops in a UN-mandated counterinsurgency mission, 2013, continuing. The insurgents are spread out across the whole of the Sahel, and some reports are suggesting that the mission is losing ground and authority: Neutral.	Tragic: although the most enormous area to police, French and British efforts at controlling insurgency in the whole of the Sahel are hampered by local politicians and, frankly, lack of interest from the international community.	**Ongoing, it demonstrates the limits of international power.**

Deployment	Rationale	*Political* Result
The United Nations currently has about twelve **PSOs** (Peace Support Operations) across the world, many of them in Africa. The UK's contributions to UN missions, demonstrates the UK's global commitment to peacekeeping.	Discretionary, although as a responsible member of the United Nations, it is essential that some countries step up to the mark in terms of PSO.	

Appendix 3. Enough to do in our own back yard?

In the text, we suggest that 'Global Britain', operating on a worldwide basis, might risk ignoring the many security threats in Europe's near abroad.

Taking a broad clockwise sweep from Svalbard to Yemen, and then on to the Spanish Sahara suggests 20 potential security problems. Consensus among European nations has always been difficult to achieve, witness difficulties of getting agreement about the Russo-Ukrainian war.

Brexit has made this more difficult, just when Britain's leadership is required. The list is not exhaustive, and these security concerns will not necessarily result in armed conflict.

What the list does illustrate is that, notwithstanding NATO, British diplomatic effort and armed force might be sorely stretched to cope with even one of these situations.

SVALBARD

According to Neil Moralee, writing on 'High Arctic Protection', the unique provisions of the Treaty of Svalbard (the 1920 Spitzbergen treaty), NATO ambiguity on the status of Svalbard, and mounting geopolitical tensions between Russia and Norway signify a realistic probability of outright violation of Norwegian sovereignty over Svalbard in the medium to long term. Moscow did not partake in the Paris treaty negotiations in 1920 because of their civil war. Oslo persuaded the allied delegation to grant Norway sovereignty over Svalbard with the concession of maritime activities to any of the signatories. While they signed the treaty in 1935, Soviet Foreign Minister Molotov made his objections clear.

In the modern era, the Russian state bolsters irredentist claims with historical narratives to legitimise violations of sovereignty.

Righting alleged historical wrongs, underpinned both the 2007 cyber-attacks on Estonia and the 2014 annexation of Crimea. The Russian Svalbard narrative centres on Moscow's perceived unfair exclusion from the 1920 Spitzbergen Treaty which has led to alleged mistreatment of the 10% to 20% of ethnic Russians who make up Svalbard's population. Following Russia's invasion of Ukraine, and their willingness to use violence to resolve what they see as historic injustices, must make Svalbard a security risk for both Norway (a member of NATO) and NATO itself.

THE BALTICS: ESTONIA, LATVIA AND LITHUANIA

Three countries little known before the break-up of the Soviet Union, they have established themselves as well-managed independent states. However, thought to be first in line in the event that the Russian Federation wants to retake the Baltics / cause trouble / punish NATO. The British Army is deployed forwards as a tripwire, which means that if they see any Russians coming over the horizon, they activate a plan, as yet confidential. Like Svalbard, Russia's invasion of Ukraine, and their willingness to use violence to resolve what they see as historic injustices, must make the Baltics a security risk for themselves (members of NATO) and NATO itself.

KALININGRAD

At the moment, the railway line from Russia (Moscow) to the Russian exclave of Kaliningrad runs through Belarus and Lithuania. In the event of Russian hostilities, they would certainly want to safeguard that route, with implications for Belarus (a Russian ally), and Lithuania (still smarting from Soviet occupation). Also, Kaliningrad is the entrance to the Baltic and thus access to Riga, Tallinn and Helsinki. The Suwałki Gap, also known as the Suwałki corridor, is a sparsely populated area immediately southwest of the border between Lithuania and Poland. Named after the Polish town of Suwałki, this choke point became of great strategic and military importance since Poland and the Baltic states joined the North Atlantic Treaty Organisation (NATO).

At the time of writing, Lithuania is trying to restrict Russian access to Kaliningrad, and the Russians have threatened dire consequences.

BELARUS

Russia has long treated Belarus as a client state, but it's not clear whether Belarus sees itself in that way. Demonstrations and riots against the current president, Alexander Lukashenko, were brutally put down.

In the event of the dissidents becoming violent, Russia may intervene to protect the established government. What might be the NATO, EU, or British reaction?

UKRAINE

This is well covered in the text, and in the supplementary chapter. At the time of writing, after 100 days of conflict, the concern now is media and compassion fatigue, with the concern that the West will not maintain its admittedly considerable support for Ukraine. NATO's reputation has been enhanced, but the longer the conflict goes on, the more gaps in NATO solidarity might appear

CRIMEA

This is covered in the main text, but in short, there is a good case for recognising Crimea as Russian, as it always was, certainly since the collapse of the Ottoman Empire, or certainly in Crimea's case the lack of will to keep the archipelago.

The Crimea is likely to become a key factor if and when Russia and Ukraine start negotiating. Most commentaries suggest that the Crimea is lost to Ukraine. The problem then becomes one of maritime rights. Extending an exclusion zone out from Crimea would severely restrict exports from Odesa, and bear in mind that Ukraine is often known as the 'breadbasket of the world', with its enormous wheat production. The Russo-Ukrainian war has already had an adverse effect on wheat prices.

THE BALKANS

Relatively quiescent at the moment but could re-ignite at any time. Anyone got a plan? Didn't think so…

GREEK/TURKISH TENSIONS

Again, could re-ignite at any time, over Cyprus, borders, marine exploration or migrants.

The 'Aegean dispute', as it is called, is a set of disagreements between Greece and Turkey over sovereignty and related rights in the Aegean and contiguous seas. This has strongly affected Greek-Turkish relations since the 1970s, and has twice led to crises coming close to the outbreak of military hostilities, in 1987 and in early 1996. Both Greece and Turkey are members of NATO, though Turkey is probably the most troublesome member.

CYPRUS
See Greek/Turkish tensions: above

LEBANON
Continuing racial, cultural and religious tensions. Economy failing; accusations of corruption directed at government, home to displaced Palestinians and Hezbollah, a Shia Islamist political party and militant group, where they are the most powerful political party. One of their goals is the elimination of the State of Israel.

ISRAEL/PALESTINE
Continuing tensions between ethnic and religious groups, which show little sign of being resolved.

EGYPTIAN INSURGENCY
In parallel with the escalation of the already ongoing jihadist insurgency in Sinai Peninsula in 2013, the pro-Muslim Brotherhood militants started violent attacks against Egyptian policemen and soldiers in Central and Western Egypt. The attacks continue to this day.

THE SAHEL

Stretches some 6,000 km from the Red Sea coast of Sudan on the eastern side of Africa to the Atlantic coast of Mauritania in the west, from Sudan, Chad, Algeria, Niger, Burkina Faso, Mali and Mauritania; Nigeria and Senegal may also be involved.

Insurgents do not respect borders, so it is a vast area to police. There have been problems with Boko Haram, a Salafist terrorist organisation based in north-eastern Nigeria, but also active in Chad, Niger and northern Cameroon. There are other terrorist and insurgent groups operating in other Sahel countries, including the Islamic State and ISIS.

MOROCCO AND THE SPANISH SAHARA

Originally a Spanish possession, the Spanish Sahara or Western Sahara, came under Moroccan control of most of the territory, including all the major cities and natural resources in 1979.

The Polisario Front, founded in 1973 to campaign for the independence of Western Sahara, supports a guerrilla struggle against the Moroccan-Mauritanian occupation.

LIBYA

Following the Joint (NATO) bombing of Libya in 2011 and the destruction of the Ghaddafi government, the country descended into warlordism. However, in 2020, the various parties signed a permanent ceasefire. It is too soon to say whether this will endure.

A PUTATIVE KURDISTAN

Would cover Syria, Iran and Iraq, but mainly Turkey, who would resist it violently, as would Iran. Syria is not in a position to do much, Iraq has already granted some autonomy to the Kurds anyway.

ARMENIA / AZERBAIJAN

have only recently (2020) come to blows: known as the 2020 Nagorno-Karabakh war, involved Azerbaijan, supported by Turkey and the self-proclaimed Republic of Artsakh together with Armenia. There is little commentary as to whether this represents a security risk to the rest of Europe. Two thousand Russian peacekeepers are now deployed.

SYRIA

Where the civil war has been going on since 2011 with little in the way of resolution. The peace conference is stagnant.

YEMEN

Continuing civil war between the Yemeni government and the Houthi armed movement. Both parties are reputedly supported by outside actors.

MOLDOVA

Currently housing thousands of Ukrainian refugees, but rather close to Russian-occupied Ukraine and with the Russian-recognised and garrisoned enclave of Transnistria along its eastern border.

Appendix 4:
The Most Notable Conventions on Banned Weapons

The following weapons are theoretically banned, but there remain many countries who have acceded to the conventions but not ratified them. However, there is great moral pressure that they should follow it nonetheless. Overall, compliance is variable. This is a partial, representative list and illustrates the scope of international agreements and the signing and ratification of each convention. In some instances, states agree to abide by the terms of the convention but not sign it. This is probably because of the difficulties of it being ratified in their parliament. In the case of non-compliance, there are only limited sanctions that can be applied for non-adherence to any convention.

This is a limited list, and does not cover such treaties or conventions to do with, for example, the Antarctic, outer space or the moon.

The Protocol for the Prohibition of the Use in War of Asphyxiating, Poisonous or other Gases and of Bacteriological Methods of Warfare, usually called the **Geneva Protocol** came into force in 1928. About three quarters of nations in the world ratified it.

The Convention on Certain Conventional Weapons was signed in 1983 and banned injurious Non-Detectable Fragments, Incendiary Weapons, Blinding Laser Weapons and demanded of the signatories that they clear unexploded ordnance.

The Convention on Cluster Munitions became effective in 2010, though only after thirty ratifications. It is notable that China, Russia, the United States, India, Israel, Pakistan and Brazil did not sign and are not bound by the convention.

The term *biological weapons* covers the deliberate scattering of toxic chemicals, bacteria or viruses in order to cause mass casualties. This has actually been used since time immemorial. In ancient siege warfare, dead dogs might be hurled into the defending city in order to spread nasty diseases. As well we know, disease has been responsible for maybe more deaths in war than weapons, though most were not caused by offensive weapons from the enemy.

The Biological Weapons Convention came into force in 1975 with almost all states acceding. There were very few non-signatories.

The Ottawa Treaty, known more elaborately as The Convention on the Prohibition of the Use, Stockpiling, Production and Transfer of Anti-Personnel Mines and on their Destruction, or more simply as the Mine Ban Treaty, came into effect in 1999. It called for signatories to stop the production of anti-personnel mines and destroy stockpiles of such mines. About three quarters of states have signed the treaty, but China, the United States and Russia have not. The United States originally agreed to abide by the provisions of the convention but, in January 2020, President Donald Trump repudiated the convention and lifted restrictions on the use of anti-personnel landmines by the American military.

Appendix 5:
Arms Control Treaties Concerning Nuclear Weapons

Conventions, agreements and treaties on conventional weapons are usually negotiated by senior officials and then signed, sometimes with great ceremony, by political leaders.

As there are only a small number of nuclear states in the world – the United Nations Security Council Permanent Five (United States, Russia, China, United Kingdom and France), plus India, Pakistan, North Korea and Israel (undeclared) – and the stakes are much higher, such treaties involve political leaders at the highest level.

There is a bewildering array of international treaties, some agreed, some ratified, and some brought into force, but here we focus on the most important treaties, some still operational, on the subject of nuclear weapons.

The Partial Nuclear Test Ban Treaty was signed in Moscow in 1963 by the Soviet Union, the United States and the United Kingdom. It was also signed by many other states, but the then nuclear states were obviously the most important. Unfortunately, a year after the treaty, China, who had not signed, conducted an atomic test and became the world's fifth nuclear power, with France as the fourth. The treaty banned nuclear tests except those underground. Nevertheless, the principal aim of the treaty was 'the speediest possible achievement of an agreement on general and complete disarmament under strict international control'. Although nearly sixty years old, this is an important provision and is still theoretically the aim of all nuclear treaties. In this, nuclear treaties have not been overly successful. The considerable reduction after 1990 in nuclear stocks was largely due to what was considered to be a better relationship between the United States and Russia, the successor state to the Soviet Union.

The Partial Nuclear Test Ban Treaty proved that international agreements on nuclear weapons could be negotiated and prepared the ground for ...

The Treaty on the Non-Proliferation of Nuclear Weapons, sometimes known as the Non-Proliferation Treaty or NPT, which became effective in 1970, was aimed explicitly at both nuclear-armed states and non-nuclear states, the objective being to prevent the spread of nuclear weapons and weapons technology, and to encourage the use of nuclear energy for peaceful purposes and in general to work towards achieving nuclear disarmament.

The NPT is the most important treaty on nuclear weapons. According to the United Nations Office for Disarmament Affairs, 'The Treaty represents the only binding commitment in a multilateral treaty to the goal of disarmament by the nuclear weapon States' and that 'More countries have ratified the NPT than any other arms limitation and disarmament agreement, a testament to the Treaty's significance.'

The Anti-Ballistic Missile Treaty, 1972, sought to restrict anti-ballistic missiles, but the U.S. withdrew in 2002, citing the need to build a national defence system, and also mentioning a possible nuclear threat from Iran.

The Strategic Arms Limitation Treaty (SALT I), fully in force by 1977, concerned the introduction of ICBM launchers and SLBM (Submarine Launched Ballistic Missiles).

SALT II, which limited ICBMs, was signed in 1979, but never entered into operation.

The Intermediate Range Nuclear Forces Treaty (INF Treaty) came into force in 1988, but President Donald Trump, citing non-compliance by the Russians, withdrew in 2019. The Russians withdrew the next day.

The Strategic Arms Reduction Treaty I (START I), which limited strategic offensive arms came into operation in 1994 but expired in

2009. Was essentially a successor to the expired SALT agreements.

START II, in 1993, sometimes known, rather clumsily, as the 'De-MIRV-ing Agreement' prohibited ICBMs with multiple independently targetable re-entry vehicles, but Russia withdrew in 2002 in response to U.S. withdrawal from the Anti-Ballistic Missile Treaty, above.

To aid verification, the **Open Skies Treaty**, which entered into operation in 2002, allowed unarmed reconnaissance flights between NATO and Russia. However, President Donald Trump withdrew from the treaty, and a Russian withdrawal quickly followed as well. The treaty was one of the most significant in terms of international efforts to facilitate the gathering of intelligence about a potential enemy's military activities.

The Comprehensive Nuclear-Test-Ban Treaty, signed 1996, which prohibited nuclear weapons testing, has never entered fully into operation. To be effective, the treaty has to be ratified by all the nuclear powers and by forty-four members of the Conference on Disarmament that possess nuclear reactors. This was achieved by 2007, except by India and Pakistan. The United States, China and North Korea have signed but not ratified.

The New START Treaty, agreed by the United States and Russia in 2011, was due to expire in 2021 and, despite President Putin of Russia wanting to extend the treaty, President Trump ignored rather than refused this request. The Russian foreign ministry accused the Trump administration of 'deliberately and intentionally' dismantling international arms control agreements and referring to its 'counter-productive and openly aggressive' approach to talks. Fortunately, the new president, Joe Biden, extended the treaty until 2026. The idea was to reduce by half the number of strategic nuclear missile launchers.

Checking that both sides are abiding by the terms of the treaty is obviously very important. The New START treaty, negotiations for which started in 2009, illustrate the complications for the two parties, in this case the United States and the Russian Federation. Inspections would be carried out by the other side, rather than any other country or international body (such as the United Nations). Each side has the right to eighteen on-site inspections per year for Type 1 and Type 2 weapons on as little as thirty-two hours' notice. Generally speaking, the New START inspection regime has been successful in terms of promoting transparency, reducing mistrust and supporting the nuclear arms control process.

This treaty, sometimes called the Nuclear Weapon Ban Treaty, is the first legally binding international agreement to prohibit nuclear weapons, with the ultimate goal being their total elimination. Although, recall that The Treaty on the Non-Proliferation of Nuclear Weapons incorporated a similar objective of 'working towards achieving nuclear disarmament'. Signatories are prohibited from developing, testing, manufacturing, stockpiling, stationing, transferring, using or threatening to use nuclear weapons.

According to the International Campaign to Abolish Nuclear Weapons (ICAN), a coalition of non-governmental organisations, all but one of the fifty-four nations of Africa, all thirty-three nations of Latin America and the Caribbean, and the ten nations of the Association of Southeast Asian Nations (ASEAN), are supportive.

No nuclear-armed nation expressed support for this treaty. Indeed, the United States, Russia and all NATO members expressed explicit opposition. Many of the non-nuclear-armed members of NATO, including Australia and Japan, also resisted such a treaty, imagining that U.S. nuclear weapons enhance or even provide their security. Similarly, the non-nuclear members of NATO claimed that the treaty would be 'ineffective in eliminating nuclear weapons' and instead called for advanced implementation of Article VI of the Non-Proliferation Treaty. The U.S., UK and France said it was 'incompatible with the policy of nuclear deterrence, which has been essential to keeping the peace in Europe and North Asia for over 70 years.' Three of the permanent members of the Security Council, United States, the United Kingdom and France issued a joint statement indicating that they did not intend 'to sign, ratify or ever become party to it'. Yet the ICAN, the International Campaign to Abolish Nuclear Weapons received the Nobel Prize in 2017! There is significant public support for negotiating, or at least starting on that path of, an international ban on nuclear weapons.

The UK's position? When the Lord Bishop of Coventry asked the government what assessment they had made of the United Nations treaty on the prohibition of nuclear weapons (House of Lords, January 2021), the government replied:

'The Government have been clear that they will not sign the Treaty on the Prohibition of Nuclear Weapons. We do not believe that this treaty will bring us closer to a world without such weapons. The Government believe that the best way to achieve our collective goal of a world without nuclear weapons is through gradual multilateral disarmament, negotiated using a step-by-step approach. We must take account of the international security environment and work under the framework of the nuclear non-proliferation treaty.'

…which is something at odds with the 2021 *Integrated Review of Security: Defence, Development and Foreign Policy: Global Britain in a Competitive Age*, which stated:

'The UK will not use, or threaten to use, nuclear weapons against any non-nuclear weapon state party to the Treaty on the Non-Proliferation of Nuclear Weapons 1968 (NPT). This assurance does not apply to any state in material breach of those non-proliferation obligations. However, we reserve the right to review this assurance if the future threat of weapons of mass destruction, such as chemical and biological capabilities, or emerging technologies that could have a comparable impact, makes it necessary.'

And also, although predictably, nuclear deterrence remains at the heart of the UK defence, the government plans to increase the maximum number of nuclear warheads from 180 to 260 – maybe in contravention of the terms of the nuclear NPT.

Appendix 6:
Nuclear Treaties

Although there were various nuclear scares during the Cold War (the Cuban Missile Crisis, Able Archer 83), the dangers of a full-scale nuclear war breaking out, other than by accident, were let's not say insignificant but controllable. The various treaties that were negotiated between the Americans and the Soviets meant that the officials concerned gained an in-depth knowledge of the other side's perspective and objectives through their own revelations, intelligence and observations. Also, the almost continuous contact reaffirmed both sides' commitment to avoiding nuclear war and to eventually lowering the number of warheads and delivery vehicles available. Both sides would, of course, warily espouse the idea of the complete elimination of nuclear weapons. There were many treaties, some more successful than others, and here we look at both those that have endured past the end of the Cold War and those that are still current today.

Partial Test Ban Treaty (PTBT, 1963), which prohibited all testing of nuclear weapons except underground, was superseded by the Comprehensive Nuclear Test Ban Treaty (1996) but this has not become fully effective

This treaty is still a basis for current negotiations.

The Nuclear Non-Proliferation Treaty (NPT), which came into force in 1970, has three aspects: non-proliferation, disarmament and the right to peacefully use nuclear technology.

Again, this treaty is still a basis for current negotiations.

The Strategic Arms Limitation Talks (1969, SALT) were in two rounds: SALT I and SALT II but the treaty (II) expired in 1985 and was not renewed. However, they did lead to the Strategic Arms Reduction Treaties (START), but neither START I (1991) nor and START II (1993)

were ratified (i.e. did not become effective).

Fortunately, a development of START I, New START, was proposed and was eventually ratified in February 2011. SALT and START were both about limiting the number of warheads in each other's arsenals, the number of delivery vehicles and also an inspection regime.

The Strategic Offensive Reductions Treaty (SORT, 2003) was a loose treaty, described as 'a couple of pages' by one commentator, and was criticised for its ambiguity. In short, Russia (which had assumed the place of the USSR) and the U.S. agreed to reduce their (undefined) 'strategic nuclear warheads'. It was superseded by the New START Treaty in 2010.

The Intermediate-Range Nuclear Forces Treaty (INF, 1987) attempted to ban U.S. and USSR land-based ballistic missiles, cruise missiles and missile launchers with ranges of 500–1,000 km (short to medium range) and 1,000–5,500 km (intermediate-range).

The Comprehensive Test Ban Treaty (CTBT, 1996) tries to ban all nuclear explosions in all environments. It has not officially come into force but has been partially successful in that neither of Russia nor the U.S. has tested any nuclear weapons since then.

The Treaty on the Prohibition of Nuclear Weapons (TPNW, 2017), sometimes referred to as the Nuclear Weapon Ban Treaty, was the first legally binding international agreement to prohibit all nuclear weapons, the ultimate objective being their total elimination. The UN General Assembly passed the resolution with 122 in favour BUT none of the nuclear weapon states nor NATO members voted

INDEX